D1356347

TAKING CARE OF BUSINESS

CLARENDON STUDIES IN CRIMINOLOGY

Published under the auspices of the Institute of Criminology, University of Cambridge; the Mannheim Centre, London School of Economics; and the Centre for Criminology, University of Oxford.

General Editors: Jill Peay and Tim Newburn
(London School of Economics)

Editors: Loraine Gelsthorpe, Alison Liebling, Kyle Treiber, and Per-Olof Wikström
(University of Cambridge)

Coretta Phillips and Robert Reiner
(London School of Economics)

Mary Bosworth, Carolyn Hoyle, Ian Loader, and Lucia Zedner
(University of Oxford)

RECENT TITLES IN THIS SERIES:

The Politics of Police Detention in Japan: Consensus of Convenience
Croydon

Dangerous Politics: Risk, Political Vulnerability, and Penal Policy
Annison

Urban Legends: Gang Identity in the Post-Industrial City
Fraser

Punish and Expel: Border Control, Nationalism, and the New Purpose of the Prison
Kaufman

Speaking Truths to Power: Policy Ethnography and Police Reform in Bosnia and Herzegovina
Blaustein

Taking Care of Business

Police Detectives, Drug Law Enforcement and Proactive Investigation

MATTHEW BACON

OXFORD
UNIVERSITY PRESS

Great Clarendon Street, Oxford, OX2 6DP,
United Kingdom

Oxford University Press is a department of the University of Oxford.
It furthers the University's objective of excellence in research, scholarship,
and education by publishing worldwide. Oxford is a registered trade mark of
Oxford University Press in the UK and in certain other countries

© Matthew Bacon 2016

The moral rights of the author have been asserted

First Edition published in 2016
Impression: 2

Published in the United States of America by Oxford University Press
198 Madison Avenue, New York, NY 10016, United States of America

British Library Cataloguing in Publication Data
Data available

Library of Congress Control Number: 2016936544

ISBN 978–0–19–968738–1

Printed and bound by
CPI Group (UK) Ltd, Croydon, CR0 4YY

General Editors' Introduction

Clarendon Studies in Criminology aims to provide a forum for outstanding empirical and theoretical work in all aspects of criminology and criminal justice, broadly understood. The Editors welcome submissions from established scholars, as well as excellent PhD work. The *Series* was inaugurated in 1994, with Roger Hood as its first General Editor, following discussions between Oxford University Press and three criminology centres. It is edited under the auspices of these three centres: the Cambridge Institute of Criminology, the Mannheim Centre for Criminology at the London School of Economics, and the Centre for Criminology at the University of Oxford. Each supplies members of the Editorial Board and, in turn, the Series Editor or Editors.

Matthew Bacon's book, *Taking Care of Business: Police Detectives, Drug Law Enforcement and Proactive Investigation,* is an accomplished account of the professional and moral worlds of police officers working within contemporary drugs policing. The title itself offers a subtle acknowledgement of Dick Hobbs' classic work, *Doing the Business,* and it is pleasing to be able to report that this, too, is a detailed ethnographic study of the working lives of police detectives. Much of the academic work on policing of the most lasting value has been based on ethnography. Sadly, and no doubt reflecting some of the less positive trends in the academy in recent decades, this breed of work has become increasingly rare—to the point where one fears imminent extinction. *Taking Care of Business* is therefore a welcome sight in a number of ways.

The book begins by noting an important paradox. Detectives and criminal investigators are the stuff of an almost immeasurable quantity of fictional portraits. Crime fiction, be it books, TV or film, more often than not translates into detective work of one form or another. Yet ironically, academic interest in this field has been occasional and often fleeting, particularly in recent times. The nature of detective work is also characterised by something of a paradox. On the one hand, it is regularly depicted as a craft, learned on the job, and often involving underhand techniques and a culture of deceit. On the other hand, from a different perspective it is also viewed as highly professional, involving quite sophisticated technological and scientific methods. Under such circumstances ethnography, with its promise of getting 'beyond the formal rules of the game', offers much.

Bacon's study focuses on two specialist detective units assigned with investigating drugs offences, in two Basic Command Units, one in the South of England and one in the North. In the main the detectives employed in such squads are experts in drug law enforcement. The nature of their working lives enables them to devote the bulk of their energies to 'utilising the art, craft and science of criminal investigation to monitor drug markets and make cases against suspected drug dealers'. If ethnographic fieldwork with the police presents many challenges, then drugs policing undoubtedly adds to them. Predictably perhaps, officers were wary of their new, young charge and his motives, and Bacon's account of the slow breaking down of barriers is hugely informative. Key in the process of getting officers to talk appears to have been 'ditching the Dictaphone'.

Whilst the study of any area of policing offers insights into the moral perspectives of officers, this is perhaps especially so of the policing of drugs. The potential futility of attempting to police something so obviously beyond the control of the constabulary also throws into sharp relief officers' attitudes toward their role and the nature and impact of police work in this area. Bacon's study shows that officers' attitudes toward drugs were predictably complex. On the one hand, and in some ways only superficially, most took the straightforward view that illicit drug use was self-evidently wrong and harmful and needed to be stopped wherever possible. Supply was always viewed as more serious than use, though 'social supply' was significantly less serious than those who were in it for profit. Yet many officers clearly had experience of drugs themselves, either personally, or via members of their families and, in practice, had a much more nuanced sense of where intervention was felt necessary. Reflecting on the fact that they would be unlikely to take action against a relative or friend, the popular sentiment appears to have been "you can't be a bobby all the time'. Thus, although they tended otherwise to take a fairly straightforward prohibitionist view of illicit drugs, they accepted that many were the source of less harm than alcohol. Indeed, the brief references to officers' attitudes toward, and use of, alcohol in this study point to an area ripe for further research.

The policing of drugs, as with much investigative activity, has changed considerably in the last decade or two. A more problem-oriented approach to policing has been promoted—under various guises—and the impact of both the National Intelligence Model (NIM) and restrictions imposed by the Regulation of Investigatory Powers Act 2000 (RIPA) are discussed in some detail. As is so common in police practice, Bacon illustrates how the best intentions of reformers are regularly mitigated by the interpretative actions and day-to-day practices of officers engaged in the investigation and enforcement of drug-related offences. In one of the fieldwork areas, for example, the approach to intelligence-led policing is described by the officers themselves as 'NIM-lite', indicating a willingness to engage in at least superficial compliance, whilst continuing to engage in elements of traditional practice. Similarly, the detectives in Bacon's study had developed a range of informal practices to circumvent the regulatory controls imposed on the use and handling of informers imposed by the much hated RIPA (known to some as 'the grim-RIPA').

The belief in the primacy of learning and practising the *craft* of policing also underpinned the occasionally disparaging attitudes that Bacon reveals some officers held toward intelligence analysis. Viewed sceptically as being 'academic', 'all about performance management' and 'pointless descriptions of what we already know', officers were especially resistant to the idea that civilian analysts might contribute toward discussions of tactical solutions in particular cases. As one officer is reported to have said, 'It's like a spectator giving advice to a professional athlete'. At heart, drugs policing comes to look like so much else in the police world. Fundamentally, as is all policing, drugs policing is about the maintenance of order. Bacon talks of regulating the drugs trade via an unwritten 'code of practice', using a suite of enforcement interventions, graded and utilised to reflect the particular local diagnoses of the problem, with an eye to both symbolic (drugs raids to send a message) and practical impact.

Dr Bacon's study of drugs policing is a significant empirical contribution to the field of police studies, and represents a pleasing return, centre-stage, of detailed ethnographic work in this area. We hope it will stimulate further, similar endeavours, and are pleased to welcome it to the Clarendon Studies in Criminology series.

Tim Newburn and Jill Peay
17 February 2016

Preface

> If you write a novel, spend weeks and then months catching
> it word by word, you owe it to both the book and to your-
> self to lean back (or take a long walk) when you've finished
> and ask yourself why you bothered – why you spent all that
> time, why it seemed so important. In other words, what's it
> all about, Alfie?
>
> Stephen King (2000, p238), *On Writing*

Deliberately altering states of consciousness is part of the human
condition and an almost universal phenomenon. Indeed, it is not
an exaggeration to claim that every second of every day, men and
women around the world are using a cosmic array of drugs and
getting 'high' for various reasons. Drugs can be a source of pleasure, have cultural value, and symbolic power. They are big business and the profits can be considerable. But so can the costs. It is
widely acknowledged that certain drugs and drug markets cause
enormous harm and need to be controlled. At the same time, it is
increasingly apparent that current drug policies are comparably
harmful in their ineffectiveness and excesses. Drugs, drug dealing, and efforts to control them are vast and fascinating topics of
great consequence that pose strenuous intellectual puzzles and
bring to the fore the complexity of defining and solving social
problems. As Kleiman et al. (2011: xxi) make clear, the issue of
drugs 'touches on poverty, disease, race, crime, and terrorism, not
always in obvious or expected ways, and thinking about drugs,
and rules about using them, forces us to consider what it means
to be fully human, and what it means to be free'. Few policy areas
are underpinned by more myths and misconceptions or generate
more heated debates.

This book aims to advance understanding of local drug law enforcement and investigative practice by offering an ethnography of
specialist detective units assigned to the task of investigating drug
offences and gathering evidence to support the prosecution of the
persons who perpetrate them. The lack of contemporary research
on detectives and drug investigations was compelling enough as a

reason for doing the legwork and the writing. There were knowledge gaps to fill and crucial questions about policing and drug control policy that needed answering. Academic justifications aside, however, this study stemmed equally, if not more so, from personal curiosity. Long before entering the hallowed halls of higher education, I was struggling to make sense of the rhetoric of prohibition, wondering where my own experiences fit into the bigger picture, and wanting to find out if media representations of cops and criminals were anything like reality. Based on extensive fieldwork undertaken in two English police service areas, *Taking Care of Business* provides an in-depth analysis of the everyday realities of the 'war on drugs' and the associated working rules, tacit understandings, and underlying assumptions that operate beneath the presentational canopy of police organizations. It also critically examines the most pertinent legislative initiatives, organizational reforms, and shifts in thinking about the values, objectives, and norms of policing that have occurred over recent decades, which, between them, have contributed to some significant changes in the ways that detectives are trained and investigations are controlled and carried out.

The book begins in Chapter 1 with a review of the existing literature on drug detectives. They are the protagonists of this story. It analyses the nature of detective work, from the origins of the police detective through to the current context of criminal investigation, and begins to consider key issues associated with changing the ways in which investigations are conceived, conducted, and controlled. It also explains why police organizations set up specialist squads to deal with certain forms of criminality and highlights the special features of drug law enforcement. The aim of Chapter 2 is to establish the parameters of policing in the drugs field and build a theoretical foundation for explaining the policing of drugs and new directions in drug control policy and practice. By critically analysing the construction of specific drug problems over time, it uncovers the logic behind some of the most pertinent governmental responses and questions whether they serve the needs of society or the interests of powerful groups. Chapter 3 reviews the literature on the illegal drug business in order to explore this subterranean world of work and play and paint a picture of what the police who deal with drugs are up against.

Moving on to the empirical components of the book, Chapter 4 answers standard methodological questions and elucidates the business involved in undertaking this particular research endeavour. It starts by considering what it means to take an ethnographic approach to social science research and explains why ethnography is both a vital scholarly enterprise in the field of police studies and the most appropriate way of penetrating the inner world of police organizations. Following this, the reader is introduced to the fieldwork settings and research participants and then walked through the chosen research methods. The discussion also contains some reflections on practical issues relating to access and acceptance that were encountered during the research process and how they were engaged with and managed. Interrogating the official organizational position on the policing of drugs, Chapter 5 delves into the police worldview with the aim of exploring and making sense of how officers perceive the drug world and their role in it, using concepts, themes, and theories from the police culture literature to help frame the analysis. Rather than presenting a monolithic view, care is taken to reflect the diversity of opinions that were expressed by detectives and a range of other police officers so as to bring out any cultural variations arising from idiosyncrasies and the distinct experiences and expectations associated with rank, specialism, and the external policing environment.

To shed some light on the organization of drug law enforcement, Chapter 6 discusses the rise of intelligence-led policing and the implementation of the National Intelligence Model (NIM). For the most part, it offers an in-depth analysis of the interactive relationship between the drug detectives and the organizational frameworks within which their formative intelligence and investigative practices were constructed and performed. Matters of substance include how the NIM has been received and the policy of 'compliance'; the significance of drug strategies, official priorities, and performance management; what constituted 'intelligence', how it entered the police intelligence system, and the routine activities of intelligence work; and the setting of operational targets. Licensing criminals, a particularly murky, morally questionable, but purportedly necessary area of policing, is the theme of Chapter 7, which considers the role of informants in drug investigations and examines how drug detectives perceived them and operated within the regulatory constraints of the police informer system. Chapter 8 then provides a detailed account of the effective realities of prohibition by examining the dynamics and dilemmas of how drug investigations are planned, authorized, and carried out after a case becomes operational. The events described are typical in that they present key features in patterns of local drug law enforcement and in processes of making cases against suspected drug dealers. Attention is given to drug warrants, covert surveillance, and test purchase operations, the tactical resolutions that were used time and again for taking care of business on the frontline. It focuses on the occupational perspective and practices of detectives, how they interpret, make sense of, and manipulate the rules of the drug game, and the ways in which they use intelligence, gather evidence, exercise power, and define success.

Finally, Chapter 9 pulls together some key findings in order to consider the extent to which detective practices were affected by the formal structural context of policing and explain why some behaviours and aspects of their culture were susceptible to change whereas others proved resistant and enduring. The discussion then moves on to make some recommendations for potentially workable alternatives to traditional enforcement strategies that are designed to stimulate further research and reconfigure the evolution of the policing of drugs. By applying regulatory theory to drug detective work, it is argued that one way forward is for the police to use their powers to beneficially shape drug markets according to the standards and purposes of harm reduction.

Acknowledgements

As I sit and look back at the ramshackle road behind me, it is humbling to think of all the people who have made this book possible and supported me through the highs and lows of the writing process. The directions, gas money, and pit stops were very much appreciated. Researchers tend to rack up a lot of debt and I've got a great many IOUs to work off.

This book has been a long time in the making. It started life as a doctoral thesis, which was completed at the University of Sheffield and funded by the Economic and Social Research Council. Although the material has been substantially reworked and developed in the intervening years, I would not have made it this far had it not been for the kindness, patience, intellectual guidance, and worldly wisdom of my supervisors: Joanna Shapland and Layla Skinns. Thanks a million. Special mention is also extended to Russell Buchan, Simon Holdaway, Bethan Loftus, Peter Manning, Megan O'Neill, Paul Ponsaers, Robert Reiner, Pietro Saitta, Teela Sanders, Toby Seddon, and Tinneke Van Camp for providing me with friendship, inspiration, comments on drafts, and candid advice about pursuing a career in academia. Any errors, omissions, or flawed interpretations are my own.

Empirical studies are made possible by gatekeepers and others in the field on whom the researcher relies to carry out the research. I would therefore like to take this opportunity to express my deepest gratitude to all of the police officers and staff who allowed me to enter their world and taught me a thing or two about real (police) work. In particular, I wholeheartedly acknowledge that without the assistance, goodwill, and trust of the drug detectives the fieldwork could not have been undertaken and would not have been as enjoyable to undertake. Names must be withheld to preserve anonymity. If you ever feel the urge to read the reason for my intrusion, I hope that you are satisfied with the story I decided to tell and do not take my criticisms too personally. Maybe one day I will be able to repay the favour.

I am grateful to Lucy Alexander and the OUP team, along with the Clarendon Studies in Criminology editors, for their efforts throughout the publication process. The author and Oxford University Press would like to thank the following publishers for permission to reproduce material for which they hold copyright: Eleven International Publishing for earlier versions of sections from Chapters 5 and 6 that appear in Saitta, P., Shapland, J., and Verhage, A. (eds.) (2013) *Getting By or Getting Rich? The Formal, Informal and Criminal Economy in a Globalized World* as 'Dancing around drugs: Policing the illegal drug markets of the night-time economy in England and Wales'; Il Mulino for earlier versions of sections from Chapters 4, 5, 6, and 8 that appear in *Etnografia e Ricerca Qualitativa* as 'The informal regulation of an illegal trade: The hidden politics of drug detective work' (1/2013); and Taylor & Francis for adapted versions of sections from Chapters 2, 5, and 9 that appear in *Police Practice and Research* as 'Maintaining order in the drug game: Applying harm reduction principles to drug detective work' (17(4), 2016). Thanks also to Stephen King and Hodder and Stoughton for their permission to use material from On Writing: A Memoir of the Craft.

Last, but by no means least, my heartfelt thanks go to Anna, my family and dear friends, for keeping me fed, watered, and relatively sane. Apologies for my general absentmindedness and relentlessly talking shop. Your love, generosity, and encouragement made it easier to see the light at the end of the tunnel.

Table of Contents

1

The Drug Detectives

As is typical for the time of year, the early morning was as dark, cold, and wet as the night before. Most days, I like to rise with the sun and will do almost anything to avoid going outside in such horrid weather conditions, but today was different; today I was up, ready, and waiting outside a police station in the centre of town for an unmarked police car to take me into 'the field'. The now familiar station wagon entered the parking lot and skidded to a grinding halt with a honk of the horn. I broke cover, ran across the puddled asphalt, opened the passenger door and jumped into the seat. 'Saddle up partner!' shouted DC Moreland—Bunk, to those who know him well enough.[1]

I knew Bunk had taken up smoking again before he opened the window and sparked up a cigarette; the lingering smell of tobacco on his clothes was a dead giveaway. 'I know! I know! I said I'd quit. I'm going to stop for the new year or else my wife will kill me before the fags do.' We chatted about his weekend away in the countryside as *The Smiths* gently played over the airwaves; he asked me about what I'd been up to lately, and wondered if I'd watched the football last night. The topic of conversation soon turned to business: the ongoing surveillance operation against a 'well-connected' heroin dealer from a neighbouring district who had the audacity to 'set up shop on our turf'. Bunk also informed me about a meeting that had taken place between the drug squad sergeant and a senior officer, the outcome of which revealed a lot about the inner workings of the police organisation and the hidden politics of drug law enforcement.

The detectives were based in a small room of a moderately sized police station, located outside a village on the outskirts of the town. Newspaper clippings of their best busts covered

---

[1] The pseudonyms used in this book have been taken from the HBO drama series *The Wire*.

the walls, prison terms were chalked up on their operations board, and family photos occupied every desk. It was usually quite cramped when 'the magnificent seven' assembled in the office for briefings and debriefings but their noticeable attempts at feng shui had created a newfound sense of space and harmony. This was the calm before the storm. 'Today's the day boys.' After three months of intelligence development and evidence gathering, the detectives were satisfied with the case they had constructed for the prosecution and convinced their target would be 'holding' when they executed the warrant. Today was 'strike day', the culmination of all their efforts, the quintessence of 'real' police work, and the substance of glorified war stories.

(Fieldnotes, Smallville)

Detectives and criminal investigations have been subjects of interest and inspiration for countless novelists, filmmakers, and 'law and order' aficionados. The newsworthiness of crime and justice matters means that hardly a day goes by without a plea to the public for information on the whereabouts of a person featured in some 'Most Wanted' campaign, a celebration of a successful enforcement operation culminating in the downfall of some notorious villain, or the gripping highlights of some high-profile inquiry or court case. Yet, although media representations undoubtedly contain elements of truth and can be valuable sources of information and symbolism, sensationalized accounts of journalists and fictional portrayals of super sleuths and mavericks—Inspector Harry Callahan, DCI Gene Hunt, and Detective Jimmy McNulty to name but a few—are, ordinarily, a far cry from reality (Mawby 2007; Reiner 2010: 177–202). Be that as it may, few social scientists have endeavoured to investigate the investigators in this country or further afield, so, alas, we know very little about who they are, what they do, or how they do it (Brodeur 2010: 185–6). Police researchers have traditionally concentrated their efforts on exposing the everyday realities of patrol work and the occupational culture of the lower ranks of the uniform branch.

This chapter reviews the police studies literature on detectives and criminal investigations in order to provide a platform on which to consider the ethnographic exploration of those specialist detective units that focus their efforts on detecting and investigating drug offences, and bringing the offenders to justice. It analyses the nature of detective work, from the origins of the police detective through to the current context of criminal investigation, attends to some of the key themes and concepts that underpin the subject matters under discussion, and begins to examine key issues associated with changing the ways in which investigations are conceived, conducted, and controlled. It also explains why police organizations set up specialist squads to deal with certain forms of criminality and pays particular attention to the special features of detective work in the field of drug control.

The Origins of the Police Detective

Criminal investigation is one of the core functions of policing and the police. Considering that the most prominent aim of police investigations has long been to detect offenders and help bring them to justice by gathering evidence that can be used for prosecutorial purposes, it is easy to see why detective work might be viewed as both the quintessence of good policing and the cornerstone of the criminal justice system. It might, then, come as a surprise to the reader to learn that the idea of attaching an investigative function to the public police service initially met with strong resistance (Emsley 1996; Ignatieff 1979). When the 'New Police' were established in England in 1829, widespread fear and suspicion of 'continental' styles of policing through networks of informants and *agents provocateurs* inhibited the formation of a plain-clothes detective branch. Brodeur (2010: 192–3) explains that investigation was 'twice tainted as a profession' because investigators were believed to be close to the criminal milieu and a threat to the exercise of civil liberties. In the face of opposition from across the social and political spectrums, the architects of the Metropolitan Police Service were obliged to construct an organizational style and image that emphasized the idea of the state police as a legitimate, accountable, and representative civilian body that policed by consent not coercion. For the most part, therefore, in the early years of 'the police', criminal investigation continued to be a principally private affair undertaken by victims of crime, freelance 'thief-takers' and agencies set up under stipendiary magistrates such as the Bow Street Runners (Beattie 2012; Zedner 2006).

However, Robert Peel's vision for policing was modified as the limitations of the preventative principle as embodied in the uniformed patrol officer became more apparent. In 1842, concerns over rising crime rates and the effectiveness of the police at dealing with serious crimes and skilled criminals prompted the force's first Commissioners to hesitantly recommend that the Home Secretary authorize the formation of a small detective unit at Scotland Yard. This, according to Morris (2007: 17), 'represented merely the bureaucratization and professionalization of the function rather than its invention', inasmuch as police officers were already acting in a detective capacity before the role was explicitly acknowledged or formally sanctioned. Detective policing of the 'dangerous classes' had continued largely unabated, and plain-clothes officers were regularly employed to catch pickpockets and observe union and political meetings (Hobbs 1988; Kuykendall 1986). What was significant about the decision to form the Metropolitan Detective Department was the acknowledgement that the investigation of certain crimes required a specialist police response. It can also be seen as recognition that the detective craft was distinct from other areas of police work.

Although Charles Rowan and Richard Mayne appreciated the need for the police to respond to reported crimes and instigate investigations, their initial reluctance to formalize or develop the practice was in part fuelled by uncertainty over how best to control and monitor the clandestine behaviour and methods of detectives. The Commissioners' apprehensiveness was surely heightened by the fact that officers assigned to 'the department' were initially permitted to pursue private investigations and were thereby at greater risk of taking an entrepreneurial approach to their work at the expense of public service. In consequence, the first police detectives were subject to close supervision and regulated through strict rules of conduct, which specifically forbade them from associating with criminals and inciting or engaging in criminal activity (Hobbs 1988; Klockars 1985; Kuykendall 1986).

The Metropolitan Detective Department was gradually expanded over the following decades, detectives were introduced to every police division, and branches emerged in the City of London Police and in several provincial forces as they developed their investigative capacity (James 2013; Morris 2007; Shpayer-Makov 2011). Furthermore, a division of labour between 'generalist' and 'specialist' detectives accompanied these new arrangements: Scotland Yard central office detectives dealt with serious crime, whilst divisional detectives investigated local criminality. Yet, in spite of this apparent acceptance, detective policing was still regarded with a general distrust, not least because of the occasional allegations and revelations of corruption. Despite reassurances of institutional control from police leaders, detectives continued to operate with considerable autonomy and problems with their probity proved difficult to remedy.

In 1877, the detectives of London were put under the spotlight when three of the four chief inspectors of the department were found guilty of accepting bribes and perverting the course of justice in the so-called 'Trial of the Detectives' (Ascoli 1979; Shpayer-Makov 2011). Following the recommendations of the ensuing Committee of Inquiry, the central and divisional detective forces of 'the Met' were reorganized into what became known as the Criminal Investigation Department (CID)—a 'totally autonomous force with a structure and hierarchy bearing little resemblance to the uniform branch' (Hobbs 1988: 41). The newly appointed Director of Criminal Investigation, a barrister called Howard Vincent, was critical of the previous system on the grounds that most officers were unsuited to the role, unable to perform their duties, and were uncontrolled by their superiors. He was given something of a free rein to reform the detective branch and endeavoured to do so by centralizing its key operations, minimizing divisional rivalries, dismissing corrupt detectives, and introducing a vetting procedure for new candidates. In hindsight, however, this classic case of 'scandal and reform' not only failed to address issues of investigator control, but in some respects made the situation worse through the creation of an independent 'firm within a firm'.[2] For James (2013: 28), the reorganization 'reinforced the detective craft and did nothing to mitigate detectives' pre-existing predilection for corrupt practices'.

Although developments outside the capital were diverse and variable owing to differences in local demand and resources, the Metropolitan model was eventually adopted throughout the service in England and Wales. The CID soon came to be seen as a distinct entity within the police organization and became both a magnet and a source of resentment for many officers, due to its higher pay, greater status, and better opportunities for advancement (Shpayer-Makov 2011). Tensions between the uniform and detective branches took root as the department set about

---

[2] 'Firm within a firm' was a phrase coined by *The Times* newspaper. It referred to the relationship between organized crime and detectives from the Metropolitan Police in the 1960s (Marks 1978).

constructing its identity and establishing ownership over investigative techniques and the prosecution of suspects. These attempts by the department to monopolize detective work and assert their autonomy were assisted by events such as the Fenian bombing campaign in the mid-1880s, during which the tactics of the 'Special Irish Squad'—the first specialist detective unit, which was later renamed 'Special Branch'—proved to be more effective than the uniform branch's preventative strategy of guarding potential targets. Likewise, the establishment of an effective fingerprinting system and the Criminal Records Office at the turn of the century led to marked improvements in the detection of crimes, which in turn accelerated the reputation of the police detective (Hobbs 1988; Maguire 2008).

It is an established practice within the history of criminal investigation that detectives respond primarily to the more serious and complex crimes, and a presumption that their specialization allows them to hold sway over the investigative areas of police work. Suspicion of covert policing has been a recurrent theme throughout this history, as has the seemingly insoluble dilemma of how best to regulate officers, who at times find themselves caught between the informal realities of their work and the formal expectations of the law and the police organization. One could even argue that misconduct and even corruption are inherent parts of the detective profession because it requires those who undertake it to operate at least partially in the shadows. Whilst there have been important breaks with the past, it will be argued in this book that the fundamentals of the detective role remain unchanged and so many of the philosophies, practices, and problems that underpin the investigation of crime in modern times can be traced back to the early development of the police investigative function.

Detective Work and Culture

The term detective is used here to describe those police officers who are members of the CID and thereby have the prefix 'Detective' before their rank to designate their certified investigative ability.[3]

---

[3] To become a fully qualified detective, police constables must pass the National Investigators' Examination (NIE), successfully complete the Initial Crime Investigators Development Programme (ICIDP), and obtain Professionalising Criminal Investigation Programme (PIP) Level 2 accreditation (Stelfox 2007, 2009).

For the most part, police detectives are employed to investigate crimes that take place in their service area and to gather evidence to support the prosecution of the persons who perpetrate them. In performing this role, detectives are actively involved in defining acts as 'criminal' as they interpret the complex web of behaviours that lead to the incidents that form their caseload and translate an opaque 'social reality' into a transparent 'legal reality' that can be neatly categorized and dealt with by prosecutors and courts. Put simply, detective work is ultimately about piecing together fragments of information in order to determine 'what happened' and 'who did it' in the eyes of the law.

'Truth' and 'reality' are subjective and relative. The investigation process is graphically depicted in Jackall's (2005: 18) engaging fieldwork-based study of how New York City detectives labour 'to transform their hard-won street understanding into convincing public proof that fixes responsibility for crime'.[4] Similarly, the research Innes (2003a) carried out with homicide detectives led him to view the investigation of crimes as the creation of 'narrative accounts', which are supported by a body of evidence that meets the legal requirements of proof and is sufficient to establish the most authoritative version of past events. These 'official' accounts of 'the incident' are designed to suppress alternative accounts and resolve the situation. Ericson (1981) argues much the same thing in his study of detectives 'making crime' within an enabling environment that allows them to operate with a great deal of discretion. This search for 'proof' rather than 'the truth' reflects the adversarial approach to criminal justice that is typically located in Anglophone common law jurisdictions (McBarnet 1981; McConville et al. 1991; Sanders et al. 2010).

The notion of police discretion refers to the autonomy of an officer to make a decision about possible courses of action or inaction independent of legal or organizational constraint (Bronitt

---

[4] Whilst studies undertaken in transatlantic jurisdictions tell us a lot about detective work in different places and are useful for comparative analyses (Ericson 1981; Greenwood et al. 1977; Jackall 2005; Manning 2004; Sanders 1977; Simon 1991; Skolnick 2011; Wilson 1978), the findings and explanations should only be tentatively applied to similar settings and situations in England and Wales. The police in liberal democratic societies face common problems that arise from their role and the constraints of legality and bureaucracy, but differences in history, culture, and the social organization of policing create variations within and between forces.

and Stenning 2011; Ericson 2007). The work of McBarnet (1981) reveals that discretion is actually part of criminal law and procedure and is enabled through indeterminate rules that allow for wide interpretive latitude and the ability to use laws to legitimate contradictory decisions. At the heart of the discourse on the scope and limits of discretion are questions about how rules relate to police decisions. Broadly speaking, the frameworks that to varying degrees structure all aspects of police work can be viewed as governmental tools that are designed to provide officers with powers and put in place hierarchical procedures and mechanisms of accountability. Internal controls over police practices are typically sought through organizational policies and procedures that are embedded into systems of reporting and auditing (Chan 2001; Dixon 1997; Ericson and Haggerty 1997). Yet, no matter how carefully prescribed these formal structures may be, they cannot, and perhaps should not, amount to an inflexible 'rule book' for dealing with the diverse range of incidents in which officers find themselves having to make sense of what has happened, and make a decision about how best to police the given situation. In his seminal essay on rules and policing, Ericson (2007) illustrates that the police have various orientations towards rules depending on both the type of rule in question and the pragmatic circumstances faced. When actually engaged in police work, he suggests that officers 'are variously ignorant of potential applicable rules, sidestep troublesome rules they think may be applicable, break rules if such action is deemed necessary to get the job done and use rules creatively to accomplish desired outcomes' (p394). Discretion provides the context in which culture can influence how officers use, manipulate, and circumvent laws, policies, and procedures that are flexible, indeterminate, or deemed situationally inappropriate for the exigencies of police work (Dixon 1997; Holdaway 1989).

Those researchers who have examined detectives at work indicate that their discretion lies in how they decide to conduct the investigations they undertake, the interpretations they make that contribute to how the 'facts' of a case are established, and the ways in which they use rules to rationalize their actions and make them legitimate (Collison 1995; Ericson 1981; Hobbs 1988; Innes 2003a; Maguire and Norris 1992; Manning 2004; McConville et al. 1991; Skolnick 2011). The detective role enables officers to operate with a significant degree of autonomy on account of the low visibility of plain-clothes work, the individualistic nature of casework, and the 'entrenched belief among CID officers that "supervision" has to be based on *trust*' (Maguire and Norris 1992: 24). Studies indicate that supervisors usually have little interest in how detectives perform their job so long as their paperwork and case files present a legitimate and accountable version of events. Accordingly, the 'mastery of paperwork and the ability to manipulate the "paper reality"' (McConville et al. 1991: 98) are seen as tricks of the trade that are both admired and required to bridge the gap between the actions of detectives and relevant legal and bureaucratic procedures. It should be noted, however, that the nature and degree of police discretion is largely dependent on context. Focusing mainly on counterterrorist investigations conducted by Integrated Special Branch departments in police forces across the UK, Lowe (2011) argues that detectives have little or no opportunity to apply discretion when applying the law in 'high policing' cases.[5]

Competing perspectives on the nature of detective work are perfectly captured by the terms 'art', 'craft', and 'science' (Tong and Bowling 2006). What little empirical research has been undertaken on the quotidian realities of detective work has tended to depict it as something of a cultural craft (Ericson 1981; Hobbs 1988; Jackall 2005; Maguire and Norris 1992; Manning 2004; Simon 1991; Skolnick 2011). From this perspective, the craft of the detective is learnt chiefly through on-the-job experience and characterized by a specific set of investigative skills and unwritten understandings about the rules of the game. It 'goes beyond academic degrees, specialized training or book learning, because all the theory in the world means nothing if you can't read the street' (Simon 1991: 18). Police notions of what makes a 'good detective' emphasize that certain officers have a natural instinct for the job and the intuitive ability to separate fact from fiction. An officer who can practise the art of investigation is typically seen as being skilled at 'reading' the signs of criminal behaviour, identifying creative lines of inquiry, resolving uncertainties, eliciting information from people 'in the know', and foreseeing strategies to avoid detection. During fieldwork, Maguire and Norris (1992: 16) found that many detectives believe the most important investigative skills are being 'streetwise' and the ability to 'mix with villains without

---

[5] For discussion of 'high' and 'low' policing see Brodeur (2010: 223–54).

crossing the dividing line of dishonesty'. Hobbs (1988) provides a colourful portrayal of the peculiar working class culture of the East End of London and shows how CID culture is influenced by the policed environment to the extent of adopting the same vocabularies and entrepreneurial styles of working. The working personality of detectives was marked out by 'deceit, evasiveness, duplicity, lying, innuendo, secrecy, double talk and triple talk' (p197). At the same time, detective work is also perceived as a science, in that detectives are 'skilled in scientific approaches, crime scene management, social sciences, the use of physical evidence, investigative interviewing, informant handling, offender profiling and managing the investigative process' (Tong 2009: 9).

Detectives are liable to see themselves as a professional elite and their role in crime control as the *sine qua non* of policing (Collison 1995; Young 1991). In fact, Bayley (1994: 57) notes that both inside and outside the police organization the work of detectives is considered 'police work par excellence'. The literature gives prominence to the cultural transition that takes place when uniformed officers move 'into clothes' (Rubinstein 1973: 399). According to Hobbs (1991: 599), the 'quicker new recruits to the CID can purge themselves of what is perceived as the plodding, mechanistic, reactive operational style of the uniform branch, the quicker total immersion in detective culture can be achieved'. A key stage in this acculturation process is when new recruits are socialized into the department and taught the 'informal code'. Innes (2003a: 17) notes that trainees and novice detectives customarily undergo some form of 'apprenticeship' or 'mentoring' with more experienced colleagues, a practice which he considers to be of crucial importance 'in relaying and transferring the tacit and informal knowledge of detective work, of how to get the job done in "the real world", and the recipe knowledge, working rules, and attitudes that will facilitate this'.

A recurrent theme in the sociology of occupations is the effect of people's work on their outlook on the world. Most occupational groups 'develop understandings about how to interpret conduct, retain loyalties, express opinions, use or abuse authority' (Skolnick 2008: 35). Such understandings are rooted in the everyday experiences, problems, and tensions of the job and transmitted across members through processes of socialization. Police researchers have identified sets of shared values and beliefs that underpin how the police view the social world, how they relate to each other, and how they interact with the public. They have tapped into a reservoir of informal norms and underlying assumptions that provide officers with coping strategies and frames of reference for how and why policing should and can be done in any situation (Bacon 2014; Cockcroft 2012; Loftus 2009; Reiner 2010). Detective culture is generally omitted from, or only fleetingly mentioned in, descriptions of police culture, which are almost always concentrated on patrol work and the lower ranks of the uniform branch. It is possible, however, to draw some generalizations from the scattering of noteworthy monographs, chapters, articles, and reports that have been written (Manning 2007). In a nutshell, the occupational culture of the CID is intensely pragmatic and oriented towards the action, danger, and excitement of crime fighting. Detectives are consistently characterized as having conservative values, an old-fashioned machismo, a strong *esprit de corps*, and a general suspicion of 'outsiders'. Another commonly identified feature of detective culture is a willingness to 'work the system', bypass formal supervisory mechanisms, and bend or break rules that get in the way of efficient criminal investigations and desirable outcomes. This practice is encapsulated in office jokes about using the 'Ways and Means Act' to achieve organizational ends or a form of justice considered appropriate by the investigating officers (Collison 1995; Hobbs 1988; Holdaway 1983; Innes 2003a; Maguire and Norris 1992; Skolnick 2011; Smith and Gray 1983; Waddington 1999a; Young 1991).

A couple of common misconceptions are that criminal investigation is a task performed exclusively by detectives and that detective work is synonymous with investigative work. In the context of the police, the word 'detective' is a noun that refers to CID officers and can also be used as an adjective to refer to their work and the organizational division or subdivision within which they are located (i.e. the 'detective branch' or a 'specialist detective unit'). 'Investigate', on the other hand, is a verb that can be understood to mean to carry out a systematic inquiry in order to find out and examine the facts of a particular incident or allegation. My point is that one need only consult a dictionary to discover that a variety of activities performed by a range of police officers and civilian staff fall under the banner of criminal investigation. The bulk of investigative work carried out by the police is actually done by the uniform branch as part of their routine duties (Greenwood et al. 1977; Stelfox 2009). When a patrol officer is sent to a potential crime in response to a report being made by a member of the public, for example, his or her role is to decide whether or not a criminal offence has taken place and, if so, conduct what Palmiotto (2013) calls a 'preliminary' investigation, aimed at establishing the 'solvability' of the case and gathering any material that is immediately to hand, such as victim and witness accounts and CCTV footage. What's more, although the 'follow-up' investigation is usually allocated to a single detective, Stelfox (2009: 50) points out that no investigations rely solely on the actions of one person. In addition to the officer in charge of the case, other police personnel such as crime scene investigators, forensic scientists, and crime analysts play important roles in the process of investigation. It is also important to recognize that various aspects of the police investigative function, traditionally reserved for warranted detectives, are now being undertaken by civilians and private security staff (Rice 2016).

Criminal investigation is generally assumed to be a 'reactive' process, an *ex post facto* inquiry that is triggered by a member of the public reporting an incident to the police and is closed when the case is solved and the suspect convicted of the offence that was being investigated. Whilst it is certainly easy to find examples that follow this pattern, Maguire (2008: 435) argues that it gives a 'highly misleading impression' of police investigations. For one thing, detectives employed in specialist squads that deal with particular types of crime often take a 'proactive' approach to their work by initiating investigations from within the police organization in response to 'intelligence' suggesting that an individual or group is criminally active. Such investigations tend to commence before the criminal act that becomes the focus of the prosecution is committed and can take place almost entirely independent of any public input. This kind of detective work usually relies on the use of informants, covert surveillance, and deceptive tactics. Having examined the work of investigation as performed in the Federal Bureau of Investigation and the Drug Enforcement Administration, Wilson (1978: 22) draws a useful distinction between 'investigation' and 'instigation' when referring to operations that encourage the commission of a crime in which the suspect will participate whilst under observation: officers who assume the role of instigator provide 'an opportunity to commit a consensual crime for a person who is ready, willing, and seeking an opportunity to do so'.

Another significant challenge to the stereotypical image of criminal investigation came when academic inquiry into the day-to-day realities of investigative work revealed that most investigations are routinely centred more on suspects than on individual offences. Indeed, Greenwood et al. (1977) criticize detectives for their inability to solve crimes unless the public provide information of a suspect or lead. In their landmark socio-legal study *The Case for the Prosecution*, McConville et al. (1991) reach the controversial conclusion that most of the investigative work they examined effectively involved the monitoring of 'suspect populations'—principally 'known' criminals—with the purpose of implicating them or their associates in criminality and constructing a suitably strong case for their conviction. Far from being an objective fact-finding mission throughout which there is complete congruence between 'the law' and 'reality', the authors demonstrate how the practice of 'case construction' involves police and prosecutors in the manipulation of rules and the creation of evidence in order to 'achieve a particular objective through the use of *the legal form*' (p11). From a 'principles of justice' perspective, this approach to investigation is open to criticism because it starts from a premise of guilt and can result in investigators not pursuing all reasonable lines of inquiry or overlooking evidence that contradicts police knowledge of events. Combined with an emphasis on crime control values, it also encourages detectives to apply techniques that violate the rights of citizens, such as 'fishing expeditions', 'under the table' bargaining, and the extraction of 'false confessions' through oppressive questioning (Maguire 2008; Sanders et al. 2010).

Detective work is a case-focused enterprise in that efforts are organized and framed by the current caseload. Much of it 'is clerical or administrative' (Smith and Gray 1983: 40). For detectives, 'the case' is not just a named file folder but 'a concept, itself a social construction, constituted by tradition, by unspoken and tacit knowledge, and by organizational processes' (Manning 2007: 395). In view of the fact that performance is measured on the basis of what are known as 'clearance' rates, CID officers typically set aside cases that have little or no chance of being solved or otherwise cleared and take no further action unless other relevant information comes to their attention (Maguire and Norris 1992; Palmiotto 2013).[6] Even those that make the cut do not carry equal weight as,

---

[6] The clearance/clear-up rate 'shows the percentage of officially recorded crimes for which one or more people have been charged, summonsed, cautioned or otherwise dealt with on the basis of an admission or reasonable evidence that they were the perpetrator(s)' (Maguire 2008: 458).

culturally, a premium is placed on 'high profile' cases and convicting 'quality villains' as the appropriate objects of investigation. The building of detective reputations rests on making 'good collars' and working cases with 'flair'. For Manning (2004: 151), flair

refers to the ability of the officer to put together the elements of a case in an intellectual fashion, to anticipate the problems that might be involved, to check out and systematize what is known and what might be known about a person or target, to carry through the investigations and execute the closure that is appropriate to the case at a given point.

Collison (1995: 41) found that the 'big busts' and exemplary displays of detective craftsmanship were 'embellished and relished in the folklore of the squad as a symbolic representation' of what 'real' detective work was all about. Case knowledge is regarded as a personal resource, a kind of property that is not easily shared with others. The ability to possess and retain knowledge unknown to others represents the supreme affirmation of the detective craft. This cultural trait contributes to the secretive, suspicious, and somewhat uncooperative nature of their working environment, reflected in 'a general reluctance to share information, jealous guarding of the names of informants, and competition to take personal credit (or "glory") for high status arrests or clearances' (Maguire and Norris 1992: 20).

Drug Squads

Drug squads are specialist detective units assigned the task of investigating drug offences and gathering evidence to support the prosecution of the persons who perpetrate them. Generally speaking, the detectives employed therein are experts in the field of drug law enforcement and spend most of their workdays utilizing the art, craft, and science of criminal investigation to monitor drug markets and make cases against suspected drug dealers (EMCDDA 2013; Wright et al. 1993). All police officers have statutory and professional obligations when it comes to the policing of drugs, but only the drug detectives are licensed to deal with them on a more or less exclusive basis.[7]

---

[7] Of the possible words that could have been used, in the course of this monograph it will be demonstrated that 'licensed' best describes the nature of drug detective work. They are authorized to police the illegal drug business, given exceptional freedom with which to get the job done, and occasionally deviate from rule, custom, or fact for the sake of artistic or literary effect.

In the drug control field, the creation of the Metropolitan Police Drug Squad in 1954 marked the onset of drug law enforcement as an operational subdivision of the CID and a new policing specialism. It was justified on the back of evidence of new patterns of drug availability and signs of an emerging drug subculture in the West End of London. As half of the first full-time two-man drug squad in the North East of England, Young (1991: 86) recounts that he was 'tasked with defining and dealing with the new social aberration of "flower power", "the counter culture", and the "psychedelic trip" '. He describes how drug detectives became 'aberrant policemen' (p90) within the organization as they pushed the boundaries of traditional police work and adopted the appearance, language, and demeanour of the drug offenders they were policing. Pritchard and Laxton (1978) offer an account of the drugs scene in the 1970s through the eyes of an officer who worked as an undercover cop, in hippie gear, posing as a squatter, a demonstrator, and a 'junkie'. Commenting on his assignment, Pritchard writes: 'I had to do a lot of things I wasn't taught at police college. And often the rule book went out the window. In fact, there is only one rule: get on with the job' (p12). As drug problems worsened in the 1980s, an era when 'war on drugs' rhetoric was reverberating on both sides of the Atlantic, the enforcement approach came to dominate drug policy and resources were concentrated on measures directed at controlling supply. Although they differed significantly in terms of organization and operations, by the end of the decade all of the police forces in England and Wales had drugs squads in place (Collison 1995; Dorn et al. 1992; Maguire and Norris 1992; Wright et al. 1993). The European Monitoring Centre for Drugs and Drug Addiction (EMCDDA) (2013) estimated that units specializing in drug law enforcement represent about one per cent of all police staff in Europe and carry out the bulk of supply reduction activities.

The organization and responsibilities of specialist squads varies between police forces and develops over time as criminal offending patterns and social priorities change. Together with drug squads, forces might have units that specialize in the policing of art and antiques, e-crime, fraud, hate crime, kidnap, money laundering, organized crime and terrorism. And I could go on. Not only do these demarcated specialisms demonstrate how police organizations use their resources to respond to policing priorities, they are also a sign of the significance the police attach to labelling and territoriality. If the police have a 'drug squad' with the specific function of policing drugs, they can claim—both internally and externally—to be doing something about the drug problem, identify who is dealing with the problem and what they are doing. Over recent decades a shift has taken place away from the dominant 'generalist' CID officer to a model of increased specialization and division of labour (Chatterton 2008; Roberts and Innes 2009).[8] By and large, the main argument for the formation of specialist squads is that certain forms of criminality 'cannot be effectively dealt with by routine responses and hence require special measures' (Maguire 2008: 442).

Challenged by the financial reductions that police forces are having to make, however, Innes (2014a: 65) notes that 'this model is rapidly being reversed, with former specialisms and squads being reintegrated and absorbed into each other'. The past decade or so has seen a substantial decline in the number of drug squads operating at both force and district level (Bacon 2013a; Lister et al. 2008). Furthermore, having carried out a survey looking at the impact of public sector budget cuts and austerity measures from a police perspective, the UK Drug Policy Commission (UKDPC) (2011) found that drug-related policing expenditure and activity was expected to fare worse than other police activities. Covert surveillance, test purchase operations, and other intelligence gathering work related to the detection of drug supply were most often mentioned by police officers as likely to decrease. There was a real concern that if such activities are curtailed it could significantly impact on the ability of the police to monitor the drug problem in their area and restrict supply effectively.

For many types of crime, the police learn about and respond to violations of the criminal law when an aggrieved citizen reports a potential offence and requests legal action. This is rarely the case for drug offences because they typically take place in secret between consenting individuals and so there is no party to the act who has an interest in being the plaintiff. Of course, in a broad

---

[8] 'Reactive' or 'general office' CID officers investigate serious crimes at the local BCU level. Chatterton (2008: vi) notes that their work is 'the hardest to categorise because they have a fluid remit but in most areas they are responsible for investigating suspicious deaths, some types of murder, serious sexual assaults, other serious assaults, cash-in-transit robberies, large frauds, aggravated burglary, and arson'.

sense, many people are victims of drugs, in that they are directly affected by the adverse consequences of problematic drug use and the workings of the illegal drug business, but in the eyes of the law one cannot be the victim of a drug offence. A person can only be the direct victim of a drug-related crime and thereby an indirect victim of the production, supply, and use of controlled drugs. Skolnick (2011: 124) clearly demonstrates that crimes 'without citizen complainants result in a structure demanding independent action on the police officer's part and therefore emphasize the craftsmanlike possibilities of police work'. In the absence of direct victims and witnesses, Collison (1995: 35) argues, 'the drug police drum up their own business and do so according to occupational, organizational, legal, and sometimes personal, imperatives and meanings—a process from which the public are largely excluded'. What this means in practice is that drug detective work is a highly discretionary form of policing; the conduct of drug investigations is largely dependent on the decisions and resources of the investigating officers.

The somewhat unusual nature of drug offences is precisely the reason that drug law enforcement has long been considered the epitome of the classic proactive or 'offender centred' approach to criminal investigation (Dorn et al. 1992; Maguire and Norris 1992). Most drug investigations are initiated from within the police organization in response to intelligence suggesting that an individual or group is involved in the illegal drug business in one way or another. Drug detectives spend much of their time trawling the streets for signs of drug market activity, 'wheeling and dealing' with informants and using covert and deceptive techniques in order to obtain information on possible operational 'targets'. When a target is selected they might proceed with the aim of preventing a drug offence from happening, but ordinarily their efforts are focused on catching a suspected dealer or dealing network in possession of a substantial quantity drugs, or engineering circumstances in which sufficient evidence can be gathered to implicate them in a specific offence for which they can be prosecuted. They might also seek to deprive dealers of their ill-gotten gains by carrying out financial investigations and seizing their assets.

Whilst there has been some relatively recent research on specific drug policing issues and evaluations of particular initiatives (e.g. Eastwood et al. 2013; Kennedy and Wong 2009; Lister et al. 2008), there are, to my knowledge, only three previous ethnographic studies of detectives specializing in drug law enforcement: Skolnick (1966/2011) studied vice control officers and other criminal law officials in a large city in California and a comparable one on the East Coast in the early 1960s; Manning (1980/2004) studied two police drug units located in a metropolitan area in the US in the spring of 1975; and Collison (1995) studied a force-level drug squad at work in a non-metropolitan area of middle England in 1990. These texts are invaluable to all those interested in the policing of drugs as they are the only in-depth, systematic, and theoretically informed analyses of the everyday realities of the drug war on the frontline, the conduct of drug investigations, and the occupational culture of the investigating officers.[9]

Skolnick's (2011) *Justice Without Trial* is a study in the sociology of law and one of the foundational classics of research on policing and the police. Despite its age, the issues of the rule of law in practice, the enduring dilemmas of policing in democratic society, the police officer's 'working personality', the patterns of drug law enforcement, and the quasi-corrupt relationship that develops between police and informants, which are all addressed in this book, remain at the core of police studies and important to public life. Skolnick's theoretical interest was in the rule of law in practice, so he decided to study the vice squad because their routine activities seemed to be central to an understanding of the police as legal actors and the tensions between law and order. His fieldwork shows that drug detective work 'is especially symbolic of an efficient professionalism to which trained and intelligent police aspire' (p105).

Narcotics officers must have a network of informers and know how to stay on good terms with them, while at the same time maintaining the strength of their bargaining position. At times, they must be able to pretend convincingly to be addicts. They must be inventive in circumventing search-and-seizure restrictions. They should have some knowledge of the various drugs in use and the legal consequences of their illegal use. Finally, they must be skilled interrogators (p108).

It also shows that norms located within police organizations are more powerful than statute books and court decisions in shaping

---

[9] Although other contributions fall short in these respects, useful information can also be found in Bowling (2010), Dorn et al. (1992), Maguire and Norris (1992), May et al. (2000), Punch (1979), Wilson (1978), Wright et al. (1993), and Young (1991).

police behaviour and that the working philosophy of the police has the end justifying the means. According to this philosophy, 'the demands of apprehension require violation of procedural rules in the name of the higher justification of reducing criminality' (p204).

In *The Narcs' Game*, Manning (2004: 24) is principally concerned with the 'natural order of control', by which he means 'the ways in which police organizations define the narcs' game, what games they play, and what the dynamics of these games are'. A key finding of the study is that drug law enforcement is constrained 'more by social, cultural and social-psychological matters of belief and practice than by the presence or absence of technical, technological, legal, or other sorts of resources' (p57). The drug units are shown to be characterized by flexible or contradictory rules and autonomous to the extent that members are distanced from the bureaucratic controls of the police organization.

Officers act without stated goals, explicit written policies, priorities, or objectives. Their policies are tacit, their operations are largely unexplicated in writing, and their activities are embedded in taken-for-granted assumptions about police work and drug enforcement. As a result, agents do not receive meaningful written guidance, and so they create and maintain latitude in defining, choosing, working, closing, and following up on cases (p89).

Manning concludes that enforcing laws 'against transactional crimes is futile, and enforcement activities do little but inflate police power, suggest to an ignorant public that something is being done, and perpetuate aspects of the police myth' (p261). The myth referred to here is our belief in the effectiveness of the police at drug control and crime control more generally. Whatever the rhetoric used to formulate intent, he continues, 'the actuality of the day-to-day work is that it is boring, unsystematic, catch-as-catch-can, and focused on obtaining immediate rewards and arresting low-level users' (pp265–6). In terms of recommendations, Manning suggests that specialized drug units be disbanded and drug enforcement thereafter carried out routinely by patrol and by detectives on a referral basis. Proactive investigations 'should be limited, selectively worked only on a closely supervised basis, and done in cooperation with other units' (p264).

In *Police, Drugs and Community*, Collison (1995) draws on rich ethnographic data to analyse the strategic, cultural, and political effects of drug policing and capture the lived reality of prohibition.

Whilst the drug detectives are shown to have much in common with their fellow CID officers, his study identifies them as an unconventional occupational group and accentuates the somewhat unconventional nature of their work. Furthermore, the apprenticeship or craft form of the learning process for new recruits to the drug squad and the implications arising from teamwork 'serves to reproduce a particular mode of working, or viewing the (drug) world, of relating to the wider organization' (p103). Drug squad work is portrayed as an internally driven entrepreneurial activity conducted in conditions of very low visibility. The detectives recognized that it was practically impossible for them to eradicate the drug market and so viewed their task as 'keeping the lid on' the local drug problem. They had a 'prevailing operational and practical sense of a normal and orderly market over which they could stamp their authority' (p169). Collison argues, however, that the approaches to drug law enforcement he observed merely net the 'little people' of the drug game and endemically produce and reproduce failure, meanwhile realizing undesirable forms of policing in a democratic society that 'can alienate communities and further close off sources of valuable knowledge and legitimating support' (p229).

Conclusion

The brief depiction of detective work and drug law enforcement presented in this chapter can be criticized for being antiquated and perhaps lacking in contemporary relevance as it relies almost exclusively on empirical studies that relate to past policing contexts and police organizations that no longer exist in exactly the same form or function in exactly the same way. Researchers have documented an influx of legislative and policy initiatives, organizational reforms, and shifts in thinking about the values, objectives and norms of policing over recent decades, which, between them, have contributed to some significant changes in the ways that detectives are trained and investigations are controlled and carried out.

During the last quarter of a century, 'the legal framework of criminal investigation has changed beyond recognition and now encompasses a range of legislation which must be mastered by investigators if they are to carry out their role effectively within the law' (Stelfox 2009: 2). Perhaps the foremost example of legislative change is the Regulation of Investigatory Powers Act 2000 (RIPA), which established a framework for regulating the powers of public bodies to carry out surveillance and covert investigations. As a consequence of RIPA, there is now guidance about the conditions under which covert methods are justifiable, the kinds of limits that should be imposed and the most effective ways of preventing their abuse by the police (Clark 2007; Harfield and Harfield 2012; Loftus and Goold 2012; Loftus et al. 2015). Scientific advances in investigative practice have been equally influential and mean that detectives must have a far broader knowledge of the techniques of investigation than was previously required. Bayley (2002) argues that the use of science in the context of DNA evidence has initiated a shift away from a 'suspect-centred' approach towards an 'evidence-centred' one. Efforts have been directed for some time at developing police 'professionalism', based on a more scientific approach to policing practice, which Tong (2009: 10) suggests 'removes some of the mythical and cultural barriers to learning and practising detective work'. Another noteworthy development has been the widespread advocacy and adoption of 'proactive' styles of policing and the expansion of intelligence beyond the remit of specialist detective units into mainstream policing (Maguire 2000; Ratcliffe 2008). In Britain, intelligence-led policing 'seems to have reached its apotheosis' with the implementation of the National Intelligence Model (NIM) (James 2013: 1).

What is unclear at present is how changes to the field of criminal investigation have affected the routine activities of officers working at the operational level of policing. Recent developments seem to be posing a serious challenge to the 'old regime' (Tong and Bowling 2006), but unless researchers are prepared to spend dedicated periods observing the norms and craft of investigation we cannot find out how reforms are implemented or play out in the station or on the streets. Police studies have repeatedly shown that reforms have habitually failed to override the cultural ways and means of the rank-and-file when they conflict with accepted wisdoms. Changes to the status quo are resisted when they challenge existing worldviews, require officers to break from established routines, and do not accord with their intuitive common sense (Chan 1997; Loftus 2009; Skogan 2008). James (2013), for example, in the first comprehensive analysis of the NIM, demonstrates that it has not affected police practice in any meaningful way on account of pervasive cultural resistance and failings in the pre-existing intelligence architecture. The early findings of Loftus et al.'s (2010) ethnographic study of covert policing suggest that RIPA has had a negative effect on operational efficiency and has been poorly received by officers engaged in surveillance operations, it being tellingly described to the researchers 'as the "cancer" of the covert world and, more humorously, as the "Grim RIPA" ' (p4).

It is evident that in order to understand the realities of policing we must go beyond the formal rules of the game and explore the environment in which it is carried out. The construction of police identities, roles, and responsibilities is significantly shaped by the social context from which they arise. In times of change, an understanding of the occupational culture is even more vital than usual, for there is a need to know how things are perceived and put into practice on the frontline if we are to see the direction in which they are going or could potentially go. Ethnographic accounts of the police are crucial to examining whether or not cultural change has taken place in police organizations. There is, then, a pressing need to revisit the policing of drugs from inside the specialist detective units assigned to the task of monitoring drug markets and making cases against suspected drug dealers.

2

Policing the 'Drug Problem'

Today's target was a black male in his late-teens. He lived on a 'problem' estate, was affiliated with some of the local gang members, and had previous convictions for drugs and violence. In other words, he was 'the usual suspect'. Intelligence suggested that he was a low-level crack dealer, who had fallen out with a rival dealer from another neighbourhood for unknown reasons. Two nights ago he had been seen by a source outside the local community centre talking big and brandishing a gun. The plan was to execute a forced-entry warrant, search his home, and find the gun. Everyone appeared to know the drill.

We pulled up round the corner from the block of flats where the suspect resided and quietly entered through the communal door. One of the detectives had contacted the housing association and arranged for it to be left unlocked. Having already seen a plan of the building, the first-through-the-door detectives ran straight upstairs and had the suspect lying face down in handcuffs in a matter of seconds. 'I ain't done nuffin'. Why ain't you listenin' to me? I'm telling ya, this is a set up!' The premises were searched, as an edited version of the situation was related to the suspect. 'I ain't done nuffin'!' A small bag of cannabis and a few rocks of crack were found in a matter of minutes, but no firearm. 'I ain't saying shit.' The officers did not seem at all surprised by this outcome; it was expected. It was 'the usual scenario'.

'What have I just witnessed?' Was this usual scenario replayed over and over on a continuous loop? Or was it a mere snippet of the long running drug control drama series? More importantly, what had I not witnessed? What was behind the intelligence, the decision-making, the methods . . . and the madness?

(Fieldnotes, Metropolis)

Whilst their contributions to cultural practices, social life, and spirituality should not be overlooked or undervalued (Escohotado 1999; Jay 2000; Klein 2008), certain drugs are widely acknowledged to be the direct and indirect cause and consequence of a great many 'problems' and are thereby regarded as a threat to society and the security of citizens.[1] Over the years, some drugs have been cast as a plague of epidemic proportions, a perfect scapegoat, and a multifarious enemy against which social campaigners and states can fight 'wars'. 'Drug' is a loaded word, one which conjures up images of danger, death, and destruction from 'dope fiend' mythology and triggers emotional reactions from parents, politicians, and the press. Gossop (2007: 1) rightly observes that the notion of 'drug taking' is 'surrounded by all manner of sinister implications which reinforce the view that the use of drugs is a strange, deviant and inexplicable form of behaviour'. Taking a similar point of view, South (1999: 9) suggests that drug users 'are seen to have placed themselves "outside" normal cultures and controls' because illegal drugs are 'exceptions to the norm of acceptable intoxicants'. They are customarily labelled as 'outsiders', abject individuals who celebrate the values of self-indulgence, their drug use emblematic of their failure to engage properly with conventional society, a deviation that must be outlawed and punished if social order is to be maintained. Those who deal in drugs are even more severely reviled and reprimanded. Many of the 'usual suspects' find themselves caught in the crosshairs for being involved in the illegal drug business in one way or another. 'Mr Bigs', drug cartels, and violent street gangs are stereotypical 'bad guys' within the popular imagination, the people who need to be rooted out and brought to justice by the police and other enforcement agencies— the infallible 'good guys'.

---

[1] Strictly speaking, a drug is any chemical compound that comes from outside the body and has an effect similar to our natural neurotransmitters, yet the contemporary usage of the term refers most often to medicinal products and illegal substances taken for recreational purposes. 'Illegal' drugs are also commonly referred to as 'illicit' or 'controlled' drugs. The term 'illegal drug', however, can be misleading, as it is the way drugs are produced, supplied, and possessed, rather than the drugs themselves, that may be illegal. Some commentators prefer the term 'illicit drug' because the substances can be described as 'illicit' when they are produced, supplied, or possessed against national or international laws. A 'controlled drug' is simply a drug that is controlled under legislation.

Raids, stop and searches, high visibility patrols, and undercover operations are everyday manifestations of drug law enforcement. The police use these tactics, and many others, across the towns and cities of this country and the next because they are key actors in the drama of drug control. Their role in this grand production is to enforce order and manage expectations in relation to the policing of drug problems in a way that reflects the unfolding dynamics of society (Collison 1995; Lee and South 2008; Manning 2004). This chapter considers the role of the police in drug control as background to the empirical study of the rationales, patterns, and priorities of specialist detective units assigned to the task of investigating drug offences and gathering evidence to support the prosecution of the persons who perpetrate them. It aims to establish the parameters of policing in the drugs field and build a theoretical foundation for explaining the policing of drugs and new directions in drug control policy and practice. By critically analysing the construction of specific drug problems over time, it also uncovers the logic behind some of the most pertinent governmental responses and questions whether they serve the needs of society or the interests of powerful groups.

Theorizing the Policing of Drugs

Drug control

The term 'drug control' is used here to refer to the social control of drugs. Broadly speaking, the concept of 'social control' is concerned with the processes that encourage or coerce people to comply with rules that maintain a sense of order and security in society (Cohen 1985; Innes 2003b). Such 'rules' include both those set by the state in order to govern individual or group behaviour and the basic values and norms of a given society or social group. Social control theories must also consider the justness of the order that a given system is capable of sustaining and the procedures appropriate for the achievement of such an order. For some, the problem with such a wide and capacious concept is that it tries to encompass everything that contributes to the reproduction of social order, which renders it too unwieldy and imprecise to be of any use, either as an explanatory or a normative tool. Others, myself included, think it is precisely this breadth which makes it an appropriate framework, as it heightens our awareness and understanding of the forms and functions of social control in diverse fields.

'Formal' means of control are generally determined by the state and organized around the enactment and enforcement of laws and regulations to govern conduct and structure responses to socially problematic behaviour. In relation to drugs, the idea of formal control relates to the international conventions and national legislation that prohibit or otherwise regulate the production, supply, and possession of certain drugs, the extensive range of programmes in different government sectors that are designed to deal with drug problems, and the agencies assigned to the task of enforcing drug laws and implementing drug policies. Different thinkers have conceived of different ways to understand the origins and subsequent history of drug control policy. There is, however, general agreement amongst researchers that the development of drug policy reveals how societies 'struggle with substances that can induce pleasure and aid the work of medicine, yet also cause enormous harm' (Babor et al. 2010: 3). The most instructive analyses explore how drug policy has been shaped and reshaped by the broader workings of the modern state and patterns of social change (Seddon 2010; Seddon et al. 2012; Shiner 2013).

A quick look at the formative years of drug control provides an insight into some of the key movers and shakers. In Britain, the first attempt to subject certain psychoactive substances to legal control was the 1868 Pharmacy Act, which gave medical professionals a monopoly over the distribution of 'poisons'. The move away from a market governed by principles of free enterprise was gradual and came about in part because of developments in the medical and pharmaceutical professions and society's increasing interest in public health reform. Early drug controls were also driven by morality and formed part of a broader disciplinary project. Power, politics, and trade have always been at the heart of drug control as well, even when policy discourses have emphasized other concerns, like health and morality. The processes of industrialization created influential groups of commercial and political elites who started to view the levels of intoxication amongst the working classes in urban areas as a social problem that posed a threat to Victorian society and the establishment of a stable capitalist order. Excessive drinking was 'incompatible with the more disciplined and regulated nature of a factory-based workforce' (Berridge 2005: 10). 'A drunken field hand was one thing', Courtwright (2001: 178–9) proclaims, 'a drunken railroad brakeman quite another. Whilst the consumption of drugs might keep workers on a treadmill, over time and in certain industrial contexts it rendered their labor worse than useless'. The discourse was much the same when the drug problem entered the international arena. Commenting on the origins of the global prohibition regime, Seddon (2013: 5) writes that the 'drivers for prohibition were complex and diverse but centred around the foreign policy and economic interests of certain powerful nations, most notably the US but also Britain and other Western European countries and, to a lesser extent, China'.[2]

'Informal' social controls, on the other hand, are embedded in the cultural fabric of societies and social groups—the shared knowledge, collective understandings, and established conventions that inform, shape, and hold to account the behaviour of individuals. Cultures and subcultures constrain us because we internalize their beliefs and values so that we can function as good citizens or as full participants. Berridge and Edwards (1981: 259), in their fascinating social history of opiate use in nineteenth-century England, describe the 'subtle and complex apparatus comprising a host of manners, conventions, traditions and folkways, with attendant systems of disapprobation for infringement of these rules and expectations, and approbation for their observation, which together will make known and felt what society expects of the individual in relation to opiate use or anything else'. Drug researchers have consistently found that the social setting in which drug use occurs and the learning processes regarding informal rules of use are among the main factors that induce control and the taking of precautionary measures (Becker 1963; Decorte 2000; Young 1971; Zinberg 1984).

---

[2] The origins of what we now describe as the 'global prohibition regime' can be traced back to a meeting in Shanghai in 1909, where delegates from thirteen countries gathered together to discuss the opium problem and the prospect of international control. A series of further gatherings culminated in the signing of the International Opium Convention in The Hague in 1912. The signatories committed themselves to regulating the international trade and enacting domestic laws designed to suppress the use of opium, morphine, and cocaine, agreeing that they should be restricted to medical and research purposes. For many, however, it was the passing of the United Nations Single Convention on Narcotic Drugs in 1961 that truly marked the onset of today's global prohibition regime with its distinctively criminalizing and punitive orientation. The present system of drug control is based upon a suite of UN treaties: the 1961 Single Convention on Narcotic Drugs, as amended by the 1972 Protocol, the 1971 Convention on Psychotropic Substances, and the 1988 Convention against Illicit Traffic in Narcotic Drugs and Psychotropic Substances (Bewley-Taylor 2012; McAllister 2000).

Viewed in this way, drug controls essentially set the legal and cultural boundaries for the socially acceptable use of drugs and thereby have a major impact upon who is labelled as criminal or deviant. Legitimacy theorists tell us that the authorities are most likely to secure voluntary compliance when formal controls accord with public values and reinforce their existing norms (Beetham 1991; Bottoms and Tankebe 2012). A significant challenge facing drug control in this respect is that public attitudes towards drug policy are far from straightforward. For instance, a recent survey of British adults revealed that just over half support the legal regulation or decriminalization of cannabis production, supply, and use. The majority still believe that the possession of illegal drugs as a whole should remain a criminal offence but are open to persuasion and debate (Ipsos MORI 2013). Another challenge is that drug policy appears to be somewhat out of step with lived realities. There is often conflict between the law and the disparate morals and customs of the many cultures and subcultures that coexist in complex societies. Behaviours that are criminal in a legal sense are not always perceived as deviant in a cultural sense and, therefore, some illegal acts are essentially nothing more than infractions of formal rules that have little or no support or relevance to everyday life. The 'normalization' thesis provides a striking example of this discordance and helps explain why some individuals and social groups choose to contravene formal means of drug control (Aldridge et al. 2011; Parker et al. 1998). In a nutshell, this body of literature describes the social changes of the postmodern era that have resulted in recreational drug use becoming an integral aspect of youth culture and to some extent accepted or tolerated by those who abstain. The implications of normalization for drug policy and the policing of drugs are monumental and have yet to be satisfactorily resolved.

Policing

'Policing' is another rather ambiguous term. Attempts to define it range from those that are coterminous with social control to those that focus only on the activities of the public police service. In an attempt to bring some clarity to the debate, Reiner (2010: 3–8) suggests that policing is best viewed as an aspect of formal social control processes which occurs universally and is expressly designed to enforce rules or otherwise maintain the security of social order through systems of surveillance and the threat of coercive sanction. A clear distinction is made here between policing and forms of control intended to produce the conditions of order, such as custom, education, family, and religion. Police scholars have also drawn attention to the symbolic dimension of policing and shown that what the police symbolize is as important as what they actually do. Policing, Manning (1997: 319) contends, 'is an exercise in symbolic demarking of what is immoral, wrong, and outside the boundaries of acceptable conduct. It represents the state, morality and standards of civility and decency by which we judge ourselves'.

Enforcing Order

There are sharply conflicting views between different groups of people about what the police should do and how they should do it. Even within small localities, a diverse range of views about policing can exist. In heterogeneous societies, which are increasingly differentiated in terms of ethnicity, age, culture, religion, social class, and sexuality, the possibilities for conflict over policing policy are increased. Patterns of policing may be based on a negotiated consensus of interests or be the result of conflict and reflect the norms and values of dominant social powers. What the following historical snapshots reveal is that the policing of drugs is ultimately about enforcing moral and social order and responding to public fear under conditions of risk and uncertainty. The specific whys and wherefores change with the zeitgeist but the overarching themes remain the same. In a penetrating analysis of drug control in the United States, Manning (2004: 254) forcefully contends that enforcement is 'a ceremony that celebrates the interests of the powerful segments of society and their views of appropriate levels and kinds of drug use, proper lifestyles and occupations, the correct place to live, and moral commitments'.

The birth of the British 'drug underground' during the Great War was a specific instance of cultural modernity. Kohn (1992: 4) argues that it disrupted several highly sensitive social boundaries under conditions of unprecedented national trauma and 'provided a way of speaking simultaneously about women, race, sex and the nation's place in the world'. An already perturbed public were given further cause for concern when stories of servicemen using cocaine and mixing with the West End underworld hit the press. At the time, the law was unclear on the nature of drug offences and designed 'to regulate shopkeepers rather than street hustlers' (p38). The London police were investigating the milieu of local criminals and undesirable 'foreigners' rumoured to be associated with the supply side of the market but were struggling to make cases that would stand up in court. When the prosecution of Willy Johnson failed, Sergeant Hedges reported that 'unless the existing regulations are supplemented, it is useless for Police to devote further time and attention' to policing drug dealers (p39). The case for new regulations was furthered by widespread concerns about bohemian lifestyles, sordid nightclubs, and xenophobic stories about men of other races using drugs as a means of seducing and enslaving young white women. Emergency measures, introduced with the passing of Regulation 40B of the Defence Against the Realm Act (DORA) on 28th July 1916, established the fundamental principle of prohibition and marked the beginning of the longstanding assumption that criminalization is the most effective way of dealing with drug problems. From then and throughout the 'Roaring Twenties' the social distribution and the policing of drugs were restricted to 'those who occupied marginal zones where ordinary conventions of morality and behaviour did not operate' (p40).

Things stayed much as they were, simmering away but not boiling over, until the social and political upheaval of the 1960s, an era when concerns about new and increasing forms of drug use led to a much greater emphasis on the role of the police and the criminal justice system. The abuse of the prescription system by doctors and certified addicts fed illegal markets in heroin and cocaine and caused alarm in policy circles. According to Young (1971), the new generation of addicts refused to conform to the 'sick role' that was reserved for them and often recommended and actively spread heroin use to others. As conventional society became increasingly hostile to the spirit of permissiveness and unearned pleasures, the state started to regard drugs as a threat to the ideologies of capitalism and the driving force behind the abandonment of moral principle and social obligation. Drug laws were enforced more vigorously. Drug squads started to appear in police forces across the country as media and political uproar about the growth of recreational drug use amongst young people prompted moral panic and the need for a decisive response. It was also thought that the organization of drug markets required a greater degree of police cooperation and centralization. In 1964, Regional Crime Squads (RCSs) covering nine regions were established as a response to concerns about organized crime and criminality being committed across force boundaries. The local police 'were seen as ill-placed to react to such crime not only because of their geographical limits but also because new degrees of seriousness and sophistication were becoming evident' (Lee and South 2008: 501). With the passing of the 1971 Misuse of Drugs Act, the government firmly rejected the calls of the 'legalization lobby'. It also rejected the argument made by the Advisory Committee on Drug Dependency in the *Wootton Report* that the moderate use of cannabis has no harmful effects in terms of health or the commission of crime and so possession of a small amount should not normally be regarded as a serious crime to be punished by imprisonment.[3]

Policing Beyond the Police

Conceived as a broad type of activity, policing is something that is authorized and delivered by a diverse array of public, private, and voluntary agencies. Indeed, it is now commonplace in academic and policy discourse to remark that policing is not synonymous with police work and that a great many individuals and organizations besides the public police service are involved in the performance of policing. To stress this reconceptualization of policing and the growth of policing beyond the police, commentators have coined new expressions such as the 'extended police family', 'plural policing', and 'security governance' (Crawford 2008; Johnston and Shearing 2003; Jones and Newburn 2006). This is a key concept to grasp when considering the role of the police in drug control because multiple agencies are involved in the policing of the drug problem. The Conservative government certainly seemed to have grasped it when they established Drug Action Teams (DATs) to coordinate local initiatives and set up partnerships to tackle local problems in their national drug strategy, *Tackling Drugs Together*

---

[3] The 1971 Misuse of Drugs Act remains the main basis of contemporary British drugs law. Under the Act, controlled drugs have both a 'Class', which determines the penalties for possession and supply, and a 'Schedule', which determines how they are regulated for medical or research purposes. The 'ABC' classification system is intended to reflect the perceived harmfulness associated with use and ensure that the severity of the punishment is proportionate to the perceived wrongdoing.

(HM Government 1995).[4] Every government strategy document and many legislative measures since have given further impetus to the police working in partnership with local authorities and engaging local communities.

Let us briefly consider the policing of the night-time economy as a case in point. For those who endeavour to police the zones in urban centres where licensed premises are densely concentrated and intoxication is the norm, their arduous task is to police drugs whilst, at the same time, respond to high levels of violence, criminal damage, and antisocial behaviour and maintain the ordered disorder of a time and place that is by its very nature out of control. There has been a significant restructuring of the organization and delivery of policing in this context following the deregulation of licensing laws and the development of partnership arrangements between key stakeholders. These stakeholders include the police, the local authorities, the licensing trade, security companies, health trusts, and resident groups. Partnership activity can take the form of anything from agreements to 'responsibilize' drinks promotions to the establishment of 'Pubwatch forums' (Hadfield 2006; Hadfield et al. 2009). Owners of licensed premises are legally required to put in place their own security measures. According to Hobbs et al. (2003: 11), the bouncers employed to work the doors 'perform an essential function in an environment that craves a very specific, malleable, and commercially functional form of social control. If their muscular presence were suddenly removed, the state police would not fill the void'. Licences ordinarily require premises to operate a zero-tolerance drug policy and often stipulate that a safe or 'drug box' be installed to store any seized drugs until they are handed over to the police. Non-compliance can lead to the revocation of the licence and the closure of the premises. Police licensing officers manage crime and disorder problems with licensed premises and, in so doing, represent 'the order

---

[4] The overall structures and goals of drug policy across the UK are guided by drug strategies, which are intended to coordinate the work of different government departments. The first comprehensive strategy was published in 1995, and between then and 2002, leadership and coordination was handled through the Cabinet Office. Since 2002, national drug strategies have been coordinated and led by the Home Office, with many local health and preventative responsibilities transferred to the devolved administrations.

maintenance interests of the state in every-night regulation of the business community' (Hadfield 2006: 165).

At a stretch, these new understandings of what policing is also cover much of the drug control work of the medical profession and a number of welfare agencies. In an interesting take on the subject, Barton (2011: 42–58) suggests that viewing medicine as an aspect of social control may allow us to look beyond medical involvement with problematic drug users from the simplistic 'treatment' model perspective and ask questions about the social, moral, and political functions performed by health care professionals in drug treatment settings. The power to prescribe substitute drugs is said to be at the heart of the medical profession's 'policing policy' in relation to drug control. Doctors are able to employ their right to withdraw prescriptions as a form of 'carrot and stick' to encourage their patients to comply with the agreed treatment plan and conform to their conception of a 'good' patient.

The Police

Police constabularies, forces, or services are specialist organizations employed by the state to keep the peace, secure the safety of the public, and act as gatekeepers to the criminal justice system. The police are only one component of the policing web; they do not monopolize the occupation of policing, nor are they the primary means of controlling levels of crime and disorder. But they do tend to be the only service agency available to respond to those in need when 'something-is-happening-that-ought-not-to-be-happening-and-about-which-someone-had-better-do-something-now' (Bittner 1990: 355). Generally speaking, members of the public call on the police in emergency situations because they alone have the capacity to wield legal powers and ultimately use legitimate force in a largely unrestricted range of circumstances.

The police are also unique in that they are considered something of a sacred organization and represent the visible face of the state, morality, and justice to the citizen. An important strand of the sociology of policing has shown that what the police symbolize is perhaps as important as what they actually do (Innes 2014b; Loader and Mulcahy 2003; Manning 1997). Through their actions and processes of communication, the police send tacit and explicit messages to a number of audiences about the nature of social relations and the quality of governance which serve to shape a sense of order and security. For example, by dealing with even minor offences in a standardized way, the police communicate to society and potential offenders that a public space is being effectively monitored and that the authorities do have the capacity and will to enforce the law. Drug dealing in deprived communities hinders their regeneration, saps community confidence, and damages the reputation of the area. Local residents may be reassured by seeing the police take visible action against drug dealers and this may have benefits in improving quality of life (Lupton et al. 2002; May et al. 2005). A policy of differentiating between offences and responding in a discretionary manner, on the other hand, can produce highly unequal outcomes, encourage the spread of anti-social behaviour, and undermine the internalization of the principles and values of the rule of law. These messages set the margins of morality by separating 'right' from 'wrong' and can thereby have a significant impact upon what behaviours are perceived as being endorsed or at least tolerated by the institutions of social control. When, for example, Mike Barton (2013), the Chief Constable of Durham Constabulary, called for an end to the 'war on drugs' in an article he penned for *The Guardian*, the lead on drug policy for the Association of Chief Police Officers (ACPO) warned him to be careful about the message on drugs that was being conveyed to the public.[5] 'We need in particular to be very thoughtful about setting clear boundaries,' said Chief Constable Andy Bliss, 'especially for young people, in relation to drugs, their misuse and criminal activity surrounding them' (Laville and McDonald 2013).

The ways in which 'control signals' are seen and interpreted depends, in part, upon how citizens think, feel, and act in relation to the police and other institutions of social control more generally (Innes 2014b). Academic research into legitimacy and 'good' policing in recent years has established that the police can strengthen people's sense of belonging to society and their normative commitment to formal controls by acting in accordance with principles of procedural justice and by wielding their power in a fair manner (Bottoms and Tankebe 2012; Bradford et al. 2014; Jackson et al. 2012). Interventions that are not seen as legitimate are likely to increase tensions between police and citizens and reduce community engagement and the flow of intelligence. The police face an uphill

[5] ACPO was replaced in 2015 by the National Police Chiefs' Council.

struggle in this respect when it comes to the policing of drugs because the laws they are enforcing are seen by many as being fundamentally unjust. Husak (1992) skilfully blends legal philosophy with empirical social science in order to demonstrate that prohibition violates the moral rights of adults who want to use drugs for pleasure. Furthermore, in his case for decriminalizing drugs, he argues that 'the general difficulty with thinking that punishment is justified in order to protect children, reduce crime, improve health, or prevent immorality is that these strategies are *overinclusive*', as the majority of drug users do not cause apparent harm to themselves or others (Husak 2002: 123). The police could counterbalance this injustice by exercising discretion and ensuring that the impositions of policing are equitably distributed across individuals and social groups. In a startling report that charts the disproportionate impact of drug law enforcement on minority communities in England and Wales, however, Eastwood et al. (2013) put forward the case that the racial disparity that exists in the policing of drugs is unjust. People from black and minority ethnic groups are overrepresented from initial point of contact through to sentencing. The authors submit that the 'benefits of reducing, or ending, stop and searches for drug possession could have a positive impact on both policing and on communities who are affected by high levels of over policing' (p49).

An early observation that strikes any researcher studying the police operating in the field is the overwhelming variety of activities that seem to fall within their mandate. Contemporary police work involves law enforcement, crime fighting, criminal investigation, public order policing, traffic control, improving feelings of safety, and so on. Given the great breadth of activities they perform, the police should not be thought of primarily as a means of crime control with the primary function of enforcing the criminal law. Police research has demonstrated across decades and jurisdictions that a minority of calls to the police for service concern crime and that most police time is spent on non-crime-related matters (Brodeur 2010: 150–64; Reiner 2010: 141–47). For Reiner (2010: 144), the core policing task is 'order maintenance', which he defines as the settlement of minor conflicts by means other than formal law enforcement. The 'craft of effective policing is to use the background possibility of legitimate coercion so skilfully that it never needs to be foreground'. This notion harks back to the classic work of Banton (1964) and his distinction between 'law officers' and 'peace officers'. When walking the beat many of the patrol officers he studied would act in accordance more with the norms and values of the policed community than the rule of law and exercise discretion in order to maintain order without recourse to legal sanction. A key idea guiding this book is that the same logic can be applied to the policing of drugs and that drug laws should only be enforced when drug offenders become 'out of order' and beyond less formal mechanisms of control.

What studies of policing on the streets have shown us is that the law is often used as a resource that can be enforced as a means of promoting order rather than a rule that must be mechanistically applied in all crime and disorder situations. In their study of enforcing order in Australia's principal heroin market, Maher and Dixon (1999: 492) show that drug laws constitute such a resource, 'providing uniformed officers with authority to intervene to disrupt drug markets and harass participants, and with opportunities to make self-initiated arrests'. They argue for a shift in policing priorities towards public health and community safety and reject suggestions that the law constrains the ability of police to subordinate enforcement to other objectives. Officers should and often do take informal action or 'turn a blind eye' when dealing with minor offences if strict enforcement is deemed unnecessary or would have harsh and counterproductive results. The majority of the patrol officers interviewed by Warburton et al. (2005: 118) said they did not always make arrests for possession of cannabis for reasons including 'the harms associated with a criminal record, the demeanour of the suspect and the time and effort spent making an arrest'. In the vast majority of minor drug offences that are committed, the criminal record is likely to cause more harm to the person than their drug use by having a negative impact on an individual's future employment, education, and ability to travel.

For the last three decades or so the overall policy trend regarding cannabis possession and minor cases involving cultivation and importation has become increasingly relaxed (Monaghan and Bewley-Taylor 2013). Since 2004, the risk of arrest for adult offenders has been markedly reduced following the introduction of the non-statutory 'Cannabis Warning' scheme and, in January 2009, the inclusion of the offence of cannabis possession in the 'Penalty Notice for Disorder' (PND) scheme. These are both discretionary forms of pre-arrest diversion. In the wake of cannabis being reclassified from a Class C to a Class B drug, ACPO (2009) officially advised officers to take an 'escalation approach' to possession offences unless there are any 'aggravating factors' present. Such factors include smoking cannabis in a public place or view and being in possession of cannabis inside or in the vicinity of a premises frequented by young people. Briefly, according to this policy, an offender should be given a warning for a first offence, a fine for a second and only face arrest, and possible jail time for a third. Following the criminalization of khat on 24 June 2014, the police were told to take a similar 'softly softly' approach to enforcing the new law. ACPO (2014: 5) guidelines state that it is important that officers retain their operational discretion, 'taking into account that khat has historically not been a controlled drug and was part of the culture for certain communities linked to The Horn of Africa'.

The War on Drugs

The so-called 'war on drugs' has dominated conceptions of drug control for decades and is central to any discussion on the policing of the drug problem. Most people would agree that the drug war should not be thought of as a war in a literal sense. To be sure, it is certainly not recognized as such by international law or governed by the Geneva Conventions. The war on drugs is a demonizing rhetorical strategy in the social campaign against certain people who use certain drugs that is designed to elicit support for repressive drug prohibition policies. Manning (2004: 13) views it as 'media resonating, and a simple and powerful morality play, a spectacle featuring notions of good and evil'. 'War' metaphors and propaganda have a dramatic appeal that plays on respectable fears, captures conservative sentiment, and mobilizes collective action. They can turn police officers into 'warriors' and the people who breach drug laws into police property and 'enemies' of the state and civil society. O'Malley and Valverde (2004: 35) suggest that the war on drugs 'has valorized the category of "drug abuse" to restore the notion of moral culpability that was at risk in discourses of addiction', thus making drug users responsible and therefore liable and punishable for their immoral and criminal activities. Drug war discourse is a means through which power and ideologies are socially constructed. Describing the policy of drug prohibition as a war invokes a state of emergency and has provided governments with a basis for asserting a range of 'wartime privileges'. War justifies the need to go beyond existing legal frameworks in the interests of security and legitimizes the use of measures that would have been deemed unjust or, at least, highly controversial in peacetime. 'Good' military strategy usually involves the decisive use of overwhelming force, whereas 'good' policing limits the use of force to a minimum. In times of war, the enforcement of order takes priority over concerns about injustice exercised by Leviathan.

The 'war on drugs' is also 'a convenient way of referring to the prevailing set of policies emphasising enforcement' (Caulkins et al. 2005: 3). Drug law enforcement has traditionally focused on reducing the size of illegal drug markets by seeking to eradicate or significantly reduce the production, supply, and use of drugs through arrests and seizures. The overarching logic of this approach is that reducing the scale of the market will reduce the problems associated with it. To make it more costly and inconvenient to acquire drugs, enforcement agencies have employed local, national and international interventions that range from eradication of crops like coca in source countries, through interdiction of traffickers at the border and in transit zones, to incarceration of domestic suppliers and disruption of retail markets. Yet, at the same time as pursuing an enforcement agenda, policymakers and practitioners have also sought to reduce both the demand for, and the harmfulness of, drug use through treatment services and the provision of education. 'War', therefore, is not an entirely apt metaphor as drug control policies contain a mix of 'warlike' and 'non-warlike' activities.

The seeds of war were planted when certain psychoactive substances were first prohibited by the international community in the early twentieth century. The outbreak of war, however, came in June 1971, when President Richard Nixon formally declared 'war on drugs' and denounced drug abuse as 'public enemy number one' following a campaign to implement a national anti-drug strategy at state and federal levels. In a historical analysis of prohibitions in the United States, Woodiwiss (1988: 170) presents damning evidence to suggest that the administration inflated the drug problem, blamed crime on drugs, and then gave the impression of firm executive action in order to deliver on its promises to restore law and order and win re-election. Drugs, in other words, became an issue through which politicians could demonstrate their commitment to morality and 'tough on crime' policy and practice.

Across the Atlantic, it was during the 1980s that the UK government began to employ war metaphors and 'fighting talk' to describe and legitimize a more punitive approach to the drug problem. The problem had transformed in scale, extent and nature, thanks largely to the increased availability of cheap heroin from Afghanistan, Iran, and Pakistan in areas of northern England and Scotland that had no previous history of heroin markets. In contrast to their predecessors, the new heroin users were mainly young and unemployed and came from the most deprived housing estates and neighbourhoods, often supporting their new habits through acquisitive crime and drug dealing (Dorn and South 1987; Pearson 1987). The heroin 'epidemic' quickly came to be seen as a major social problem at a national level. In May 1985, the House of Commons all-party Home Affairs Committee issued a report based partly on the lessons they had learned from a 'fact-finding' trip to the US, which was accompanied by a barrage of rhetoric that was remarkably close to that of American anti-drugs crusaders (Woodiwiss and Hobbs 2009: 119). Later that year, Prime Minister Margaret Thatcher visited the customs area at Heathrow airport and publicly warned drug traffickers that '[w]e are after you. The pursuit will be relentless. We shall make your life not worth living' (Woodiwiss 1988: 222). True to her word, the government came down hard on the people responsible for the importation and domestic supply of drugs, pumped exorbitant amounts of money into the enforcement effort, and gave policing agencies new and far-reaching powers. The 1985 Controlled Drugs (Penalties) Act, for example, increased the maximum terms of imprisonment for drug trafficking, with a life sentence being made a potential punishment for Class A drug supply. The National Drug Intelligence Unit (NDIU) was established in the same year as a joint police and Customs intelligence service, and specialist operational 'drug wings' were added to the Regional Crime Squads following the adoption of the structural and operational model for tackling drug distribution as set out in the 'Broome Report' (ACPO 1985). Asset confiscation was brought in by the 1986 Drug Trafficking Offences Act, giving the police the power to trace and seize the assets of persons found guilty of an offence that are suspected or shown to be derived from crime and shifting the burden of proof from the prosecution to the defence.

In the 1990s, the drug situation in Britain underwent further significant changes. New outbreaks of heroin further spread its geographical reach across the country, while crack cocaine started to enter into the repertoire of some drug users. But perhaps the most significant transformation occurred in the area of the everyday experiences and encounters of young people with drugs. The Tory government witnessed the 'normalization' of recreational drug use, the rise of 'rave' culture and the associated moral panic over ecstasy (Collin 1997; Redhead 1993). By the summer of 1988 raves were regular events in urban and rural areas and attracting attention from politicians and the police. Tabloid reports condemned acid house as a front for drug distribution and the 'stiffest penalties' were justified for 'those responsible for this gigantic exercise of hooking our youth on drugs' (Collin 1997: 97). The Entertainment (Increased Penalties) Act 1990 brought in fines of up to £20,000 for the organisers of unlicensed events and thereby pushed event organization into the hands of large commercial promoters with the money required to pay for licences and policing. It became illegal to hold, wait for, or attend a rave with the passing of the 1994 Criminal Justice and Public Order Act. As unlicensed events were being legally suppressed, the leisure and alcohol industries were attempting to hijack the various dance scenes that grew out of rave culture and situate them within licensed premises. Rather than removing drugs from the equation, they became 'a central dynamic of the contemporary night-time economy with cultural products being moulded to complement their use, and the commercial viability of some dance-oriented venues being dependent upon their chemically induced ambiance' (Hobbs et al. 2003: 227). The official 'no drugs will be tolerated' stance in such venues is invariably a façade that remains intact because the proceeds are 'channelled into the pockets of corporate investors and used to drive the economic renaissance of post-industrial cities' (Hadfield 2006: 60). This clearly indicates once again that the prospect of amalgamation and capital can be just as important as concerns over health, morality and social order in driving the drug control agenda.

New Labour largely continued where the Conservatives had left off. Throughout his term in office, Tony Blair became closely involved in drug policy, repeatedly argued that a war on drugs was needed to protect society, and littered his speeches with the usual warmongering rhetoric (e.g. 'threat', 'menace', and 'scourge') (Buchanan 2010; Stimson 2000). The Government's promise to tackle drugs and get tough on the causes of crime also led to the development of a new infrastructure of drug treatment embedded within the criminal justice system (Seddon et al. 2008, 2012). Following the piloting of drug testing in police custody suites and within certain parts of probation work, a pivotal moment in the so-called 'criminalization of drug policy' was the introduction of the Drug Interventions Programme (DIP), which aimed to bring together the range of drug interventions that had been accumulating up to that point in a relatively piecemeal fashion and to provide more coordinated and joined-up provision to drug using offenders. The more punitive and coercive elements of the programme were extended through the 'Tough Choices' initiative. Under the 2005 Drugs Act, the police are empowered to impose drug testing on arrest for detainees who are arrested in relation to 'trigger offences' and direct those who test positive for opiates and/or cocaine to have an assessment with a drugs worker.[6]

The Post-War Era

Many policymakers, policing practitioners, and members of the public view blanket prohibition as a functional prerequisite of social order and the only workable policy option. For those who hold this view, the war on drugs approach to drug control–the draconian laws, snowballing arrest rates and mass incarceration of drug offenders–is justified in order to protect children, reduce crime, improve health, and prevent immorality. McKeganey (2011: 90–1) argues that without robust enforcement the drug trade 'will flourish and may in time acquire such acceptance, and such financial resources, that it shifts beyond the regulatory power of the state'. Others would argue that such views are based on a myth because drug control is and always has been 'beyond the state' (Garland 2001: 123).

Yet, if the purpose of prohibition is to stifle the production, supply, and use of those substances deemed to be 'dangerous', close down the illegal drug business, and ultimately create a 'drug-free society', most reasonable people would concede that it has not only failed but cannot succeed. In fact, there is evidence that increases in expenditure have actually been associated with rising consumption and declining prices, the precise opposite of what would be

---

[6] The list of 'trigger offences' was initially set out in the Criminal Justice and Court Services Act 2000 but has since been amended and added to by subsequent legislation. Broadly speaking, they include the types of acquisitive crime that are believed to be connected to problematic drug use (e.g. drug supply, theft, robbery, and burglary).

expected if tough 'law and order' interventions were being at all effective as a market reduction instrument. Drug markets have proven to be resilient and adaptable to actions taken by the authorities. Over the years, enforcement agencies have suppressed the 'low-hanging fruit' and achieved some remarkable operational successes against 'Mr Bigs', organized crime networks and violent street gangs, making many arrests and seizing tons of drugs, but, despite this, drug problems persist and continue to worsen. The available evidence suggests that, whilst enforcement can have a marginal impact on local markets and change the conditions confronting buyers and sellers, it cannot cut the steady flow of supply to the streets or reduce the prevalence of drug use in the community. It also suggests that higher levels of enforcement produce diminished returns and that any benefits tend to be short-lived and disappear once an intervention is removed or ceases to operate (Mazerolle et al. 2007; McSweeney et al. 2008; Reuter and Stevens 2007; UKDPC 2009).

Another strong criticism of the war on drugs is that it actually causes a range of significant harms in its own right. Whilst it can be difficult 'to disentangle the harmful effects of drug use from the deleterious consequences of drug control' (Stevens 2011: 5), the damaging impact of prohibition on aspects of crime, security, civil liberties, human rights, public health, and social inequality has been extensively documented (Kerr et al. 2005; Rolles et al. 2012; Werb et al. 2011; Wood et al. 2009). These costs result not from drug use itself, but from 'a punitive enforcement-led approach that, by its nature, places control of the trade in the hands of organised crime, and criminalises many users' (Rolles et al. 2012: 5). Enforcement can, for example, lead to violence as displaced dealers clash with established ones or subordinates and competitors fight over who will fill the gap that has been left in the market. Enforcement activity has also been shown to have a negative impact on public health by encouraging users to adopt risky practices in storing, transferring, and administering their drugs in order to avoid detection and deterring them from visiting drug treatment services for the very same reason. Despite acknowledging these problems, however, there has been no systematic evaluation of whether the intended consequences of prohibition outweigh the 'unintended consequences'. Led by the Transform Drug Policy Foundation, and supported by over a hundred NGOs and civil society groups, the Count the Costs initiative (http://www.countthecosts.org) aims to fill this knowledge gap by reviewing the substantial body of research and scrutinizing the negative impacts of the drug war in seven key policy areas: undermining development and security and fuelling conflict; threatening public health and spreading disease and death; undermining human rights; promoting stigma and discrimination; creating crime and enriching criminals; deforestation and pollution; and wasting billions on ineffective law enforcement.

Drug war rhetoric has fallen out of favour in the political arena due to its increasingly obvious failures and there is now a growing consensus amongst governing elites that current approaches to drug control have been ineffective and actively counterproductive. A series of high-profile reports has pushed the reform agenda right to the forefront of public debate (Global Commission on Drug Policy 2011; Home Affairs Select Committee 2012; Home Office 2014). The case for reform has been articulated many times over the last few decades, but only recently have we started to see serving politicians and senior police officers stand up and tell the unpalatable and politically unpopular truth. Britain is losing the war on drugs 'on an industrial scale', former Deputy Prime Minister, Nick Clegg, claimed as he called for a reform of drug laws (Williams 2012). For the most part, according to Chief Constable Mike Barton (2013), 'politicians, professionals and the media collude in the fiction that we are winning the war on drugs, or if not, that we still have to fight in the same way'. He calls for a more honest debate and says that decriminalizing drugs would cut off the income stream of criminal gangs and help solve the worsening problems of addiction. Over the past decade, further weight has been added to the case for reform as 'a new wave of countries have moved toward the decriminalisation model, suggesting growing recognition of the failures of the criminalisation approach and a strengthening political wind blowing in the direction of an historic paradigm shift' (Rosmarin and Eastwood 2012: 11).

There is some evidence that drug law enforcement has been quietly moving towards a 'post-war era' for quite some time. Dorn and Lee (1999) show that a more practical and potentially achievable 'community damage limitation' approach is slowly but surely beginning to replace the 'heroic but politically risky "war" stance' (p97). Increasingly, they demonstrate, with particular reference to British localities, the national level, and the European Union, that the police are developing strategies in partnership with the most appropriate agencies, defining their mission in terms of being responsive to the needs of local communities, and scaling down expectations by redefining their aims and modifying the criteria by which success is judged. Having charted the impact of competing government agendas, Parker (2006: 38) similarly argues that the 'strategic changes and about-turns so evident in a decade of dealing with the country's drug problem are primarily a product of realisation. The war on drugs rhetoric and eradication targets are long gone as we have come to realise we can only manage UK drugs "around the edges" to reduce harm and contain problems'.

Against this backdrop of uncertainty, reform, and revolutionary rumblings, the concept of 'harm reduction' has moved to the foreground of drug control and some policing agencies appear to be choosing to rethink and redevelop their enforcement strategies and tactics to focus on managing drug markets in a way that minimizes the various associated harms (Caulkins and Reuter 2009; Felbab-Brown 2013; Stevens 2013; UKDPC 2009).[7] Harm reduction is a principle that has been widely accepted as an important pillar of the health policy response to drug use but has less frequently been applied to policing. The school of thought that underpins this movement advocates that the ultimate aim of drug control should be to reduce drug harms and that the wider purpose of drug policing should be to ensure the safety of the community by reducing harms to its members. According to Stevens (2013: 2), a harm reduction approach can be justified on both pragmatic and ethical grounds because it emphasizes a concern for 'what works' and reflects 'the emphasis of both international human rights treaties and rationalist morality on the legal and moral imperative for states to act in ways that support human rights'. In contrast to other policing strategies, the application of harm reduction principles to the policing of drugs is somewhat radical in that it attempts to tackle the inimical aspects of drug markets without necessarily requiring a reduction in the quantity of drugs being sold or used. To work effectively, such an approach requires the explicit recognition that drug laws are resources, discretionary powers that can be enforced as a means to an end rather than rules that must be enforced come

---

[7] The adverse consequences of drug use and distribution and the unintended consequences of prohibition are many and varied. For comprehensive lists of these drug-related harms see: Caulkins and Reuter (2009: 20); MacCoun and Reuter (2001: 106–7); UKDPC (2009: 44).

what may. 'For enforcement to suppress a particularly noxious part of the market', Caulkins and Reuter (2009: 16) submit that 'it is not necessary to make the submarket or that selling practice uneconomical; it is only necessary to make it uncompetitive relative to other, less noxious forms of selling'. Harm reduction encourages academics, policymakers, and practitioners to 'think outside the box' and consider a smorgasbord of ways and means for policing drug problems in the context of prohibition. It also offers a framework for taking into account both the benefits and costs of enforcement interventions. Consultations undertaken by the UKDPC (2009) found some evidence that the police have been learning the lessons of research and a widespread view amongst enforcement personnel that they should have a harm reduction role, although the extent to which this approach has been recognized and embraced varied considerably across forces and regions.

Decriminalization is widely acknowledged to be a potentially effective step in the right direction since the 'most direct way in which the police can reduce harm is to stop imposing criminal records and other punishments which harm people' (Stevens 2013: 6). Focused-deterrence strategies, selective targeting, and sequential interdiction efforts against the offenders who are causing the most harm to communities are being increasingly embraced as promising enforcement alternatives to zero-tolerance approaches to drugs and crime (Braga and Weisburd 2012; Felbab-Brown 2013). Examples of targeting specific individuals or groups identified as being particularly harmful are assertive outreach schemes such as Operation Reduction in Brighton and Operation Iceberg in Kent (UKDPC 2009, 2012). In these schemes, street-level dealers, who have been identified as user-dealers, are approached and offered the opportunity to enter a programme of treatment as an alternative to arrest and prosecution. An evaluation of Operation Reduction suggested that it was a cost-effective way of rehabilitating individuals and reducing their offending (Brown et al. 2008).

Conclusion

Policing the 'drug problem' is about enforcing order and managing expectations in a way that reflects the unfolding dynamics of society. It is a complex and delicate issue, a veritable Pandora's box, a balancing act between conflicting interests in a field that is awash with confusion, contradiction, and controversy. Conceptions of order and the appropriate modes of achieving it are context specific and tend to correspond to the interests and situational requirements of dominant institutions and social and political groups. Local cultures and their diverse morals and customs also play a crucial role in selecting which behaviours are perceived as problematic and influencing how they are responded to.

Owing to a multi-layered and widely debated combination of liberal governance, moral entrepreneurship, and paternalistic concern, ever since the onset of prohibition the habitual regulatory response to potentially harmful psychoactive substances taken for recreational purposes has been to label them as 'dangerous drugs' to be controlled through the processes of criminalization. Prohibition is grounded in the classic deterrence model in that it aims to alter behaviours by deterring those convicted of drug offences and other potential offenders. By criminalizing drugs and emphasizing enforcement, the state has put the drug problem into the hands of the police and the criminal justice system. Being a high-profile area of priority and specialization, the war on drugs has often led the way in reshaping the police organization and stimulating innovative and invasive laws and policing techniques. In effect, then, it might be argued that governments and enforcement agencies have used the failures of prohibition to their advantage in order to make their mechanisms of control more powerful and far-reaching. If history has taught us anything it is that power, politics, and trade, the ideologies of capitalism, and the 'law and order' agenda have always been at the heart of drug control, even when policy discourses have emphasized other more laudable concerns like health and morality. But the reasons for controlling drugs cannot always explain the forms that regulatory attempts have actually taken. Another lesson from the history books is that control efforts have too often been framed by unwarranted generalizations from worst-case scenarios that seldom conform to the realities of drug use or supply.

What is evident from the preceding discussion is that the police play multiple roles in the long-running drug control drama series. Over the years they have played the hero, the villain, and the damsel in distress, written the script and forgotten their lines, directed the production, designed the set and done the editing. They have brought drug offenders to justice, disrupted the market, and protected people against themselves, encountered the counterculture, fought in a war, and worked in partnership to reduce the harmfulness of drug use through treatment services and the provision of education. They have criminalized countless citizens and enforced 'unequal laws within an unequal social order mandate against unequal peoples' (Brogden and Ellison 2012: 20). And the show must go on. It must go on because drugs are prohibited and it is the duty of the police to enforce the law and bring offenders to justice. It must go on because drugs are connected to a range of crime and disorder problems and it is the duty of the police to reduce crime and maintain social order. It must go on because drugs are a cause of public concern and it is the duty of the police to reassure the public and respond to their calls for service. But it need not go on in the same way. Now more than ever there is an appetite for change and a more balanced and comprehensive evaluation of the wider impact of current enforcement strategies and tactics. For too long we have had deterrence at the price of injustice. 'Justice', Husak (2002: 13) argues, 'should not be conceptualized as a *goal* our policies should try to achieve, but as a *constraint* that limits what we are allowed to do in pursuing our objectives'. The ultimate aim of drug control should be to reduce drug harms and the wider purpose of drug policing should be to ensure the safety of the community by reducing harms to its members. Until the global prohibition regime is overthrown, police services should be governed by the principles of harm reduction and only use tactics that are experienced by the community as being fair, lawful, and effective. They are a visible face of the state to the citizen and have a symbolic function in terms of representing what is just and sending messages about social expectations.

3

The Illegal Drug Business

The town centre of Metropolis was a vibrant hive of ceaseless activity, every scene an almost perfect picture of the hustle-and-bustle of contemporary urban life. Everywhere I looked, people of all backgrounds and personalities were going about their business, living out their lives.

This inner-city ward was also the setting for an illegal drug market and all that goes with it. The drugs, the sex, the violence—they were all there, bubbling away below the surface. There had been a 'gang-related shooting' a couple of days ago, at an outpost of one of the public housing estates located just a short walk from the transport interchange. A couple of drug dealers had been arrested; a copious amount of crack cocaine and cash had been seized. Eruptions from the underworld were a regular occurrence, part and parcel of the natural environment. If you went down the 'wrong' street or ran into the 'wrong' person there was always the chance that your world would get turned upside down. Where you draw the line depends on your outlook and what you're looking for.

I'd read about the drug world before entering the field... seen the movies, got the t-shirt. Let's just say I was naïve but not entirely ignorant. The cops had told me about their territory, given me guided tours by car and on foot. They'd given me the police view of the streets, told me titillating stories about criminal characters, cringeworthy crimes, and celebrated cases. They'd warned me about where not to go and what not to do. I wondered if I would see the streets in the same light without my police escort, if my experience would be everything like I was told to expect. I wondered how the people viewed their world, the local residents and the transient inhabitants—with love, fear or contempt?

I loitered with intent around the market stalls and street corners, watching for signs of drug market activity, waiting for something to happen. As I watched the world go by,

I wondered how many people were involved in the drug game, and how many more were affected by it, for better or worse. I observed several 'users' clustering together, precisely where the police had told me they tended to cluster. I recognized some of them from their mugshots on the walls of the police stations; others I judged on the basis of their appearance, behaviour, and acquaintances. I noticed a gaunt down-and-out with train tracks running up and down his arms, waiting for the man. 'Others' were quite openly smoking cannabis. 'Wanna bit of puff?' 'Wanna smoke?' It's all in the eyes and that slight nod of the head. Maintain eye contact, if only for a second. Slap an expression of knowing and wanting on your face and chances are you'll be given an invitation to treat. No one else seemed to notice... Well, notice anything out of the ordinary.

(Fieldnotes, Metropolis)

A threat to some, an opportunity for others, and a potential lifeline for those facing hardship, the illegal drug business is an everyday feature of social and economic life in urban and rural settings throughout the world. Drug markets of one kind or another are a deeply embedded characteristic of past and present societies. They are at one and the same time a source of gratification and a thorn in the side of those who experience drug problems. This chapter provides a narrative review of the research literature that has contributed hugely to our knowledge of the realities of this subterranean world of work and play. It thereby paints a picture of what the police who deal with drugs are up against. An understanding of markets for illegal drugs underpins any scholarly discussion of drug control policy and the policing of drugs. By the same token, an understanding of drug markets should also underpin any policies and policing interventions that aim to regulate them.

Illegal Drugs and the Informal Economy

Defining the drug business

Many perspectives can be used to enhance our understanding of drug markets since what we are dealing with is a subject area that encompasses a range of academic disciplines. For many commentators, a good starting point is the recognition that the buying and selling of illegal drugs largely follows the same basic economic principles as the buying and selling of any other tradable commodity (Pearson and Hobbs 2001; Ruggiero and South 1995; Ruggiero 2000). All commodities are produced and distributed in markets that are driven by the forces of supply and demand under conditions of competition. The term 'market' is used to refer to the abstract relationship between buyers and sellers and the physical place where transactions occur. A strict economic approach allows drugs to be stripped of any moral overtones and seen only through the calculating eyes of the economist.

Another useful orienting perspective is to interpret 'the illegal activities associated with drug use and distribution as *work*' (Ruggiero and South 1995: 4). Remunerative crime can be viewed as a way to earn a bit of extra cash, an occupation, or an occasional enterprise, and explained through concepts such as apprenticeship, employment, professionalism, and specialization. Like regular workers, offenders and other irregulars enter into workplace relationships, develop their skill sets, and experience variable levels of job satisfaction. Based on six years of fieldwork in an upper-level drug dealing and smuggling community, Adler (1993: 147–8) made the following observation:

Drug dealers organized, planned, and executed their ventures in similar ways to other businessmen. They relied on an occupational body of knowledge which new recruits had to learn. A modicum of business acumen was required for success. It was also important to have contacts and networks of associates. Finally, dealers' occupational involvement took the form of a career, with the same entry, socialization, and retirement stages found among all workers.

Taking this economic/work approach, drug markets and the people who operate therein are best conceived as falling within the 'informal economy'. Other examples of somewhat comparable informal economic activities include cigarette bootlegging, employing illegal immigrants, gambling, prostitution, selling counterfeit or stolen goods, and unlicensed street trading.

The concept of informal economy is introduced with caution as it has been the subject of much contention, and considerable vagueness of definition remains (Beckert and Wehinger 2013; Saitta et al. 2013; Shapland et al. 2003). This is complicated further by the great many adjectives that are used to denominate its myriad related activities—'criminal', 'hidden', 'illegal', 'irregular', 'shadow', and 'underground' to name but a few (Williams

2004: 2–5). In contrast to the formal sector, which is typically identified with forms of wage employment and declared earnings, the informal economy can be broadly defined as those forms of economic activity that escape most state regulation or otherwise fall outside its sphere of influence and protection. Put differently, it includes the provision of goods and services that are unregistered by or deliberately concealed from the authorities in order to avoid the burdens of tax, social security, and/or labour law obligations.

What is considered 'informal' is largely dependent on the decisions of the state with regard to its social, economic, and fiscal policies (Shapland and Ponsaers 2009). States, in other words, create and shape the informal economy through their law and policy frameworks and enforcement mechanisms. When a government decides to regulate or prohibit an economic activity, that activity may be drawn out of the formal economy and into the informal economy. In relation to drugs, it is worth reminding ourselves that for much of the nineteenth century drug markets throughout Europe and North America operated in accordance with the liberal ideology of free enterprise and were subject to little external regulation (Berridge and Edwards 1981; Courtwright 2001; Jay 2000). Alternatively, if governments decide to deregulate or legalize criminalized activities, they may become legally regulated and taxable, as recently happened when the states of Colorado and Washington voted to remove the prohibition on recreational marijuana markets (Drug Policy Alliance 2015a, 2015b; Pardo 2014). Historical components and cultural influences cannot be ignored when studying the processes of criminalization and the parameters of the informal economy.

Drug dealers

For present purposes, 'drug dealer' is used as a catchall term for persons who buy and sell drugs illegally. This includes 'distributors', 'peddlers', 'pushers', 'sellers', 'smugglers', 'suppliers', 'traders', 'traffickers', and other such nouns. Notwithstanding the apparent diversity of the actors known to be involved in the illegal drug business, almost without exception such persons are criminalized and labelled as 'drug dealers', a term which conjures up an array of typically negative images, from Pablo Escobar and the Medellin Cartel to the faceless villains lurking in the shadows outside school gates or hustling on street corners. Drug dealers, Coomber (2006: 1) contends, are 'one of the most despised groups in contemporary western society and rarely engender any sympathy or concession to their character'. His book demonstrates that when subjected to greater scrutiny, however, many common assumptions are found to be inaccurate and overly simplistic. Reviewing the research-based evidence, he shows that there is hardly a common type of drug dealer and that many dealers are actually 'relatively ordinary individuals, with ordinary thoughts, feelings and even morals' (p167). If we are to deal with drugs in a meaningful way we must first break down our preconceived notions and dispense with unhelpful stereotypes and scapegoating.

One of many misunderstandings is that studying the drug trade and other aspects of the informal economy is little more than a study of those who live on the margins of society. On the contrary, empirical research has revealed that informality is by no means limited to the 'lower' classes or the need for basic subsistence. Williams and Windebank (1998) found that the most common form of informality for the 'skilled' and the 'professional' was to add informal business to formal work 'on the side'. In fact, the literature suggests that workers are more likely to obtain informal employment through existing networks in the formal workplace, rather than be the stereotypical benefit claimant or immigrant working for cash-in-hand. Adler (1993) encountered irregular and full-time drug traders from a wide range of occupational backgrounds, from those working in and around the night-time economy, to actors, realtors, and students. Dorn et al. (1992) came across financially solvent regulars who began to deal in drugs as a 'sideline' when the opportunity arose. They demonstrate how legitimate businesses can provide 'cover' for drug trafficking and actually facilitate it through access to premises, transport, and other resources useful for distribution activities. By bringing together ideas from routine activity theory, social network theory, and opportunity theory, the research of Kleemans and van de Bunt (2008) illustrates the importance of social relations, work relations, and work settings to organized crime. Based on an analysis of Dutch police investigations of criminal groups, they conclude that legitimate occupations that involve social interaction, international contacts and travel methods, as well as individual freedom, movement, and discretion, present greater opportunities for criminal activity. In the drug business, such occupations are shown to include airline staff members, baggage handlers, and haulage firms.

Yet, whilst people from all walks of life are involved in one way or another and for a variety of reasons, the literature strongly indicates that a great many, particularly at the street level, are marginalized individuals who live in conditions of socio-economic deprivation and work informally as a means of survival—though not all would categorize themselves as 'survivors'. Venkatesh (2013: 146) shows that the call girls, drug dealers, and immigrants he studied 'never thought of themselves as victims seeking to overcome great odds for a few bread crumbs. In their eyes, they were pursuing an American dream in the Big Apple just like anybody else'. Informal economic activity seemed to offer a means of escape from the constraints and exploitation levels that are often present at the bottom stratum for employment in the formal economy. Having interviewed people involved in local drug markets, May et al. (2005: 39) found that:

For many young people, working a 40-hour week for what they considered to be a pittance signalled a lack of real choice. Some of them believed that selling drugs offered greater financial rewards, better job opportunities and also possibilities for 'promotion'—all of which they perceived to be unattainable goals in the legitimate employment market.

This is not to say that the informal economy enables those who are poor to escape their poverty. Drugs can make the well-off wealthier or transform rags to riches, but in reality most dealers make very little money (Caulkins et al. 1999; Levitt and Dubner 2005; Levitt and Venkatesh 2000). A detailed analysis of the financial activities of an entrepreneurial street gang led Levitt and Venkatesh (2000) to the conclusion that drug dealing is not particularly lucrative and for those on the lowest rung of the gang hierarchy hourly wages are no better than the minimum wage.

Areas of persistent poverty provide fertile ground for the development and establishment of drug markets because the local social structures can facilitate or even normalize law breaking as a strategy for 'getting by' (Anderson 1999; Bourgois 2003; May et al. 2005; Venkatesh 2006). In his study of the social and cultural dynamics of life in the inner-city ghetto areas of Philadelphia, Anderson (1999: 29) notes that parents tacitly accept their youngster's drug dealing because they get some of the money for help with household expenses. Even the crimes committed by drug users in order to generate money to support their drug use can be cast in a positive light. Johnson et al. (1985: 115), in their study of the economic behaviour of heroin users, submit that 'their crimes and productivity in the underground economy create real values and economically benefit more persons than suffer losses'. Their acquisitive crimes, for instance, supply the market for stolen goods and thereby meet the demand for consumer products that are otherwise out of reach.

Entry into the drug business seems to require little capital or skills beyond those which are acquired from a familiarity with the trade and its members (Adler 1993; Matrix Knowledge Group 2007; Taylor and Potter 2013). Knowledge of prices, purities, and availability is almost common knowledge in the information age and the informal 'rules' of the game are easily learned through differential association (Sutherland 1947). Whilst this relative ease of entry might suggest that drug dealing is easy money, a major drawback is that 'off the books' activities replace absent structures or take over perceptions of economic possibilities, preventing workers from turning 'legit'. According to Sandberg and Pederson (2009: 115), street drug dealers 'do not stand much of a chance in the legitimate economy. They do not possess the necessary skills, relevant work experience or cultural capital'. Many of the upper-level dealers and smugglers studied by Adler (1993: 134) possessed the necessary forms of capital but still 'knew it would be difficult to find another way of earning a living. They feared that they would be unable to account to prospective employers for their years spent in illicit activity'. Work in the formal sector increasingly requires formal evidence of competence—including no criminal record (Farrall et al. 2010). New entrants into the labour market without any, or many, formal qualifications struggle in this respect. The young, for example, those excluded from school, and those coming out of prison, are likely to view the informal economy as being a less demanding and more realistic option. Getting work in either sector, however, requires both capacity and access to social networks. Shapland et al. (2013) found that it was equally difficult for young offenders, having decided to desist from crime, to find formal or non-criminal informal work because they were lacking in these departments.

The High Life

Although the informal economy approach highlights the 'business' aspects of illegal drug markets, it fails to provide a complete explanation of what motivates people to enter and remain in the trade because it treats crime like any other line of work. Money is not the only motivation. Sufficient weight must be given to the lifestyle that might accompany certain types of deviant occupation. Indeed, Hobbs (2013: 229) argues that 'it is as unwise to disregard hedonism as an aspect of illegal market engagement, as it would be to ignore the coke-addled, helicopter-riding lifestyles of hedge-fund traders in a consideration of the occupational culture of financial service workers in the City of London'.

There appears to have been an acceleration in the search for the 'high life' since passing into the era of neo-liberal capitalism. One change that is of particular relevance to the current discussion is the shift away from the primacy of production towards a new emphasis on consumption and the rise of the 'consumer society'. Against this backdrop, Hobbs (2013: 159) comprehensively demonstrates that the 'generic adoption of entrepreneurship as both a central ideological prop and a pragmatic strategy of post-industrial society has assisted in the consolidation of both legitimate and illegitimate interests around a central theme of wealth accumulation'. Choices about consumption have become central to the construction of identities and consumption itself has become a form of social competition between individuals. In *Criminal Identities and Consumer Culture*, Hall et al. (2008) provide an outstanding analysis of the impact of neo-liberal capitalism on crime and working class cultures in the North East of England. Their ethnographic data reveals that the lives of most young criminals revolve around consumer symbolism. The individuals they spoke with 'appeared to believe whole-heartedly that the good life should be understood in terms of the acquisition and conspicuous display of commodities and services that signified cultural achievement in the most shallow of terms' (p48). This tendency, the authors go on to argue, 'is not an ethical or proto-political response to a life lived under harsh social circumstances, or a hybrid "sub-cultural" reworking of mainstream "values", but rather a general cultural injunction created by the market economy and filtered through the ideological apparatus that supports advanced capitalism and its liberal democratic system' (p62).

Drugs dealers are also motivated by a desire for status, power, and respect in their cultural milieu. Adler (1993: 151) notes how dealers and smugglers derive standing and self-worth from their drug trafficking and the fact that they were top-level professionals.

Some even broke their rules of secrecy to reveal their occupation to outsiders. At the other end of the market, Pearson (1987: 122) talks about the promise of becoming 'a figure of some real local standing' which is held out to heroin users who contemplate selling their wares. Collison (1996) likewise suggests that, for young male offenders, drug use, drug dealing, and other forms of criminal 'graft' function as sources of credibility and respect and serve as important cultural and emotive resources for scripting a particular masculine identity on the street. He explains how a dismantling of working-class masculinities following Britain's de-industrialization has left working-class youths in a state of anomie. In search of an anchor, they cobble together 'super-consumerist' identities based on crime and fast living. Drawing on the work of Bourdieu (1990) and Bourgois (2003), Sandberg and Pederson (2009) offer a theoretically sophisticated analysis of young black men dealing cannabis in Oslo, based on the concept of 'street capital'. This concept is used to capture 'the knowledge, competence, skills and objects that are given value in street culture. It is masculine in its essence, and values violence, retaliation, fashionable clothes and the attraction of females. Most importantly, street capital is a form of legitimate power that is relational and has the capacity to generate profit' (p168). A dealer might also aspire to acquire 'subcultural capital' for being in the know and being known as a person who knows how to get things. Also drawing on Bourdieu, Thornton (1995) originally developed this notion through research on the British 'rave' scene and related music style. She was interested in shedding light on the cultural mechanisms of constructing meaning, which allow the members of 'club culture' to see themselves as 'underground' and 'hip', and the ways in which they are able to raise their status and climb the clubbing hierarchy.

A final spin on the high life is that people become involved in the illegal drug business because of their involvement in drug use. At the street level, dealers of drugs such as heroin and crack are often dependent users who sell drugs to supply their own habit. No surplus profits are made and drugs are often used as currency (May et al. 2000; Pearson 1987). There is evidence of collective action and a sense of community within drug-using populations. In their study of drug markets and law enforcement, Dorn et al. (1992) identified 'mutual societies' as networks of user-dealers 'who support each other and sell or exchange drugs amongst themselves in a reciprocal fashion' (pxiii). Such methods of distribution are shown to exist for all drug types. The authors also identify 'trading charities' as distinguishable enterprises involved in the drug business because of ideological commitments to drugs. Largely associated with the heyday of the 'hippies', the ideologically motivated drug dealer 'ties involvement in the supply of drugs to a particular facet of their social life and *socialising* within it'. The 'goal of profit accumulation is subsidiary to, or strongly tempered by, a commitment to or enjoyment of the social and cultural aspects of using the drug and the context in which this is done' (p10). Whilst these peaceable dealers have been somewhat overrun by capitalists and criminals, subsequent studies have shown that their outlook lives on in parts of the drug world. Potter (2010), for example, in his ethnographic study of domestic cannabis cultivation, found that many growers are motivated more by ideological positions associated with cannabis than financial considerations. Taking an economic sociology approach, Sandberg (2012: 1148) argues that many cannabis markets 'cannot be understood without seeing the importance of cannabis culture and the symbolic association between cannabis and anti-business and non-commercial norms and values'.

Academic inquiry has revealed that the significant majority of recreational users get their drugs through 'social supply' networks of relatives, friends, and friends of friends (Duffy et al. 2007; Jacinto et al. 2008; Parker 2000; Taylor and Potter 2013). Most social suppliers tend not to see themselves or be seen by others as 'real' drug dealers; they see their role as 'facilitative, as sorting or helping out friends and acquaintances' (Parker 2000: 67). 'Real' dealers are considered to be those suppliers who sell drugs in order to make a profit and are unknown to their customers beyond the dealing transaction. This is not to say that social suppliers do not profit from their drug market activities. Indeed, in recognition of this definitional issue Coomber and Moyle (2014) attempt to develop and extend the concept of 'social supply' to 'minimally commercial supply'. The body of literature on the subject also reveals how social suppliers might 'drift into dealing' or make a profit driven move to become a drug dealer (Jacinto et al. 2008; Murphy et al. 1990; Taylor and Potter 2013).[1]

---

[1] 'Drifting into dealing' reflects broader ideas of how people 'drift' into delinquency through a series of gradual escalations of deviant behaviour (Matza 1964).

The High Price

Money

For what they are—a bunch of natural substances, chemical derivatives, and synthetic products—illegal drugs are tremendously valuable per unit weight. The best way to appreciate fully just how valuable drugs are is to compare data on prices for different drugs and commodities in regular commerce. In the absence of prohibition, most illegal drugs would probably cost much the same as their legal counterparts, but are instead worth at least their weight in gold (Caulkins and Reuter 1998; Reuter and Greenfield 2001). Globally, it has been estimated that the annual size of the market at the retail level could be as much as US$320 billion, or around 1 per cent of global GDP (UNODC 2005). Unpublished internal Home Office calculations suggest that there are 300 major importers into the UK, 3,000 wholesalers, and 70,000 street dealers, generating an annual turnover of £7–8 billion (Matrix Knowledge Group 2007: 2).

Drug prices fluctuate with changing market conditions and vary dramatically by location. During the Australian 'heroin drought', for instance, which occurred because of a combination of factors including the disruption of major trafficking networks through enforcement efforts, the price of heroin increased from around A$40 to A$300 per gram (Degenhardt et al. 2005; Weatherburn et al. 2003). In terms of geography, Babor et al. (2010: 70) call attention to the strong positive correlation between retail prices and per capita GDP for most drugs. This, they explain, is partly because residents in high-income countries are able to pay higher prices. It can also be explained by the fact that such countries are generally farther from producing regions. As with all commodities, the price of drugs increases the closer they get to the end consumer, owing to mark-ups at each stage of the supply chain (Matrix Knowledge Group 2007; Pearson and Hobbs 2001).[2]

[2] Commentators regularly split the drug trade up into market levels, which basically correspond to the main stages of the drug supply chain (i.e. production, importation, wholesale, middle market distribution, and retail). Each level is relatively distinct, in terms of the actors involved, their social organization and methods of operation. The most striking differences between the links in the chain are the price and the quantity of the commodities being traded. However, it is necessary to stress that these neat divisions should not be rigidly applied as they are simplistic reflections of a fragmented, fluid, and flexible reality.

The 'high price' relates not only to the monetary costs of the commodities being produced and distributed but also to the non-monetary risks to the people involved in the drug business. Some costs that legal businesses face are actually much lower or not applicable to illegal businesses precisely because they escape most state regulation or otherwise fall outside its sphere of influence and protection. For instance, drug dealers do not pay taxes or conventional customs duties and cannot be held to account for acting in breach of any commercial, consumer, or labour laws. Product illegality also means that marketing, packaging, and storage costs are negligible (Caulkins and Reuter 1998; Caulkins et al. 1999). What drives up the cost of producing and distributing illegal drugs is 'compensation' for actual or potential risks. The drug world is a hostile entrepreneurial environment in which there is a constant risk of arrest, imprisonment, and confiscation, not to mention being ripped off, set up, or killed by colleagues, connections, and competitors. Sellers generally have the upper hand in terms of bargaining power as they are selling a relatively scarce commodity for which there is considerable demand. The most popular theory quantifying risk compensation suggests that dealers demand compensation equivalent to the expected value of the non-monetary risks they face (Reuter and Kleiman 1986). This compensation might take the form of increased price or reduced volume or purity. Enforcement activities thus impose extra costs on drug dealers in much the same way as regulation impacts on legitimate businesspersons.

Risk management

Precisely how drug dealers perceive or manage risk is little known or understood. Risk aversion seems to be the norm, though a degree of tolerance is inevitable as complete aversion is in tension with the trade itself. As one might expect, some individuals go to great lengths to protect themselves and their assets, whereas others are more inclined to take risks, this perhaps reflecting 'personal preferences for excitement, challenge and... achievement against the odds' (Dorn et al. 2005: 10). On the basis of in-depth interviews with high-level drug smugglers incarcerated in the US federal prison system, Decker and Chapman (2008: 133) argue that risk tolerance was typically based on age and life stage concerns, including family, finances, and status in the community.

More importantly, they found that risk calculation 'was hardly representative of the "criminal calculus" suggested by rational choice or deterrence theorists' and challenge the assumption that decision-making processes take the form of rational cost-benefit analyses. For the smugglers they interviewed, risk management meant trying to find a 'comfort zone' (p151) in which they believed that the odds of getting away with the crime were in their favour. This state of mind was achieved by engaging in a series of precautionary measures that were believed to reduce the risk of being detected or held legally liable. Other criminal actors have been found to rely more on blind faith or a tot of Dutch courage. Collison (1996: 434) argues that few young offenders 'stop long to calculate the risks but rather trust in a mystical invincibility, hope for a run of good luck or fate, simply do it, and sometimes use drugs to situationally erase risk'. Research has also demonstrated how some criminals are prone to act in economically irrational ways. Katz (1988: 132) observed that the careers of persistent robbers show us not the 'precise calculations and hedged risks of "professionals", but men for whom gambling and other vices are a way of life, who are "wise" in the cynical sense of the term, and who take pride in a defiant reputation as "bad" '. Such unpredictable behaviour is difficult to anticipate and build into a comprehensive model of risk management in the illegal drug business.

If drug dealers are to survive and prosper they need to understand the mechanisms of the criminal justice system and the 'ways and means' of the drug law enforcers who are employed to disrupt their business and deprive them of their liberty and ill-gotten gains (Adler 1993; Decker and Chapman 2008; Dorn et al. 1992; Jacobs 1996, 1999; Johnson and Natarajan 1995; Matrix Knowledge Group 2007; Ruggiero and South 1995). Savvy dealers might monitor the activities of enforcement agencies through the use of surveillance, tracking, and detection equipment. Knowing about enforcement tactics and the legal requirements of proof enables them to evade the law, develop effective counter-strategies, and avoid ties to evidence. Some dealers are known to engage with corrupt criminal justice professionals, as business associates or through bribery or blackmail, in order to access information or secure 'favours'. The more prosperous might also need accountants and lawyers to help maintain or set up a legitimate front for their criminal activities and launder their proceeds in the formal economy. That being said, the interviews conducted by the Matrix

Knowledge Group (2007: 39) with prisoners convicted of 'serious drug-related offences' suggest 'unsophisticated money laundering techniques with a tendency to use friends and family, for example by investing in their businesses or bank accounts'.

The risks associated with the illegal drug business compel most dealing enterprises to remain small and operate covertly through closed distribution networks, depriving them of opportunities to exploit economies of scale or market power (Dorn et al. 1992; Matrix Knowledge Group 2007; May and Hough 2004). In 'closed' markets access is limited to known and trusted participants. An unknown buyer needs someone to introduce or vouch for them before they can make a purchase. Communications and transactions need to be sufficiently difficult to detect, penetrate, and decipher, so as to avoid giving enforcement agencies the opportunity to gather intelligence and piece together evidence. The division of labour and dissemination of information on a need-to-know basis can also help in this regard. Dorn et al. (1998) provide evidence of well-capitalized, risk averse 'Number 1s' (principals/organizers), who were 'cut out' from the riskiest aspects of drug importation by 'Number 2s' (trusted associates/managers). The more risk tolerant organizers and managers were more 'hands on' and directly involved in the organization of logistics and the recruitment of 'Number 3s' (e.g. transporters and corrupt officials). As in the formal economy, the literature clearly shows that the riskiest tasks in domestic and international drug markets are left to unskilled labourers, those 'mass' criminals who are 'interchangeable, replaceable, powerless, moveable, dependent' and almost inevitably poorly paid (Ruggiero and South 1995: 127).

Retail level markets are markedly different in some of these respects, owing to the existence of 'open' and 'semi-open' marketplaces (May and Hough 2004; McSweeney et al. 2008). There are no barriers to access in open markets. They tend to operate overtly in geographically well-defined areas at specific times, and dealers will generally do business without a prior introduction provided the buyer 'looks the part'. Semi-open markets are based in and around pubs and clubs and are believed to make up a significant part of the recreational drug distribution systems of the night-time economy. Where the retail market is structured, dealers might employ 'runners' to supply drugs directly to users. Johnson et al. (2000: 34), in an article drawing on an exceptional ethnographic study of drug distribution in New York City, explain how sellers established new tactics in response to increased police pressure. Well-grounded fears of police 'buy-bust' tactics led them to be cautious about selling to any person who was not a 'regular' or previously known customer. They significantly reduced the number of visible police targets in public spaces and many used cloned cellular phones to maintain contact with customers and fill orders. 'Steerers' and 'touts' directed buyers to private premises, 'middlemen' completed the transactions, while 'lookouts' were on guard against police activity and any other signs of trouble.

Researchers have discovered that the foremost concern of drug dealers is not law enforcement per se, but 'how trust and order are maintained in an illicit market where contracts cannot be legally upheld' (Pearson and Hobbs 2001: 27). Taylor and Potter (2013) describe a number of advantages that can be gained from only doing business with friends or highly trusted and recommended individuals. For customers, they suggest, friendship and trust helps ensure that the product received is of good quality and quantity. For dealers, it acts as a form of 'insurance against the risks of legal repercussions and against the risks of advancing credit' (p401). The evidence-base emphasizes the importance of previous criminal activity, serving time in prison, and having a reputation for being reliable and discreet (Adler 1993; Decker and Chapman 2008; Matrix Knowledge Group 2007; Pearson and Hobbs 2001). Owing to the global, profitable, and somewhat unpredictable nature of the marketplace, however, those who study drug markets are increasingly finding evidence of dealers working with people from outside their trusted networks when there are mutual interests at stake. Ruggiero and Khan (2006) studied the prevalence of consortia formed by South Asian groups operating in the UK with overseas partners based in drug-producing zones. They found that family and mono-ethnic networks are unable to distribute to wider markets than their own local outlets because 'their capacity to form commercial alliances, at home as well as abroad, is hampered by a form of business provincialism' (p482). Whilst kinship, ethnicity, and direct commercial links continue to be important they are increasingly overshadowed by inter-ethnic networking and market dynamics.

Systemic violence

By operating outside the law, the actors involved in the illegal drug business have no recourse to the rights and resolutions offered by the criminal and civil justice systems. Whilst trust and mutual interest help ensure the maintenance of amicable working relationships, in otherwise unregulated markets outlaws are required to put in place their own safeguards and resort to their own methods of aggressive competition and enforcement. Violence, then, or at least the threat of violence, is often regarded as a key characteristic of illegal market activity and an integral part of life for those involved in this line of work (Goldstein 1985; Pearson and Hobbs 2001; Reuter 2009). Brute strength, physicality, and a reputation for violence represent forms of cultural capital that, when fused with entrepreneurial acumen, create masculinities suited to a highly competitive illegal marketplace (Ellis 2015; Hobbs 1995, 2013; Winlow 2001). With this in mind, it seems logical that people with the greatest experience and proficiency in violence are more likely to be attracted to the business than pacifists or pushovers.

In the absence of property rights, prime real estate for selling, which for legal businesses would usually be allocated to the highest bidder by whoever currently owns it, goes instead to whichever dealer can most effectively intimidate his or her competitors. On the basis of interviews with adult males imprisoned for firearms offences, Hales et al. (2006) submit that drugs are the most significant factor underlying the illegal use of firearms. Firearms possession was reported in relation to personal protection, territorial disputes, and robberies. May et al. (2005: 22) similarly found that those dealers who carried a weapon often did so because they felt they needed protection from being robbed by other drug market players. Being criminals themselves, such individuals are reluctant to report being victimized for fear of exposing their own illegal activities (and probably would not be taken seriously even if they did make a complaint) (Jacobs 2000; Jacobs et al. 2000; Topalli et al. 2002). The drug dealer/robbery victims interviewed by Topalli et al. (2002: 340) were in general agreement that direct retaliation was the ideal 'method of exacting a satisfactory, if informal measure of justice'. Generally speaking, however, overt acts of interpersonal violence are considered 'bad for business' as they attract unwanted attention from the authorities and can lead to avoidance and retaliation in the marketplace. Pearson and Hobbs (2001: 42) suggest that beatings, stabbings, and shootings, as opposed to the implicit threat of violence, are 'best understood as a result of market dysfunction and instability'. This means that enforcement can thereby be viewed a causal factor in drug-related violence because it disrupts and destabilizes the market (Moeller and Hesse 2013; Reuter 2009; Werb et al. 2011).

Trends in recent scholarship are challenging the assumption that violence is 'systemic' and 'normatively embedded in the social and economic networks of drug users and sellers' (Goldstein 1985: 503). Indeed, Reuter (2009: 275) argues that 'illegal drug markets are generally peaceable' and 'illegality itself is insufficient to generate high levels of violence in a market'. Different drug markets have vastly different levels of associated violence and the norms of drug dealers are not universally violent. Having studied individuals operating in the upper echelons of the drug trade, Adler (1993: 119) found that '[o]stracism was considered sufficient retaliation for burns, rip-offs, security violations, and other disreputable behavior'. Taylor and Potter (2013: 403), to give another example, demonstrate that threats of violence were available as a 'last resort', but that not one supplier interviewed had taken this route of debt enforcement. The extent of violence that is directly related to the drug business is thus greatly exaggerated.

For Coomber (2006: 117), 'much of what passes for drug market violence is in fact often the "culture of violence" that many of those involved in the drug trade live by anyway'. In many deprived urban areas, where faith in the institutions of the state has been eroded by decades of discrimination and neglect, violent behaviour is reinforced through interaction with marginalized cultures that equate self-dignity and respect with an ability to physically defend and take care of oneself (Ellis 2015; Hobbs 1995, 2013; Winlow 2001). It is for this reason inappropriate to attribute economic rationality to all of the violent acts performed by individuals who 'are obligated to respond to a perceived slight of self, or to family with the same level of ferocity and commitment as they would to a threat to their commercial viability' (Hobbs 1995: 122). To make sense of violent crime, it is imperative that scholars explore the everyday lives, biographies, and subjectivities of the perpetrators, and how they interact with their socio-cultural and economic conditions.

The Drug Distribution Web

The use of the word 'web' to describe the organization of drug distribution is intended to stress the fact that the various components of the illegal drug business do not form an integrated whole and generally operate independently from one another with few coordinating mechanisms. It is also a playful recognition of the growing role of the Internet in providing an innovative mechanism for global marketing and sales. The recent emergence of markets in 'novel psychoactive substances' has been greatly facilitated by online trading and discussion forums (Seddon 2014; Walsh 2011). Furthermore, Griffiths et al. (2013) suggest that ready access to scientific information on chemical synthesis has allowed entrepreneurial chemists to stay ahead of the regulators by manipulating chemical structures and evading the law. This trend is certainly not limited to 'legal highs'. Indeed, the online 'cryptomarket' *Silk Road* was devoted primarily to the sale of illegal drugs (Aldridge and Décary-Hétu 2014; Barratt 2012; Barratt et al. 2014; Martin 2014).

(Dis)organized crime

Drug markets are complex and fluid social structures that are made up of a great many diverse dealing enterprises and collaborative partnerships. For the most part, commentators seem to converge around the idea that marketplaces are populated by a multitude of small groups and individuals operating in a highly decentralized manner that might best be described as 'disorganized crime' (Reuter 1983a). Some drug dealing groups have a durable core of principals, whereas others are loosely linked, operate on an intermittent basis, and organize their activities around specific business ventures. Different group members undertake different roles and subsidiary members are recruited as and when they are needed to perform particular tasks. Freelancers run their own operations or sell their services without allegiance. And then there are the irregulars, those who are involved in the informal economy in a variety of positions, drifting around seeking opportunities on a relatively precarious basis (Curtis and Wendel 2000; Dorn et al. 1992, 2005; Matrix Knowledge Group 2007; Pearson and Hobbs 2001).

In contrast to popular images of 'organized crime', empirical research has revealed that the constraints and consequences of illegal market activity are hardly conducive to the formation of stable hierarchical enterprises, and so, in reality, 'there is no person, no mafia, no cartel organising the market overall' (Dorn et al. 1992: 203). Corporate-style distribution infrastructures do exist in the UK and elsewhere but they tend to be impermanent and capable of exercising only a limited degree of control over a given market or geographical territory (Edmunds et al. 1996; Hobbs 1998, 2001; Lupton et al. 2002; May et al. 2000, 2005). Such forms of distribution are much more prevalent in drug-producing and transit regions which suffer from corruption, internal conflict, and weak institutions (Dorn et al. 2005).

Drug dealers and other market players construct drug markets through networking and connecting sellers and buyers who are spatially and socially scattered. Studies of illegal enterprises consistently show that social networks are critical to their understanding, and crucial determinants of their performance and sustainability (Morselli 2008). A significant consequence of the network character of the drug business is its resilience. To be sure, eliminating individual players, or even entire groups, within a sophisticated distribution network has limited impact on the ability of the network as a whole to distribute drugs as there are multiple alternative connections. Another consequence is adaptability. Networks seem to be more conducive to the threatening and variable nature of illegal markets, making it easier for drug dealers to roll with the punches, to diversify and create or exploit new opportunities, such as multi-commodity trading and 'commodity-hopping' (Hornsby and Hobbs 2007; Pearson and Hobbs 2001).

Uncovering the structure of connections among individuals involved in drug dealing enterprises through the application of network analytic techniques contributes to our understanding of how the illegal drug business functions. In turn, this enables analysts to identify vulnerabilities in different types of criminal organization and can lead to more effective policymaking and enforcement interventions. Based on a case study of an investigation conducted by Montreal Police, the Royal Canadian Mounted Police, and enforcement agencies from various other countries, Morselli and Petit (2007) assess how enforcement intensity affected the structural features and inner workings of the targeted transnational cannabis and cocaine importation network. The principal data source comprised information submitted as evidence during the trials of participants in the 'Project Caviar' network. Rather than arresting the participants, the investigation sought to manipulate the network by seizing the drug consignments that united them. The study reveals that enforcement controls are integral to shaping criminal networks and that networks become less orderly when intensively controlled on account of the 'emergence of an environment of discontent and mistrust' (p128). In a like manner,

Natarajan (2000, 2006) studied wiretap records gathered in the course of prosecuting drug dealing organizations in New York City. Her work provides a valuable insight into their structure, the roles of individual members, the network of contacts among them, the extent of communication within and between subgroups, and the degree to which they are geographically concentrated.

A 'glocal' marketplace

Although there appear to be shared market characteristics across time and space, the research literature strongly indicates that drug markets are shaped by the actors involved in the trade, the commodities being traded, and the socio-economic and cultural context of the market setting. Massari (2005: 8), for example, the coordinator of the Gruppo Abele research project on synthetic drug markets in Amsterdam, Barcelona, and Turin, noted that 'the pharmacological characteristics of the drugs purchased, the consumption patterns associated with them and the embeddedness of drug use in particular subcultures and social contexts, all deeply influence the ways these substances are made available to final users'. The illegal drug business is a global phenomenon that manifests itself as a tangible process of activity at the local level (Curtis and Wendel 2000; Hobbs 1998, 2001; May et al. 2005; van Duyne and Levi 2005). Each market is unique, with different organizational forms and business practices that are intrinsically bound up with the culture, economy, geography, history and networks of local communities.

Researchers have drawn a significant amount of attention to the symbiotic and parasitic relationships between formal and informal economies along trade routes (Ruggiero 2000; Shapland et al. 2003; Shapland and Ponsaers 2009; Saitta et al. 2013). Using the Netherlands as a case study, Farrell (1998: 21) argues that 'variations in European drug trafficking routes and markets are falsely attributed to drug policies when they are primarily driven by variations in licit routine activities'. Drug trafficking is said to be a 'side-effect' of economic and commercial trade patterns. This is why the port of Rotterdam acts as a key transit point for the drug markets of Western Europe: the large volume of shipping reduces the risk of interception, and the country's geographical position and transport infrastructure facilitates further distribution. This also helps explain why London, Birmingham, Manchester and Liverpool are the major drug importation and distribution hubs in the UK, and why ecstasy typically arrives from Holland and Belgium through the ports of Dover, Felixstowe, and Harwich (Pearson and Hobbs 2001). Research on domestic supply networks is predominantly urban-centric, in that it assumes the major conurbations act as nerve centres for wholesale distribution, from which the markets of other cities are supplied, which in turn operate as regional centres supplying smaller urban and rural areas. But there are exceptions to every rule. After pondering over why two towns had developed significant yet unexpected roles in the middle market, Pearson and Hobbs (2001: 40) attributed it to the fact that each town was 'conveniently situated close to a major port, with links by both the rail network and motorway systems to North and South, together with easy cross-country East-West motorway links'.

Most of the drugs coursing through the veins of the domestic drug using population originate overseas. Taking into account the geographical determinants of the global drug trade, it is easy to see why 'the vilification, persecution and victimization of various ethnic groups for real or imagined associations with drugs has been a strong constant of drug control history' (Ruggiero and South 1995: 110). Not only do such associations seem logical, as international trafficking is dependent on links with dealers in drug producing countries and those countries situated on drug supply routes, but they also find support in the enduring popular belief that organised crime is a 'alien conspiracy' and that 'outsiders' are responsible for bringing drugs and drug problems into 'our' society (Hobbs and Antonopoulos 2013; Woodiwiss and Hobbs 2009). There are many examples of mono-ethnic supply networks and foreign dealers travelling from abroad to ply their trade in domestic markets. Having analysed a range of law enforcement intelligence sources, Pearson and Hobbs (2001: 20) confirm that there is evidence of Turkish trafficking networks based in London with family links extending back to Turkey. Likewise, the fact that Colombia produces and exports the lion's share of the cocaine consumed worldwide gives credence to the claim that Colombian traffickers control most of the bulk shipments into the country. Kinship and ethnicity remain vitally important in maintaining viable nodes in international networks. Yet, although certain ethnic groups are known to be heavily involved in the importation of specific drugs, commentators stress that it is extremely difficult for any group to hold sway due to the diversity of local marketplaces and the kaleidoscopic nature of the business. Ethnicity only seems to be a business asset when there are international trade routes and migration flows to disguise the movement of drugs.

In his ethnographic account of Colombian drug entrepreneurs operating in the Netherlands, Zaitch (2002: 143) suggests that Colombia's 'powerful market position has been the result of their ability to "place" and trade the cocaine overseas'. Apart from drugs destined for domestic consumption, 'nobody would sell cocaine in Colombia that could otherwise be more profitably sold in Miami or Rotterdam' (ibid). But being in possession of a commodity for which there is a large demand is only lucrative if a buyer can be located and a deal negotiated. 'Traquetos' were used to bridge the gaps: individuals or small flexible networks based outside Colombia, whose foremost role was to act as cocaine envoys by seeking out and doing business with distributors in transit and destination countries. When forging links with potential buyers, Bovenkerk et al. (2003) found that the manipulation of ethnic reputation—'playing the cartel'—could work to their advantage by establishing credibility more easily. On the other hand, some interviewees felt like they were 'the double targets of the international war of drugs and the restrictive migrant policies' (p33), which left them in an unpropitious position since many non-Colombian traders refused to work with them to reduce the risk of law enforcement intervention. In the end, it was found that Colombian traders were very active at the import level, but they do not monopolize the cocaine trade and their role diminishes drastically as the drugs move down the supply chain.

Given their 'advantageous position' in domestic markets, empirical studies have shown that established indigenous drug dealers 'are often in a position of some strength when negotiating prices with importers' (Ruggiero 2000: 42). This is principally because they are well integrated in their countries, understand their political, judicial, economic, and social conditions better, and are therefore more difficult for the police to identify. Indigenous dealers have tended not to be directly involved in the act of importation, preferring instead to take control of drugs upon entry into the country or designating the task to hired smugglers. However, an emerging deviation from this tendency is what Pearson and Hobbs (2001: vii) have termed 'leap-frogging', which involves domestic traders 'making direct contact with intermediaries to warehousing systems in mainland Europe and importing modest loads on that basis, thus leap-frogging more traditional systems of bulk importation and wholesale trade'. Although there is still only sparse knowledge available, this development signifies that ethnic links to source and transit countries might be diminishing.

The extent to which ethnic minority involvement in the drug business is a function of access and opportunity or a reflection of social exclusion is much debated and in need of further interrogation (Murji 2007). Illegal activity by some minorities can be interpreted as an adaptive mechanism that is a direct response to their marginal economic status and limited social and cultural capital in host societies. In their literature review of drug trafficking and ethnic minorities in Western Europe, Paoli and Reuter (2008: 22) argue that this is true particularly 'for recent undocumented immigrants, who have few opportunities to find a job in the legal economy and, as a result of restrictive policies adopted by most Western European states, are de facto forced to find menial jobs in the informal and illegal economies'. Wider social disadvantages are reflected in the less favourable trading positions occupied by non-indigenous participants in the drug trade: ethnic minorities tend to be disproportionately present at the least remunerative and most risky levels of drug distribution, predominately working as mules in cross-border activity and as street sellers in open markets. Commenting on the Brixton drug economy, Ruggiero (1993) suggests that white native dealers prevent 'foreigners' from establishing stable enterprises at the retail level and consolidating any degree of control over middle market distribution, either by competing against them or by informing the police of their activities or of possible immigration offences. Furthermore, he suggests that the end consumers may also contribute to the creation of these 'internal barricades', since they 'prefer to buy from white dealers rather than from black ones, the former, in their view, possessing more "business ethics" than the latter' (Ruggiero 2000: 42). In these respects, the drug trade reproduces some of the worst aspects of the formal economy, most evidently exploitation and racism.

Conclusion

The illegal drug business is an everyday feature of social and economic life in urban and rural settings throughout the world. This chapter has reviewed the most germane research literature in order to explore this subterranean world of work and play and paint a conceptual picture of what the police who deal with drugs are up against. The picture that emerges is of a ubiquitous phenomenon of the utmost complexity that is in need of control albeit all but uncontrollable.

Although there appear to be shared characteristics across time and space, drug markets are largely shaped by the actors involved in the trade, the commodities being traded, and the socio-economic and cultural context of the market setting. As May et al. (2005) suggest, therefore, effective strategies for tackling local drug markets have to be built on a rounded understanding of the relationships that exist between the markets and their 'host' communities and then tailored to tackle the specific problems that emerge as significant. The drug business is a source of employment, a way to earn money 'off the books', experience unbridled hedonistic materialism, and resolve problems stemming from structures that discriminate against some, or are unfair or unable to provide everybody with at least a minimum income. A handful of prospectors make profits hand over fist, but the prospect of untold fortune does not hold true for most who follow the gold trail. Drug markets can provide 'outsiders' and those on the margins with more status, power, and respect than they would be able to attain through legitimate work and conventional ways of living. They can also act as social forums for cultural interaction that are based on friendship, an ideological commitment to drugs, and to non-commercial norms and values. At the same time, however, some markets are a cause of widespread public concern and some are associated with high levels of crime and disorder. Violence, insecurity, and neighbourhood decline are just a few of the negative effects that the drug trade can have on individuals, families, and communities.

Drug laws and enforcement interventions attain and maintain the structural consequences of illegality and profoundly influence the operations of drug dealing enterprises. They keep the 'high price' in place, rule out the ability to advertise, compete openly or exploit economies of scale, and deprive the actors involved of the rights and resolutions offered by the criminal and civil justice systems. These market conditions are supposed to suppress the drug trade, but they also create a high risk of organized crime and exploitative work situations and conditions owing to the lack of legal remedies. For those who decide to throw caution to the wind and become embroiled in the drug distribution web, the constant risk of arrest, imprisonment, and asset confiscation from one side of the law, and abuse, theft, and violence from the other, is an occupational hazard that imposes hefty costs on doing the business. Be they organized criminals with extensive criminal involvements, businessmen who are otherwise relatively law-abiding, marginalized individuals just trying to make ends meet, or drug users who sell drugs to fund their own use, if they want to survive and prosper in the drug business they are required to operate covertly, trade using closed distribution networks and put in place their own risk management strategies and enforcement techniques. Criminalization has a tendency to breed criminality and so, by prohibiting drugs and subjecting the drug trade to aggressive policing, the state has actually made the drug world more criminal than would have otherwise been the case.

4

Investigating the Investigators
Research Methodology

> I went down into the under-world of London with an attitude
> of mind which I may best liken to that of the explorer. I was
> open to be convinced by the evidence of my eyes, rather than
> by the teachings of those who had not seen, or by the words
> of those who had seen and gone before.
>
> Jack London (2007, p4), *The People of the Abyss*

I remember these words from the early days of fieldwork, the
formative period of my academic career when I still feared my apparent lack of knowledge, skill, and direction more than the tick-
ing clock counting down to my thesis submission deadline. They
were written by Jack London in his preface to *The People of the
Abyss*: a classic, moving, and eye-opening account of the time he
spent living amongst the deprived and depraved in the East End
of London at the turn of the twentieth century. The day I started
reading this book had been long, hard, and trying. As would soon
become a force of habit, I found myself in another unfamiliar pub
having a solitary drink before my train journey home, reflecting on
a number of methodological issues and attempting to make sense
of what was happening in the drug game. The answers were not
at the bottom of the glass, so I moved onto another and started to
give serious thought to admitting defeat and finding a new line of
work. It was becoming increasingly difficult to suppress the sense
of futility, the feeling that my research was on the road to nowhere,
and that academia was perhaps above and beyond me after all.
'You are a police researcher,' I tried to convince myself. Breathe.
Repeat mantra. At a time when I was feeling dejected and con-
fused, these words gave me some much-needed clarity. From that
moment onwards, I assumed the role of an explorer in the police

world, following in the footprints left before me on the way into uncharted terrain. By carrying out empirical research, I was gaining an insight into the police organization and the occupation of policing, visiting areas both on and off the beaten track in order to discover the unknown, and ultimately produce an ethnography of the everyday realities of police detectives, drug law enforcement, and proactive investigation.

The purpose of this chapter is to answer standard methodological questions and elucidate the business involved in undertaking this particular research endeavour. It starts by considering what it means to take an ethnographic approach to social science research and explains why ethnography is both a vital scholarly enterprise in the field of police studies and the most appropriate way of penetrating the inner world of police organizations. Following this, the reader is introduced to the fieldwork settings and research participants and then walked through the chosen research methods. The discussion also contains some reflections on practical issues relating to access and acceptance that were encountered during the research process and how they were engaged with and managed. Research ethics and various *in situ* ethical dilemmas, experiences, and decisions are discussed in Bacon and Sanders (2016).

An Ethnographic Approach

Reflecting on his own experience in the foreword to *Heaven and Hell*, Huxley (1956) submits that the mescaline user 'comes to a new and better understanding of the ways in which those other minds perceive and feel and think, of the cosmological notions which seem to them self-evident, and of the works of art through which they feel impelled to express themselves'. With or without psychedelic assistance, the doors of perception are unlikely to open for the ethnographer as they did for Huxley, yet the desired outcomes are strikingly similar.

Ethnography is a voyage of discovery into the 'symbolic world', the study of culture and how meaning is produced, distributed, and understood in everyday contexts. Culture is usually conceptualized as a complex ensemble of norms, values, and beliefs held in common by a collectivity that emerges in response to problems of external adaptation and internal integration (Geertz 1973; Schein 2004). Ethnographers become immersed in a particular setting, group, or organization for a prolonged period of time. They enter certain aspects of the lives of 'others', learn to speak their language, appreciate their customs, and see reality through their eyes. 'Being there' allows them to observe daily activities, social interactions, and spectacular events as they naturally occur, form close relationships with their research participants, share experiences, have conversations and conduct interviews at the opportune moment or when the opportunity arises. This closeness, familiarity, and reciprocal acquaintance also facilitates the collection of relevant artefacts, documentary sources, and visual images. Extensive fieldwork that combines several qualitative methods is carried out in order to gather detailed and nuanced material that describes and explains perspectives and behaviour in terms of cultural patterning. In their writings, ethnographers bring the symbolic world to life in a manner that can be rendered intelligible to the reader, give a voice to those who are researched, and communicate the story of the research experience. They attempt to provide an authoritative account of the people in question and make their culture visible through interpretative representation (Atkinson et al. 2001; Fielding 2008; Hammersley and Atkinson 2007; Hobbs and May 1993; Wolcott 1990; Van Maanen 1988).

'Social action', Manning (1997: 37) writes, 'like poetry, is ambiguous. It can be read or interpreted in a variety of ways and at several levels of meaning'. Far from being a neutral channel of communication, the 'self' of the ethnographer is the research instrument, the lens through which the social world is seen and the person with whom research participants interact. Ethnographers construct reality through their idiosyncratic interpretations of it. Their findings are shaped by social processes and personal characteristics. There is a tension, then, 'between the naturalism characteristic of ethnographers' methodological thinking and the constructionism and cultural relativism that shape their understanding of the perspectives and behaviour of the people they study' (Hammersley and Atkinson 2007: 10). For the sake of methodological robustness and rigour, it is therefore necessary to address the effects of the researcher on the data through 'reflexivity'. In short, to take a reflexive approach to the production of knowledge is to reject 'the idea that social research is, or can be, carried out in some autonomous realm that is insulated from the wider society and from the biography of the researcher' (p15). What this means is that the researcher must have constant epistemic awareness. They must learn to recognize how they affect the research process and how their research affects both them and the social phenomena being researched. They must also recognize that there are no 'theory-neutral' facts and that all empirical observations are approached through some kind of theoretical understanding (Bottoms 2008; Layder 1998).

The ethnographic approach to social science research has a long history in criminology and has been the principal strategy used to establish the foundational work in the field of police studies (Manning 2014; Reiner 2015). In terms of legacy, many concepts, themes, and findings that have become central tenets of the sociology of policing have their origins in the wave of pioneering ethnographies that started to emerge in the sixties and spanned several decades (e.g. Banton 1964; Bittner 1970; Cain 1973; Holdaway 1983; Manning 1977; Punch 1979; Reiner 1978; Rubinstein 1973; Skolnick 1966; Westley 1970).[1] These classic monographs interrogate the role of the police in society, the everyday realities of police work, the structure of the police organization, and the occupational culture of the police, issues that are always relevant and persist even when contemporary concerns in policy and practice are at the forefront of the research agenda. They set the key questions for those who followed in their wake and remain a source of inspiration and valuable lessons for police scholars around the world and across the generations.

From an empirical standpoint, ethnography has proven unparalleled for penetrating the inner world of police organizations and examining the working rules, tacit understandings, and underlying assumptions that operate beneath the presentational canopy of institutional frameworks (Loftus 2009; Manning 2014; Marks 2004; Reiner and Newburn 2008). Speaking as both social scientist and serving police officer, Young (1991: 15) submits that it requires a great deal of fieldwork 'to reveal much about the unspoken agenda which determines many aspects of police practice'.

---

[1] *Police Work* (Manning 1977/97) is routinely included in lists of classic police ethnographies but is not viewed in the same light by the author. He writes that the book 'is based upon extensive fieldwork but is not an ethnography. Nor is it a description of day-to-day police work. It is not a comprehensive review of the literature on policing but is an attempt to articulate a perspective on policing as an activity, as an organization, as a set of symbolic repertories and situated actions, as a source of myth, drama, and commonsense theories of social conduct' (1997: 32).

All other methodological approaches are to varying degrees unsuitable for achieving this end as the methods employed 'rely on some sort of account offered by the police themselves (whether in interviews or official documents and statistics), the veracity of which is often precisely the question being studied' (Reiner and Newburn 2008: 354). Such accounts are selective presentations that do not necessarily depict actuality accurately or entirely, attempts to convince listeners and observers of a particular image or truth that should not be taken at face value. Interviews allow police officers to candidly express their views and assert their values but can only ever produce recollections of past events. The moment is always lost and the explanations given are often designed to create an impression and present police activities in a favourable light. Furthermore, one-off interviews may not provide an adequate tool for understanding the occupational culture because assumptions are often not readily available to conscious thought and as a result they 'can fail to tap into deeper levels of cognition' (Marks 2004: 870). Goffman (1959: 13–4) argues that 'the "true" or "real" attitudes, beliefs, and emotions of the individual can be ascertained only indirectly, through his avowals or through what appears to be involuntary expressive behaviour'. Mission statements, policies, and codes of conduct are best understood as indications of aspiration or strategic intent rather than precise descriptions of the ways in which the police truly operate. They are political documents, intentional expressions made by police administrators to communicate the 'organizational front' or 'official culture', techniques of establishing and maintaining control over the symbolic meanings of policing and the police that are oriented towards legitimating existing practices publicly (Jermier et al. 1991; Manning 1997). Documentary records of intentions, what transpired, and why it transpired as it did are filtered versions of police work, artificial renderings designed to construct a legitimate and accountable reality (Hobbs 1988; McConville et al. 1991). Remarking on the cynicism surrounding paperwork, Manning (2004: 232) suggests that both of the drug units he observed 'dismissed their own records as accurate portrayals of their work'. It is worrying, then, that trends in funding, career prospects, and government evaluation systems do not seem to favour ethnographic research (Manning 2014). Quantitative surveys, systematic reviews and evaluations of policing initiatives all serve a purpose, but unless we understand the nature and influence of the occupational culture we cannot hope to understand the realities of police work or the impact of law, policy, and reform on operational policing.

Goffman's (1959) analysis of social life as a theatrical performance offers an insightful conceptual and metaphorical toolkit for analysing the discrepancies and interactions between the formal and informal aspects of organizations (Manning 1997, 2008a). In particular, the distinction he makes between 'front stage' and 'back stage' behaviour is a simple but effective way of explaining how people act in a variety of social settings, perform various roles and engage in forms of 'impression management'. Basically, the front stage is where actors present themselves in the guise of a character and give the appearance of adhering to certain standards that have meaning and legitimacy to the 'audience'. When performing a routine on the 'front stage', the behaviour of rank-and-file officers, for example, might be framed by what the organization requires in bureaucratic terms and delivered in a way that responds to their interpretation of the expectations of the public or their colleagues and supervisors. The 'back stage', on the other hand, refers to low visibility or off-duty situations in which police officers are able to step out of character, express themselves in an informal manner, and act in accordance with their cultural ways and means and personal preferences. It is here that 'the capacity of a performance to express something beyond itself may be painstakingly fabricated; it is here that illusions and impressions are openly constructed' (Goffman 1959: 114). According to Manning (1997: 43), the police 'engage in the selective systematic presentation of their activities, and take special care to manage or control access to and knowledge of back regions. This protects that which they conceal, such as organizational secrets, plans, and the less-than-laudatory features of organizational life'.

By immersing themselves in the police world, ethnographers are attempting to obtain the 'behind-the-scenes' access that will enable them to observe the norms, values, and beliefs that embody the identity of the police and assist them in dealing with problematic conditions that arise in their job and organizational environment. Following this longstanding tradition of research, my study of drug detectives strongly verifies the need for researchers to examine the front and back regions of police work in general and drugs policing in particular. In so doing, the aim is to comprehend 'the conduct of the police within the logics of the insider as well as with the perspective of the outsider' (Fassin 2013: xii). As Manning

(2004: 1) suggests in his study of drug law enforcement, ethnography is the most appropriate approach 'for drawing connections between the meanings and activities of naturally occurring events and the outcomes and consequences of official dramas of control'.[2]

The Field

The empirical data that informs this book derive from extensive ethnographic fieldwork undertaken in two English police service areas, during which I was primarily concerned with the routine activities and occupational culture of specialist detective units assigned to the task of investigating drug offences and gathering evidence to support the prosecution of the persons who perpetrate them. Such units might be perceived as a 'team', a social organization that exists to play a particular part in the drama of drug control, a 'set of individuals whose intimate cooperation is required if a given projected definition of the situation is to be maintained' (Goffman 1959: 108). In total, ninety-six days were spent in the field between April 2008 and May 2010. So as to preserve the anonymity of the police forces and those police officers and members of staff who participated in the study, the research settings have been given the pseudonyms 'Metropolis' and 'Smallville'. Both locations were coterminous with the geographical boundaries of a district—or, to use the police terminology of the day, a Basic Command Unit (BCU)—of the associated constabulary and selected to provide variation in local context.[3] That being said, the

---

[2] Academic justifications aside, if I'm honest I always wanted to do an ethnography and become an ethnographer. From what I understood of ethnography, 'the apparent freedom from rigid methodological rules associated with fieldwork and the blissful disregard that many ethnographic writers displayed for high-flying abstractions in their papers and monographs seemed to provide a wonderful excuse for having an adventurous good time while operating under the pretext of doing serious intellectual work' (Van Maanen 1995: 2).

[3] 'The police service' of England and Wales is not a single entity, but rather consists of a number of police 'forces', each of which has its own organizational structure. Generally speaking, within each police force, the headquarters houses the strategic managers and a number of operational and organizational support departments. The personnel working at headquarters are responsible for setting and coordinating force-wide strategy, policy, and procedure. They also allocate resources and support and monitor the BCUs (also known as boroughs, districts and divisions). BCUs deliver basic policing services—patrol, response, investigation, and partnership work—within a fixed geographical area (e.g. a borough,

routines of police work resulted in the observations being concentrated in the areas where the police dealt with the most drug problems and the police stations where key participants spent most of their time.

Being an in-depth study of a limited number of cases that are relatively small in scale, ethnographic work is regularly criticized for its lack of representativeness and generalizability (Hammersley and Atkinson 2007: 233–4). Although I am cautious about making general conclusions and believe that researchers must respect the particularity of research settings, I agree with Bowling (2010: 19) that 'it is the task of the social scientist not simply to document and explain patterns of policing in a specific village or city but to generalize to all such rural or urban settings simply enough for the data collected in one place to provide the basis for descriptive or explanatory lessons to be drawn elsewhere'. Their task, in other words, is to connect a personal research experience with a general field of knowledge. The problem, Fassin (2013: xvii) argues, 'is not to know whether the police act identically everywhere, within a national territory or across borders, but whether the type of relation they have with a certain public, the way in which political incentives influence their practice, the effects of various systems of evaluation and sanctioning on their conducts, or the justification they provide for their deviant behaviors are generalizable'. With this in mind, by analysing similarities and differences in drug detective work between diverse police service areas, and providing an account that engages with the existing academic and policy literature, this study offers a resource that readers can use to understand new situations in similar settings.

Research settings

Metropolis is a borough of a city in the South of England. Being one of the largest inner-city boroughs, it is home to a multitude of local, national, and international businesses, transport gateways, and cultural attractions. Yet despite this apparent prosperity, Metropolis is

town, or city). Each BCU has its own headquarters. This is the base for the divisional command team and the divisional operational and support departments. It is from here that the divisional commander oversees the delivery of policing in the local policing units. These are smaller geographical areas in which teams deliver response and community policing (Mawby and Wright 2008).

a deprived area with high crime and unemployment rates. Parts of the borough are trendy, affluent, and bear the signs of many years of gentrification, whereas others are dominated by rundown public housing estates built during the era of post-war redevelopment. Throughout the fieldwork stage of the research project, Metropolis had a dense population of over a quarter of a million. Around half were aged between twenty and thirty-nine. A similar proportion of the residents were from a diverse range of ethnic minority communities, a third of them having been born outside the UK. Afro-Caribbeans were by far the largest minority group, though there were also Asian, Eastern European, and Portuguese neighbourhoods of noteworthy size. Relations between the police and local communities have been notoriously poor for decades, not least because of the turbulent history of rioting and disorder in the area.

By contrast, Smallville is a town in the North of England. In the industrial heyday of Britain, it was an area characterized by coal mining, manufacturing, and the production of iron and steel. However, with the processes of deindustrialization the town decayed, and subsequent recessions have resulted in further closures and redundancies in many of the few remaining industries. Recovery and regeneration were slow to start and still have a long way to go. A major problem has been that the main industries of Smallville are those in serious decline at a national level, whilst the main sectors of the national economy are severely underrepresented. Many of the communities have been ravaged by years of social inequality. Anyone who walked the streets of the town centre would be struck by the mass of boarded up shops and closing down sales. Long-term unemployment rates have always been higher than the national average and it remains one of the lowest paid regions in the country. Smallville had a disproportionately white population of just over 250,000 during fieldwork, spread over a geographically expansive aggregation of villages and vast tracts of rural England.

The police

The detectives of the Smallville 'drug unit' were tasked with investigating suspected drug dealers on an exclusive basis.[4] Their base of

---

[4] The terms 'squad', 'team' and 'unit' were used interchangeably, but the sign on their office door clearly identified them as a 'unit'.

operations was a small room of a moderately sized police station, located outside a village on the outskirts of the town. The station acted as the intelligence centre of the district, as it housed the intelligence unit, the source unit, the financial investigation unit and the whole proactive investigation department (which consisted of the drug squad, the burglary squad, and the vehicle theft squad). During fieldwork, the drug squad was made up of seven detectives—the self-proclaimed 'magnificent seven': one detective sergeant; five detective constables; and one trainee detective constable. Membership changed only slightly when the trainee detective left to work in 're-active CID' and another officer was temporarily assigned from the force-level 'serious organized crime unit'. The squad operated under the management of the head of the proactive investigation department, a detective inspector who reported to the detective superintendent in charge of divisional operations. Plans were put in motion by middle management to disband the drug squad as the fieldwork was coming to a close, with the intention of merging the separate squads of the proactive investigation department into a generalist crime squad. Not only did this unforeseen event provide a great opportunity to observe the initial stages of organizational restructuring and speak with those involved in and affected by the change, it also added a natural end to my time in the field.

Before fieldwork commenced in Metropolis, I learned that the drug squad had become the 'firearms team' a few years earlier. Whilst the detectives employed therein remained the foremost drug investigators in the district and spent most of their time policing drugs, their focus was now on firearms offences. Being aware of the substantial decline in the number of drug squads operating at both force and district level over the past decade, I saw this as an opportunity to compare the routine activities and occupational culture of a drug squad with a specialist detective unit that had previously specialized in drug law enforcement but was now primarily concerned with drug-related crime. Towards the end of the fieldwork period their focus changed to gang-related crime and the firearms squad was rechristened the gang squad. The firearms squad occupied the top floor of a small police station, which they shared with a Safer Neighbourhood Team (SNT) and a team of school liaison officers. It generally consisted of around eighteen officers (no less than fifteen and no more than twenty): one detective inspector; three detective sergeants; ten detective constables; two trainee detective constables; and two uniformed officers on attachment. There were a number of personnel changes over the course of the research process, but, thankfully, most of the key participants remained in place. These changes actually turned out to be fruitful because they enabled me to observe the socialization of new recruits into the group. Officers were split into a reactive and a proactive team: the former responded to firearms-related incidents and calls from the public about potential firearms offences, whereas the latter specialized in investigating firearms offences and suspected drug dealers. Each team operated under the management of the detective inspector, who reported to the superintendent in charge of divisional operations.

Given that the drug detectives were situated within an organizational context, their world and work featured regular interaction with other social actors, which made it impossible to study them in isolation. Thus, in order to provide a comprehensive account of how drug law enforcement and proactive investigations were performed in the station and on the streets, it soon became apparent that I would have to cast the net wider and study the parts played by their colleagues as well. For instance, owing to the centrality of intelligence units to intelligence-led policing and the National Intelligence Model (NIM) business process, I decided to observe their routine activities and interview intelligence officers and civilian analysts. Likewise, to get a broader understanding of the role of the police in drug control it was necessary to study a range of ranks, units, and shifts and their involvement in the policing of drugs. This included interviewing officers employed in force-level specialist detective units and carrying out observations of management meetings and the practices of the uniform branch. So, whilst the detectives of the Smallville drug squad and the Metropolis firearms squad were the key participants, as the research progressed I laboured to contact and, where possible, work with those police officers and staff who emerged as germane to the focus of the inquiry (see Table 4.1). This practice is referred to as 'purposive sampling' in the research methods literature. Once in the field, however, participants were mostly gathered using 'snowball sampling', whereby existing participants are used to make connections with other potential participants. Sample selection and construction was ongoing. By observing who the drug detectives interacted with, asking them who they thought I should talk to, and taking note of the names on their paperwork, I was able to construct a social network of the key actors involved in the investigatory process and the policing

Table 4.1 Research Participants

Force Level		Research Method	
Metropolis	Smallville	Observed	Interviewed
Drug Unit	Serious Organized Crime Unit		✓
	Intelligence Unit		✓

BCU Level		Research Method	
Metropolis	Smallville	Observed	Interviewed
	Middle Managers	✓	✓
Firearms Unit	Drug Unit	✓	✓
	Reactive CID	✓	✓
	Intelligence Unit	✓	✓
	Source Unit		✓
	Financial Investigations Unit		✓
	Response Teams	✓	✓
	Safer Neighbourhood Teams (SNTs)	✓	✓
	Licensing Unit	✓	✓
	Drug Interventions Programme (DIP)	✓	✓

of drugs. The main problem with this method of sampling is that using the networks and suggestions of a small group of people is likely to result in a sample that is unrepresentative of the population and, thereby, a distorted view of the social world under study. To overcome this shortcoming, the staff directory was also consulted so as to ascertain the roles and responsibilities of police personnel and identify those who occupied relevant organizational positions. An advantage of studying a bureaucratic organization such as the police is that it is almost always possible to find out who officially does what, where they are located, and how best to contact them.

Research Methods

The chosen methods offered the most appropriate and useful re-search tools available as they enabled me to describe and explain patterns of police activity, access the features of the occupational culture, and examine the ways in which drug detectives experience, interpret, and structure their everyday working lives. By bringing together multiple methods, the data reveals different dimensions of police investigations and the policing of drugs and enriches understandings of the multifaceted and complex nature of detective work and legal processes. The technique of 'triangulation' was used in order to corroborate findings and assess the validity of the data and the principles of 'thematic analysis' were employed throughout (Boyatzis 1998). Many aspects of the police world doubtless remained hidden or eluded me. In the end, it 'will be for the reader to judge whether the account offered here is accurate, reliable, and compelling' (Bowling 2010: 21).

Observation

The research primarily comprised over five hundred hours of direct observation of ordinary police work both on and off the streets, everything from meetings, briefings, and administrative duties to covert surveillance operations, the execution of drugs warrants, and court proceedings. Not being a functioning member of the police service, an 'observer-as-participant' role was adopted because it was the only available option (Gold 1958). That being said, it is 'increasingly accepted that the most faithfully-negotiated overt approach inescapably contains some covertness, in that, short of wearing a sign, ethnographers cannot signal when they are or are not collecting data' (Fielding 2008: 272). Eavesdropping became a forte of mine, and I regularly excused myself to scribble down notes in a toilet cubicle. Whenever possible, the dedicated periods of fieldwork corresponded with the working hours of the drug detectives, from raids at dawn to the endless hours of a nightshift. Care was taken to ensure that the research captured the range of activities taking place, temporal variations in behaviour were taken into account, and time was equally divided and alternated between the two research settings.

When carrying out fieldwork, I limited myself to 'observing, listening, formulating a few questions, engaging sometimes in mundane conversations and, ultimately, trying to comprehend what was going on' (Fassin 2013: 24). At times it felt as though I was trying to observe too much, wasting time taking note of who made the coffee, who made jokes and who made a show of their flatulence. But when the purpose of the research is exploration one must be careful not to dismiss or undervalue the little things that contribute to the bigger picture. Following Loftus (2009: 208), I distinguished two types of data as pertinent for accessing the features of the occupational culture: the ways actors talk spontaneously about aspects of their occupation provide an important insight into their values and beliefs; and how they deal practically with real situations conveys a great deal about the norms and craft of routine policing. Every so often participants would volunteer explanations as to why they acted in a particular way, but more often than not I would make inferences or simply ask them during the course of naturally occurring conversations. Like Skolnick (2011: 29), I found that 'the most informative method was not to ask predetermined questions, but rather to question actions the police officer had just taken or failed to take concerning events or objects just encountered, such as certain categories of people or places in the city'. The process of discussing created an air of informality when opinion seemed to be more openly expressed.

In using observation and informal conversation as my principal research methods, most of what I learnt in the field was systematically recorded by way of fieldnotes. Writing fieldnotes is in many respects like keeping a diary or logbook that contains personal impressions and 'a running description of events, people, things heard and overheard, conversations among people, conversations with people' (Lofland and Lofland 1995: 93). For the most part, I use the actual words of the police as 'the "situated vocabularies" employed provide us with valuable information about the ways in which members of a particular culture organize their perceptions of the world' (Hammersley and Atkinson 2007: 145). Not only do fieldnotes act as a source of data and a powerful memory aid, but they are also vital to the reflexivity of the project in that they allow the researcher to express their emotions and reflect upon the research process and their role in the formation and interpretation of data. Taking on board the recommendations of Emerson et al. (2001: 353), I took the view that fieldnotes 'are writings produced in or in close proximity to "the field". Proximity means that fieldnotes are written more or less *contemporaneously* with the events, experiences and interactions they describe and recount'. Detailed fieldnotes tended to be written up at the end of the working day or as soon as possible thereafter, before engaging in further interaction. Given that I wanted to be as unobtrusive as possible, pen rarely touched paper when in the company of the police. In the field I was heavily reliant on 'mental notes' and would only make 'jotted notes'—'little phrases, quotes, key words, and the like' (Lofland and Lofland 1995: 90)—at inconspicuous moments. However, although I consider it to be impractical and methodologically unsound to make notes when observing officers doing police work or interacting with their colleagues, I found that complete note taking abstinence was not always possible or preferable. Research participants often expected me to write down what they were saying, perhaps because they wanted to make sure that I got the 'facts' right or felt that they were making a particularly noteworthy point. A golden rule of mine was to be descriptive rather than analytical and never write down anything that I would not want my participants to read.

Ultimately fieldnotes cannot precisely capture everything that is seen or heard, nor can they contain all of the information that is stored inside the head of the researcher. Ethnographers learn more in the field than is ever contained in the written record. Their writings are a selective, subjective, and purposeful representation. For Hammersley and Atkinson (2007: 142), what is recorded 'will depend on one's general sense of what is relevant to the foreshadowing research problems, as well as on background expectations'. Owing to the conditions in which they are written, fieldnotes usually require editing prior to dissemination so as to remove irrelevant material and produce a coherent and readable account. They were reordered and substantially rewritten as I selected and moulded them with some analytic or representational purpose (Emerson et al. 2001). The excerpts that appear throughout this monograph are polished versions of the notes that were produced during fieldwork. Whilst some verbal data were written down verbatim, many of the quotations are a précis of what was said. Only very occasionally was I required to recall events, people, and conversations from memory, when there were gaps in the narrative or the descriptions and initial impressions were lacking. On numerous occasions participants were actively chased up to clarify various points of uncertainty and validate their comments, claims, and accounts of events. Most of the factual materials of this book have been read in one state of draft or another by the police personnel involved and they have generally responded by saying that the portrait is fair and accurate.

Interviews

Along with the relatively unstructured 'interviews as conversation' (Burgess 1984) that were integrated with the observations, another strand of methodology comprised fifty semi-structured interviews with key individuals within the participating police services. Interviews took place in a variety of locations and ranged in duration from thirty minutes to three hours. The process of interviewing was useful for focusing on specific topics, testing the veracity of observations, and asking questions aimed at isolating and capturing individual perspectives towards the job, the working environment, and the field of drug control. Furthermore, the interview settings, which included cafeterias, cars, offices, and pubs, allowed participants to reflect upon personal experiences and express themselves without the presence of their colleagues. The first phase of interviewing involved 'elite interviews' and group discussions with middle managers in order to comprehensively discuss the aims and outputs of the project and facilitate access to potential research participants. Analogous interviews were then carried out with the relevant line managers and supervisors. For the most part, interviews with frontline officers and police staff were reserved for those whose routine activities were not observed. Before leaving the field, a series of exit interviews were conducted in order to discuss and corroborate the findings of the study and arrange for future contact and dissemination.

With the exception of a handful of interviews that spontaneously took place following chance encounters, interview schedules or aide memoires, which contained a logically ordered list of broad topics and specific questions to be covered, were always prepared in advance. Preparation was shaped by the research questions and the likely content of the interview and constructed to set a loose agenda. Schedules and questions were rewritten and rephrased as I learnt from experience, and were naturally modified to reflect the progress of the research. The intention was to encourage discursive accounts, allow for interviewees to speak freely, and reveal the meaning of their actions or the reasons for their attitudes in their own terms, rather than in response to directive questioning. Accordingly, I adopted an open, conversational, and flexible style of interviewing, following issues and tangents as and when they came up and exploring topics that were not anticipated but turned out to be important.

To ensure that I had a complete and accurate record of all that was said, the first few interviews were recorded using a digital audio device. Yet, going back over those transcripts now, it seems fairly obvious that this recording technique altered the dynamics of the interaction, inhibited the flow of conversation, and induced self-censorship. Interviewees were prone to stay on the front stage and seemed reluctant to express personal opinions or say anything that might be considered controversial. The same officers spoke much more candidly during informal conversations. One interviewee actually advised me to stop using a Dictaphone because 'hardly any cops will give you the answers you want on the record'. Writing about this issue, Innes (2003a: 287) suggests that tape recording his interviews 'would have precluded some of the frank and open discussions about sensitive material and issues that were enjoyed by the researcher'. So I ditched the Dictaphone and opted for note taking instead, which meant that interviews were not recorded verbatim and at times I was focusing more on writing than on observing the appearance, body language, and demeanour of the interviewee.

Documents

In order to interrogate the 'organizational front', understand the legal and policy context surrounding the investigations under observation, and examine how such frameworks structure the work of detectives on the frontline, it was crucial that I analysed the relevant statutes and internally and externally published police documents. Government departments and the police generate and consume huge amounts of documentation that should not be overlooked by ethnographic researchers. Documentary analysis enabled me to describe and analyse 'official' definitions of the situation and how the police present themselves and their work. It also provided an insight into police powers, strategic priorities, operational activities, management structures, and mechanisms of accountability.

Preliminary analysis of publically available documents was undertaken prior to the commencement of fieldwork. These included drug laws, national drug strategies, legislation designed to govern police investigations, and 'professional practice publications', which are designed by police practitioners, the Home Office, and other criminal justice stakeholders for internal consumption but can also be accessed externally via the internet or upon request. During fieldwork, the primary source of such publications was the National Policing Improvement Agency (NPIA).[5] There are four types of professional practice publication: 'codes of practice'; 'guidance'; 'practice advice'; and 'briefing papers'. Codes of practice are commissioned by the Home Secretary and are intended to promote the efficiency and effectiveness of the police. Once published, police managers are obliged to implement the codes and ensure that the prescribed practices are adopted. Guidance documents are commissioned by ACPO and/or the Home Office and developed through comprehensive consultation with stakeholders to identify 'good practice'. Compliance with guidance is mandatory and is embedded into Her Majesty's Inspectorate of Constabulary (HMIC) inspection frameworks. Practice advice is commissioned by ACPO and/or the Home Office and is produced primarily to assist practitioners by promoting good practice. Unlike guidance, the implementation of advisory publications is discretionary.

Internal police documents were identified and accessed through interviews and observations. These included role profiles, training manuals, crime data, force drug strategies, intelligence reports, analytical products, warrant applications, surveillance logs and interview transcripts. The most informative and revealing sources were the 'case files' kept by detectives that documented the process of investigation from the instigation of an operation through to the close. They typically contained information used by the police during the course of investigations, actions performed by the investigating officers, and evidence gathered. Furthermore, I am convinced, like Brodeur (2010: 198-9), 'that it is courting failure to interview criminal investigators (and intelligence officers) without

---

[5] Established by the Police and Justice Act 2006, the NPIA was a non-departmental national policing organization that acted as a central resource to the police service, working for ACPO, the Association of Police Authorities (APA), and the Home Office to improve the delivery of policing. It subsumed the work of, and replaced, the Central Police Training and Development Authority (Centrex) (including the National Centre for Policing Excellence (NCPE)). As part of its remit, the NPIA was required to develop policing doctrine. Since leaving the field, the NPIA has been abolished and by December 2012 all functions had been transferred to the Home Office, the Serious Organized Crime Agency (SOCA), and the College of Policing. SOCA was itself replaced by the National Crime Agency as a feature of the Crime and Courts Act 2013.

being thoroughly acquainted with their work and without being in a position to question...the claims they make in the course of an interview'.

Negotiating Access

When I first decided to carry out the research, I had no 'foot-in-the-door' access. Being an 'outsider outsider' (Brown 1996), I was not part of the world I intended to study, had no personal connection with any potential participants, and no official status or academic credentials that mandated police co-operation. For me, the identification of potential 'gatekeepers' and the negotiation of formal access were facilitated by existing relationships between academic colleagues and senior police officers in Metropolis and Smallville. Although they expressed a willingness to sponsor and assist in the research project, my initial points of contact were properly concerned about whether or not I could be trusted with sensitive information, what picture of the police world I would paint, and how the findings would be disseminated. As they were in total control of the fieldwork at this stage, they decided to block off certain lines of inquiry. For instance, my original intention was to focus on force-level drug law enforcement, something called for by Pearson and Hobbs (2001: 56) to better understand the 'growing "void" of enforcement activity and intelligence in what might be thought of as the "middle" of the domestic market'. This request was immediately declined for 'security reasons', as was the request to carrying out observations of the routine activities of the source unit, interview informants, and analyse the associated paperwork. After these issues were ironed out in a face-to-face meeting, permission was granted and a provisional research bargain agreed.

Following the formal access meetings, the senior officers put me in touch with the drug detectives and helped set the wheels in motion for brokering another deal. This experience taught me that formal access might be the first hurdle into the organization but it certainly does not translate into a backstage pass or guarantee acceptance and assistance. The following fieldnote extract illustrates this point:

Today I met with the detective sergeant of the Smallville drug Unit—'DS Daniels', or 'Cedric' on a good day—to discuss the research aims and negotiate access. Naively, since management had already given me the green light, I assumed that this meeting was merely a formality and that things would run relatively smoothly from hereon in. I was sorely mistaken. Upon arrival at the police station, the receptionist informed me that DS Daniels would be indefinitely late. No explanation was forthcoming. So I signed in, sat myself down in the waiting area and nervously awaited his arrival. After just over an hour of breathing exercises and thumb twiddling, the security door opened and out strode a monster of a man to greet me. His burly build, blank expression, and unremitting eye contact made me very apprehensive. Silently, he escorted me into an empty room and closed the door behind us. The discussion that followed was an interrogation in all but name, throughout which I felt more like a suspected criminal than a supposed researcher. DS Daniels was standoffish, told me quite frankly that he was disinclined to facilitate my research, and unable to see any potential benefits in doing so whatsoever. However, regardless of his personal feelings on the matter, he said he would assist me because 'the chief' had requested his compliance. Whilst I was relieved to have access, I knew that unless I could win over the drug detectives and find some common ground the project was doomed from the get-go. (Fieldnotes, Smallville)

Although access to the drug squad had been officially granted, DS Daniels employed various tactics to slow the research process down and deter me from returning. Despite my punctuality, I was often kept waiting, put on hold, or told to call back later. Painstakingly written emails received belated responses or disappeared into the ether. On the day that fieldwork was set to commence with the squad, he informed me that, due to an ongoing operation, I would have to spend a couple of weeks working with the intelligence unit instead. When observations finally started, he insisted that I could only come in once a week and would not be able to accompany them on all of their endeavours. For the first month or so I felt like an unwelcome stranger, marginalized by my status as an outsider and suspected 'challenger' (Holdaway 1983: 71–7).[6] There were a great many cautious glances, whispered conversations, and meetings behind closed doors. On the whole, I was accommodated but kept at a distance, as the detectives investigated this so-called researcher who was watching their every move and asking disruptive, intrusive, and potentially incriminating questions. Under

---

[6] Researchers are typically regarded as 'challengers' in the sense that they are 'in a position to pierce the secrecy and protection of the lower ranks' and gather information that might be used to criticize the police and thereby challenge their authority and legitimacy (Holdaway 1983: 71).

such circumstances, I found it difficult to obtain anything other than superficial or stage-managed data that was beset with lies and partial truths and came to realize that the researched have power of life and death over the research.

Ethnographers must be accepted by those they are researching and this can be a lengthy process that requires patience, perseverance, and providence. The days in the field passed as they always did, the drug game lived on, and in time the thaw set in and the inner world of the drug detectives began to reveal itself. Before long, I found that officers were willing to speak candidly in my presence and teach me the ways of the force. 'Trust is unlikely ever to be complete' (Reiner and Newburn 2008: 354), but spending extensive periods in the field, being open about the focus of the research, sharing common experiences, and enduring whatever trials, tribulations, and initiation rituals arise helps form and maintain good relationships. If a researcher wants their participants to be honest and genuine with them the least they can do in return is reciprocate.[7] It is unwise and practically impossible to be a constant researcher. Indeed, it is of the utmost importance that researchers get to know their participants as people, rather than seeing them simply as contacts and sources of information. 'Hanging around' and chitchatting made it easier for the police to run character checks and become more familiar and comfortable with my research and presence in their lives. Like a number of other police researchers, I found going for an off-duty drink to be an effective method of breaking down barriers, becoming a *de facto* member of the group and revealing rich data. The pub was where the detectives of Metropolis drunkenly swore me in as a 'deputy sheriff', where I witnessed some of the most regrettable dance moves known to mankind, and where I was told about the sordid sex stories of the CID. Dedicated as I am to my work, on occasions I found myself in the same situation that Hobbs (1988: 6) did

---

[7] When asked, I was open about the focus of the research but not usually required to be specific. This is a useful distinction when it comes to the ethical principle of informed consent. The research was explained in general terms to make it understandable and acceptable to the researched. Like Van Maanen (1978a: 334), 'I do not believe it is ethically necessary, nor methodologically sound, to make known specific hypotheses, background assumptions, or particular areas of interest'. For example, I rarely mentioned that I was taking note of discriminatory attitudes or the harmful effects of drug law enforcement for fear that it would impact on natural behaviours or bring the research to a grinding halt.

during his study of detectives, waking up in the morning with a hangover 'facing the dilemma of whether to bring it up or write it up'. Evidence of my acceptance included being referred to as a 'colleague' or 'mate' and asked to join social activities. Some participants disclosed details about their personal lives and past drug use, others gave me entry codes so that I could let myself through locked doors, allowed me to print out or photocopy documents, or browse on the police intranet without supervision or restriction. This breaking down of barriers is when the researcher is able to move from the front to the back stage. Furthermore, it also helps counter a recurrent criticism of observational research. No matter how inconspicuous the researcher strives to be, when an overt role is adopted they have an impact upon the research setting as participants modify their behaviour in response to being studied. The longer the research goes on, however, the more difficult and perhaps the less important it is for the observed to maintain any pretences or conceal aspects of their world, especially when the act they are engaged in is more important than the fact that an outsider is observing them.

5

The Police on Drugs

Be they knowledgeable, ignorant, or somewhere in between, everyone seems to have an opinion on drugs and how best to deal with them. Though I tried to remain neutral and keep my thoughts, viewpoints, and private life to myself, from the outset some of the detectives were under the impression that I was 'one of those idiots who thinks drugs should be legalized'. Furthermore, a few of them assumed that I was or had been a recreational drug user. I couldn't help but wonder whether their assumptions were based on their attitudes or prejudices towards the student population. Or maybe the opinions they held about the academic profession and those who sit on the left of the political spectrum had caused them to jump to conclusions. Maybe their reasons were more personal and related to the fact that I 'looked the part' or exhibited the 'tell-tale signs' in my mannerisms and character traits. Maybe the obligatory background checks had revealed something incriminating or at least implicating enough to warrant their reasonable suspicion. Or maybe I had completely misread the situation and failed to appreciate their sense of humour.

As time progressed, it transpired that most police officers viewed recreational drug use as a relatively normal part of university life. It was taken for granted and a matter of fact that 'students' spend much of their time in the pub and some of their time experimenting with drugs. Their views on this particular subject matter could have been based on their professional experience of policing students or their personal experience of being a student. They could equally have less to do with the job and more to do with the stories and stereotypes that are embedded in popular culture. Outside the office of constable, the association between getting high and higher education is common knowledge and might even be considered a rite of passage. Whatever the case may be, this clear case of stereotyping got me thinking about how perceptions and preconceptions impact on police attitudes and the delivery of policing

(Fieldnotes, Smallville).

Police researchers have identified sets of shared values and beliefs that underpin how the police view the social world, how they relate to each other, and how they interact with the public. Police culture, Campeau (2015: 2) argues, 'is *used* by officers as a *resource* to make sense of their occupational lives'. Taken collectively, the 'core characteristics' revealed in a longstanding tradition of police research—sense of mission, action orientation, cynicism and pessimism, suspicion, isolation and solidarity, conservatism, machismo, racial prejudice, and pragmatism (Reiner 2010: 118–32)— are widely considered to encapsulate the 'dominant' culture of the police.[1] These characteristics are said to arise as officers adapt to the demands of the police role, the constraints of legality in modern liberal democracies, and the wider social, economic, and political conditions of policing.

Police culture lies at the centre of much research and theorizing about policing and the police because it is thought to exert a considerable influence over the attitudes and behaviours of police officers. Another proposition that remains central to understandings in this area is that the occupational culture of the lower ranks has proven to be stubbornly resistant to changes in policing and capable of undermining organizational reforms. Interrogating the official organizational position on the policing of drugs, this chapter delves into the police worldview with the aim of exploring and making sense of how officers perceived the drug world and their role in it, using some of the most pertinent concepts, themes, and theories from the police culture literature to help frame the analysis (Bacon 2014; Chan 1997; Cockcroft 2012; Loftus 2009; Reiner 2010). The cultural lens is focused on the drug detectives of Metropolis and Smallville. It looks, for the most part, at the spontaneous talk they engaged in with their colleagues, their comments and explanations about the job, the drug problem, and the state of humankind, the things they said in private, in the course of their work, and in the communal areas of police stations where officers congregate to 'shoot the shit'. And let us not forget the slurred statements and

---

[1] The adjective dominant is used here not only to capture the powerful influence of this cultural core over police officers and the occupation of policing, but also to imply that it dominates perceptions of police culture. Sklansky (2007) goes so far as to say that preoccupation with the dominant culture has resulted in a sort of 'cognitive burn-in' that obscures variations in police culture and policing styles.

amazing revelations that were haphazardly taken down over a pint or two. Rather than presenting a monolithic view, care has been taken to reflect the diversity of opinions that were expressed by detectives and a range of other police officers so as to bring out any cultural variations arising from idiosyncrasies and the distinct experiences and expectations associated with rank, specialism, and the external policing environment. The data presented really highlight the importance of observations, informal conversations and interviews as methods of gaining an insight into the complex and at times contradictory reality of police values and belief systems.

The relationship between talk and action is far from straightforward and by no means easy to fathom, but by looking at what officers say we might also learn something about the craft of policing and the everyday realities of police work. Commentators have developed the concept of 'canteen culture' as a means of explaining the gap between the privately expressed views of police officers and what they actually do in practice (Fielding 1994; Hoyle 1998; Waddington 1999b). The 'canteen' symbolizes the places where officers socialize when off-duty, where they have a catch-up with friends, spread gossip, and share information about recent goings-on. Such talk is revealing but does not always speak the truth and should not be taken as a statement of fact. For Hoyle (1998: 75), canteen culture 'allows officers to articulate their fears, and vent their frustrations and anger' about the role of the police and the demands of operational policing. She stresses that, whilst attitudes certainly have some impact on behaviour, they do not cause police officers to behave in a particular way or necessarily correspond to their practices. Through storytelling, whether the anecdotes are tall tales or short ones, the police are said to affirm their worldview, give meaning to their experiences, and demonstrate their competence to an audience of their peers. Stories also allow officers to learn about the unknown, express opinions on subjects about which they know very little, and recount past events in which they played no part (Shearing and Ericson 1991; van Hulst 2013).

Drugs

Controlled substances

When asked directly for their views on drugs, most police officers were resolutely anti-drugs, in that they were against the use and supply of *illegal* psychoactive substances. 'Everyone knows drugs are bad news; they're illegal for good reasons' were the words of one detective. This comment summed up the views of the majority. Drugs were invariably said to be 'bad', 'damaging', 'dangerous', 'harmful', 'problematic', and 'serious'. The 'bad news' usually featured stories of petty and serious crimes, harrowing tales of addiction, and regular bulletins about the harmful effects that drugs have on individuals, families, and communities. The 'good reasons' for legal prohibition were explained in much the same terms. 'Drugs are illegal because they're damaging to society'—for the police this truism was just common sense. So too was the implication that drug laws exist to preserve social order and protect the public. They rarely questioned the authority of the law and tended not to go beyond empirical matters in their explanations. They didn't know much about the philosophical underpinnings of prohibition or the history of drug control policy. They didn't need to. Their job was to enforce the law. Criminalization was seen as the natural governmental response to the drug problem because it provided the police with the power to maintain the security of social order. This is but one of many examples of the 'conceptual conservatism' that Reiner (2010: 131) describes in his account of police culture, 'the very pragmatic, concrete, down-to-earth, antitheoretical perspective which is typical of the rank and file'.

The legal status of a drug was of great significance to the police by virtue of their unique position of enforcing the law in a liberal democratic society and the fact that upon their appointment they had sworn to uphold it. As Skolnick (2011: 54) said in *Justice Without Trial*, 'the fact that a person is engaged in enforcing a set of rules implies that the person also becomes implicated in *affirming* them'. The differences of opinion, however, and the differential rates of enforcement that were revealed through fieldwork, and are discussed further below, reflect an ambivalent form of affirmation. The following was typical of the sentiment expressed on the record:

For me there's no difference between the controlled drugs, they're all illegal and it's my job to enforce the law. (Detective Sergeant, Smallville)

During the long conversation from which this short quotation is taken the 'Serg' discussed differences in the legal classification of controlled drugs, the different laws, offences, and penalties; he was knowledgeable about the chemical composition of different drugs, their pharmacological effects, markets, and the associated risks. He was a perfect example of a dedicated professional and ardent law enforcer who had acquired this knowledge through specialist training sessions and independent research because it helped him do his job. 'If it was up to me and we had the resources it'd be as simple as "you break the law and we take you in". It's that black-and-white.' Like many other officers, the 'boss' of the Smallville drug squad exhibited a number of authoritarian personality traits, including political conservatism, a strong sense of morality, a rigid dichotomizing style, and an intolerant, punitive attitude towards deviance from conventional values and traditions. For the authoritarians, the role of the police in drug control was usually conceptualized as a simple matter of law enforcement. In their eyes it essentially boiled down to the fact that people who use or supply drugs are acting in contravention of the law and it is their job to enforce the law and bring offenders to justice.

Alcohol

This 'black-and-white' mentality is all the more obvious when one considers police attitudes towards legal psychoactive substances. Police officers certainly did not think of alcohol as a drug in the same sense as its illegal counterparts—'it's not even in the same league', being a typical comeback when I suggested that it was. Many preferred to refer to alcohol as an 'intoxicant' rather than a 'drug' simply to highlight this artificial distinction. This lack of reflexivity is paradoxical, but perhaps protects officers from cognitive dissonance. As one officer put it:

I don't understand why anyone would want to take drugs. I enjoy a drink every now and then, but drugs...now that's a different kettle of fish. (Detective, Smallville)

From what I heard and observed, drinking habits have changed since Hobbs (1988) studied detectives doing the business in the East End of London. Detective work was rarely conducted in licensed premises anymore and so alcohol no longer 'provides a strategic prop in the dramaturgical presentation of the urban detective' (p196). Far from being seen as a demand of the job, drinking whilst on duty is strictly prohibited.

It's a social thing isn't it, to go for a drink after work or get pissed up and have a laugh for a mate's birthday. There's always a few who can't handle it or take it a bit too far, but I think everyone's been there once or twice. (Detective, Metropolis)

In the course of the fieldwork I went for after-work drinks with police officers, nights out to celebrate a job-well-done, or any other excuse. I've seen drug law enforcers refused entry into venues for being too drunk and be asked to leave for the very same reason. I've tried to keep up and missed trains home, woken up at the end of the line and struggled to vividly recollect the inebriated events of the night before. And then there was the sobriety, hard work, and wholesome entertainment. For me, the place of alcohol within police culture simply reflects the culture of drinking that pervades British society (Hadfield 2006; Hobbs et al. 2003; Measham and Brain 2005).

Alcohol may well be a substance that police officers regularly use and abuse, but on the streets of the night-time economy the magnitude of alcohol-related crime and disorder presented them with an arduous task.

Up until tonight I had never really tried to observe the streets of the night-time economy from a police perspective, having only ever experienced the highs and lows of nightlife as a customer of the pubs and clubs that are concentrated in and around most urban centres. Tonight I undertook my first Friday night of fieldwork with the police officers assigned to the task of patrolling the night-time high street of a town in the North of England, an experience which enabled me to see that when the 'beer goggles' are replaced with an academic lens things can look very different indeed. The bright lights, pleasure-seeking masses, and plentiful supply of leisure activities and consumables might provide the public with the perfect place in which to enjoy themselves and let off steam, but to the police it is a policing nightmare within which the occurrence of crime and disorder is an absolute certainty. Before the sun went down, the officers assured me that within a matter of hours there would be more sights, fights, and frights than they could possibly handle. They also assured me that among the neon signs, music events, and drinks promotions of the commercial infrastructure, people would be distributing and consuming illegal drugs. 'Drugs are everywhere these days,' I was told with an air of cynicism and concern, as the police geared up to confront the consequences of our binge-drinking culture. (Fieldnotes, Smallville)

During nightshift observations with the uniform branch, the duty groups, neighbourhood teams, public order vans, and response units working in urban centres, most of their time was spent dealing with drunk and disorderly behaviour and waiting for the violence to 'kick off':

> If we actually stopped and searched everyone who we suspect has drugs on them, we'd get nothing else done, and when we do find something it's usually a few pills or a bit of coke. In that situation, I'd prefer to just seize the drugs and give them a caution, but that kind of policing's hard to justify...It takes a long time to get them through custody and do all the paperwork, and we need all the officers we can get on the streets in case it kicks off. (Police Constable, Smallville)

Similar sentiments were expressed by the patrol officers interviewed by May et al. (2002, 2007) in their studies of policing cannabis possession offences. The police would strategically position themselves in and around the 'hotspot' areas: the stomping grounds of the 'weekend warriors'; the nightlife events that tended to attract 'a certain type'; the usual venues at 'chucking-out time'; and the cashpoints, takeaways, and taxi ranks. For all intents and purposes, the 'binge drinker' was the problematic drug user of the night and the primary drug control concern of the police. This finding captures the irony of the police gearing up for the consequences of alcohol-related disorder whilst seeing drugs as the negative.

The official position is that 'party', 'recreational', or 'soft' drugs are illegal and will therefore be policed like any other drug, but unofficially the police recognized that the law does not reflect important distinctions between drugs, drug markets, and drug problems. For example, a common belief within the organization was that people fuelled by cannabis or ecstasy cause less crime and disorder than those fuelled by alcohol. When asked why they thought this was the case, officers alluded to the pharmacological effects of the drugs, the types of people that tend to use them, and the fact that consumption and distribution tended to be contained within particular settings. Shortly after having issued a fixed penalty notice for being drunk and disorderly, an officer disclosed that 'we know a lot of drug use goes on in the gay clubs down the road, but they rarely cause us any trouble so it's not that much of a problem'. These subjective and situational notions of 'trouble' and 'problem'—as well as displays of stereotyping—demonstrate that perceptions of crime, priorities, and the police role are dominant features of the occupational mindset. Here, we see that 'soft' drugs are not 'hard' enough for the crime-fighter mentality of the police and so are routinely relegated to the lower end of officers' 'sense of crime hierarchy' (Loftus 2009: 92).

'Legal highs'

To further illustrate the significance of legal status, let us now turn to the issue of those novel psychoactive substances that have become commonly known as 'legal highs'. Before it was outlawed in April 2010, mephedrone was rarely encountered by the police aside from when officers working the streets of the night-time economy carried out routine arrests and stop and searches. In appearance, it looks similar to any other 'white powder' drug, so they were quite within their rights to detain the persons they suspected of possession, confiscate the substance, and send it away for forensic analysis, despite any protestations of innocence. Though I never observed it firsthand, officers told me it was a frustrating time: people were 'acting like we couldn't touch them', some 'even had the cheek to demand their drugs back', and those found in possession of controlled drugs would regularly claim that the substance was mephedrone in an attempt to deceive the police. Their frustration was symptomatic of their loss of control and plainly signified the importance of authority and respect to their culture.

With only a few exceptions, the police officers I worked with found out about mephedrone through the news media rather than the job—even those who specialized in intelligence and the policing of drugs. When I first asked the Smallville drug squad about it in November 2009, one of the detectives said: 'Mephedrone? I think you mean methadone, Matt. I thought you were supposed to know about this type of thing.'

DS Daniels was able to fill them in, as he received weekly newsletters and regular emails from government agencies about drug trends and emerging issues. 'It's one of those new legal highs', he explained, 'nothing for us to worry about'. The subject didn't get mentioned again until January, when the same detective started up a conversation with: 'I read something about that mephedrone you mentioned a few months back in the paper the other day. It's a plant food isn't it? Why would anyone want to take plant food?!'

As is characteristic of a pragmatic culture, these findings suggest that police officers are generally only interested in or knowledgeable about the problems that fall within their immediate occupational remit. Given that the principal role of the police in drug control is law enforcement, when mephedrone was legal they either did not know what it was or knew but did not consider it to be a police problem. Because the detectives were not required or empowered to do anything about it they were caught unawares and almost nothing was done. The whole organization seemed to have a 'wait and see' attitude:

If I'm honest we're all hoping it will just blow over. If it doesn't the government will probably make it illegal, and then we'll start policing it. (Senior Officer, Metropolis)

Even after the ban, the detectives were ambivalent and reluctant to take on the 'meow meow' problem. They were waiting to see what the impact of criminalization would be and hoping that the drug would simply disappear when the surplus ran out:

For us it's not an issue; the media made a mountain out of a molehill. In reality mephedrone isn't even that much of a problem, and unless it becomes one we're not going to look into it. (Detective, Smallville)

An exception to the rule was in Metropolis, where the force intelligence unit had a dedicated drugs desk in place to monitor the information highway for movements and murmurs in the drug world. As soon as the plans to ban mephedrone were announced by the then Home Secretary, Alan Johnson, on 29 March, the unit set about producing a 'problem profile' of the available information surrounding the use and distribution of the drug. During interview, the author of the profile, a senior analyst, told me that 'someone from upstairs' had asked him to do it 'so it looks like we've been doing something'.

Drug Use

'Are you experienced?'

As expected, I came up against quite a lot of resistance when asking officers if they had ever taken drugs themselves. I learnt to gauge their reactions to the question, their taken aback expressions, wondering eyes, and occasional stumbles—'watch them squirm', to put it like a cop. Some thought it was a trick question and that I should have known the answer was incontrovertibly, 'No!'. Others were more suspicious of my motives, perhaps thinking that I was secretly working for management, the government, or the press. It was a question saved until the latter days of fieldwork, one which was generally reserved for those officers with whom I had developed sufficient rapport to feel comfortable enough to speak with them about our private lives. A few actually jumped the gun and spoke about their drug use experiences without prompting.

The overwhelming majority of police officers claimed to have never been anything other than drug free. Not one officer confided that they were currently or occasionally using drugs, and hardly any admitted to having used drugs in their former police life. A few spoke candidly about their cannabis consumption, for instance, a few more owned up to having dabbled in the rave culture of the early 1990s, and one or two of the older generation declared that they were once young hippies. They did not regret the choices they made but still felt the need to offer justifications by using clichés such as 'everyone experiments when they're younger' or it was 'just something everybody did':

When I was at university I smoked quite a bit of hash; that's a normal part of student life, isn't it? We had a lot of fun and didn't do anybody any harm. It's something you grow out of... Now, I'm a copper with a family. (Detective, Metropolis)

I don't want my kids doing it, but I do think experimenting with drugs is a part of growing up. Let them get it out of their system when they're young, and most of them will grow up to be responsible adults... I'd be a bloody hypocrite if I said otherwise, wouldn't I? (Detective, Metropolis)

Those who confessed to previous transgressions tended to exhibit relatively liberal attitudes towards drug use and control. This observation finds support in the work of Warburton et al. (2005: 123), who found that those officers who had used cannabis at some stage of their life were more likely to take informal action against drug offenders than those who had not. So too did the significant minority who said they personally knew people who took drugs recreationally or had taken drugs in the not so distant past:

I know people who take drugs; I've had good times with them and heard all their stories about mad nights out. It never really appealed to me though, I'm happy to stick with the drink. (Police Constable, Smallville)

It's not like they do it in front of me, they know better than that! The way I see it is it's their choice. In the end they're only hurting themselves. (Detective, Smallville)

I've got friends who've smoked cannabis for years. They started out in the 60s, thinking it was liberating and mind-expanded and all that... They won't touch alcohol when we meet up for a drink; they haven't for years, they think it's much more dangerous. (Senior Officer, Metropolis)

Of these officers, most expressed their disapproval of such behaviour and said they had expressed it to those concerned. None of them had ever taken formal action against a relative or friend for taking drugs, however, nor did they say that they ever would. A popular sentiment was that 'you can't be a bobby all the time'. If anything, it was thought that 'a quiet word' was all that was needed if they got 'out of line' by overindulging, behaving in an impertinent manner or neglecting the performance of their duties in the home or the workplace. The police had a strong sense of solidarity and camaraderie; they valued trust, loyalty and unity, believed there was a need to support and protect colleagues, family, and friends, even if that meant condoning their mistakes and misbehaviours.

When off-duty officers tried to suspend judgement, they said they would usually overlook what they considered to be 'tolerable' or 'ignorable' drug use. The following fieldnote illustrates this point:

When I arrived this morning the squad were chatting about what they had been up to over the weekend, so I grabbed myself a cup of tea and joined them. Like most weekends, Bunk had spent Saturday night in the pub. 'You'll never believe it,' he exclaimed, before proceeding to tell us about how he'd 'clocked' a group of young men he didn't recognize 'obviously doing coke'. He surreptitiously watched them for a while longer—the far from discreet 'hand-overs', excessive number of trips to the toilet, and severe case of the sniffles confirmed his suspicions. 'What did you do?' the detectives asked. 'Well, I didn't want to get involved myself like—I'd had a few and we were having a good night. But I don't want that kind of thing going on in my local, so I called it in.' (Fieldnotes, Smallville)

Clearly Bunk felt reluctant to exercise his powers in front of his friends and neighbours. Maybe he didn't want the reputation for being the authoritarian cop of the village; maybe he didn't think there was a pressing need for an enforcement intervention; or maybe he just wanted to have some time off. Whatever his motives, he had the autonomy to assess the situation and decide how to act. Would he have acted differently if he had known the group of men? Would he have passed the information on to his colleagues if it was not his local pub? A little light was shed on the latter question some time later, during a night out to celebrate a promotion:

After a few too many hours drinking we found ourselves in a city centre nightclub. Bunk and I were shouting towards each other over the music when a man emerged from the crowd and tapped him on the shoulder. I leant in to try and hear what was said. 'Alright pal, have you got anything?' said the wide-eyed man. Bunk looked surprised and amused by what was happening; he asked the man to repeat his question and then told him that he should ask someone else. The man persisted, so Bunk took out his wallet and flashed his badge. 'I said you're asking the wrong guy mate.' Needless to say the wide-eyed man left with great haste. 'Can you believe that?' laughed Bunk, 'I'll bet that scared the shit out of him!' (Fieldnotes, Smallville)

From a legal standpoint, a police officer is always on duty and bound by the rules and regulations set forth by the organization that employs them. An off-duty officer should report minor violations to an on-duty officer and should only use their powers of arrest when there is an immediate need to prevent a serious crime or apprehend a suspect. The findings presented here indicate that this does not always happen in relation to drugs. It doesn't happen because police officers exercise extensive discretion in how they enforce the law. Moreover, it doesn't happen because there are tensions between the demands of the job and the realities of everyday life, and police officers are reluctant to police their social networks and the places where they socialize. To demand that they do so would be an unenforceable and unreasonable invasion of their privacy.

'Problem' drug users

When asked for their thoughts on people who take drugs, the police were inclined to think first of the stereotypical 'addict'. Although it was widely recognized that addiction is a deeply complex phenomenon, one which affects people from all walks of life and is associated with a broad range of medical, legal, and social problems, from a police perspective it manifested itself in the form of the 'problem' drug user and was typically conceptualized in terms of crime and disorder. The link between drugs and crime was a simple matter of fact. Officers have learned from experience that those individuals heavily involved in using heroin and crack are also heavily involved in property offending and drug distribution:

Let's be honest, druggies are scum, aren't they? From what I've seen during my service, they're either criminals, potential criminals, or just fucking stupid. There's no more to it; you don't need to study them to know that. (Detective, Smallville)

How else are they supposed to pay for it? They're spending over a ton on gear a day and it's not like they've got a job or a winning lottery ticket is it. (Detective, Metropolis)

In the police worldview, there was a significant difference between problem drug users and people who use drugs recreationally:

Most people don't let drugs take over their life, it's an every now and again sort of thing. (Detective, Metropolis)

I'd say it's common knowledge that heroin is a line you don't cross. (Detective, Smallville)

Although this black-and-white distinction oversimplifies the diverse nature of contemporary drug consumption and implies conceptual conservatism, it provided the police with a useful tool for labelling, sensemaking, and operational prioritization. The police certainly did not see recreational users as model citizens, no matter who they are, what they do, or where they live, because upstanding members of the community do not take illegal drugs. However, for the most part recreational drug use was not perceived as being causally connected to acquisitive or violent crime, and so, unlike the addict, 'every now and again' users were not labelled as criminals or targeted like the usual suspects. Being relatively in control of their drug use and able to pay for it through legitimate sources of income, recreational users were considered to be out of order but not out of the ordinary. Their risky behaviour was irresponsible but their desire to have an ephemeral break from the shackles of everyday life was natural and permissible.

Most of the people that take drugs like ecstasy do it socially on a night out. Sure it's illegal, so we can't just let it be, but most of them aren't committing any other crimes. (Detective, Smallville)

We know it's quite normal for some young people to take drugs. I don't approve of that sort of behaviour, but that's just the way it is. (Detective, Smallville)

At worst, recreational users were earmarked as potential criminals, owing to the popular belief in the 'gateway' theory.[2] Speaking about cannabis use, one senior police officer explained:

Smoking a bit of cannabis might seem fairly harmless at first, but softer drugs are a gateway to harder drugs—that's a fact. Once a week becomes every other day, then every day, and before you know it they're after a new high.

Other than the significant weight that problem drug users were believed to add to the otherwise heavy police workload, the main cause of contempt was that they are 'dirty', 'weak', 'lazy, unemployable scum':

Addicts are disgusting! I hate having to deal with them. Some of them don't even bother to clean the shit out of their pants. (Detective, Metropolis)

The main problem I have with them is they don't work; they just steal and cheat the system while the taxpayer has to bail them out. All they do is sit around all day taking drugs waiting for the next hand out. (Detective, Smallville)

The way I see it is everyone's got an "inner-policeman". With most people the sirens go off in their head and they don't take drugs... Addicts have lost their self-control. (Police Sergeant, Smallville)

These assumptions and generalizations about addicts stand in stark contrast to police notions of respectability and the discipline, hard work, and successful achievement of conventional goals that they value. Addiction was seen as a failure to cope with life and warranted no sympathy because it was a self-inflicted condition and the result of poor choices. Furthermore, the strong association between addiction and the economically marginal provides evidence of the 'class contempt' that Loftus (2009) found in the daily narratives and interactions of the police in Northshire. She argues that police cultural knowledge is 'infused with class themes and orientated officers towards those whose bodily appearance and comportment betrayed their class origins' (pp183–4). People who are addicted to drugs and part of the unemployed 'residuum' were judged to be lacking in morals and social worth

---

[2] The gateway theory is an attempt to explain how people progress from legal to illegal drugs and then from 'soft' less harmful to 'hard' more harmful drugs. It has had widespread popular appeal and retains an influence in policy and practice despite there being little evidence to suggest that there is a pharmacological basis for the progression (Coomber et al. 2013: 95–9).

and constructed as the embodiment of disorder and distaste. They were, in other words, placed firmly into the category of 'police property'. According to Reiner (2010: 123), this categorization is applied to 'low-status, powerless groups whom the dominant majority see as problematic or distasteful. The majority are prepared to let the police deal with their "property" and turn a blind eye to the manner in which this is done'.

Believe me, people don't feel kindly towards drug addicts. They don't care what we do with them; just so long as we get rid of them from near where they live or where their kids go and play. (Senior Officer, Metropolis)

The stories I heard rarely described the characters, drug scenes, and social contexts in a Dickensian fashion, the tellers instead opting for a black comedy approach to the 'toothless crack whores' of the red-light district, the woman who was caught on camera inserting heroin into her anus, and the time that an addict vomited on an officer as he was being handcuffed. For some, humour was a mechanism for coping with the harsh realities and hostile environments they were exposed to on a regular basis (Waddington 1999b; Young 1995). 'You've got to laugh Matt,' said a detective after noticing that their mocking impressions of the 'filthy skaghead' in custody were not having the desired effect. 'Most of these poor bastards have lives so sad you can't take them too seriously.' And then there were those officers who simply exhibited bad taste and a lack of empathy:

During the search of a run-down property in a run-down part of town, the sniffer dog—'Buster', for the sake of animal anonymity—defecated on the kitchen floor. The tenants were being detained in the living room at the time, so were unaware of this little accident. The dog handler chuckled, got a magazine from the table and strategically placed it over the foul to hide it from view. He looked across at me smiling: 'They'll probably not even notice it in this shithole.' To be fair, it was one pile amongst many in an otherwise filthy environment, and there wasn't exactly an abundance of cleaning products to hand. But still, I thought it was common courtesy to at least inform the known users and suspected dealers of the presence of the shit. The shit that summed up the dog handler's opinion of them and sent a symbolic message about their place in society. (Fieldnotes, Smallville)

Police officers tended to dehumanize addicts when they talked about them by making their drug use their defining characteristic. This was despite the fact that they knew most of the 'local faces' by name and saw them so frequently they were almost like 'old friends'. As Van Maanen (1978b) suggests in his classic essay on the 'asshole', labelling people in such ways—'crackhead', 'druggy', 'junky'—serves a purpose in guiding police action, establishing social distance between the police and their segmented audiences, helping police officers make sense of seemingly meaningless behaviour, and providing an expressive outlet for them to let off steam. Lister et al. (2008: 47) also came across this practice in their study of street-level drug policing. When discussing their experiences of being policed, many drug users said they considered this labelling process to be a form of unnecessary and unwarranted 'moral censure', which added to the 'level of antagonism' some of them felt towards the police.

Some police officers nevertheless recognized that contemptuous 'othering' was inhumane, stigmatizing, and counterproductive. They took into account the fact that addiction could be the result of genetic weakness or physical or psychological dependency and appreciated that many individuals used drugs to escape from the boredom, desperation, and exploitation that comes with poverty and social exclusion. A few even expressed great sympathy for the plight of the addict, and felt frustrated that they could not do more to prevent the 'worst-case scenario' from happening:

'I've seen people destroy themselves on drugs. It can be painful to watch.' Joe proceeded to rummage around in the files on his desk and produced a campaign poster that was designed to encourage members of the public to call *Crimestoppers* with information about drug dealers. 'This woman,' he pointed to the first photo, 'was only eighteen when she came over from Romania. I don't know why she ended up here, but she soon ended up on crack and working the streets'. The series of custody photos provided a graphic display of the degenerative effects of problematic drug use on her physical appearance. 'I spoke with her a few times; she seemed nice, was pleasant enough to talk to... I think the last picture was taken a month before she died; she was picked up in the town centre for soliciting. It's such a shame. (Fieldnotes, Metropolis)

Joe was a celebrated and respected detective sergeant with over twenty years policing experience. He had worked in a variety of frontline roles but had spent most of his service investigating drug markets and handling informers. This meant he had spent more time with drug users than most of his colleagues. More so than most, he knew that for every nasty piece of work there is an ordinary person who 'got themselves hooked and can't find a way out'.

He also knew that sustaining a drug habit is hard work, that life on the margins is tough, and that people in such circumstances are often misunderstood, mistreated, and unfairly vilified. On the occasions that I observed Joe dealing with drug users he always called them by name, treated them with respect and appeared to be sympathetic and genuinely concerned for their wellbeing. When I commented on his admirable but unusual demeanour, he acknowledged that 'what most police officers don't see is that [drug addicts] are just people like you and me, only they've made some bad choices and are down on their luck'.

Whilst in the field I only came across three police officers with personal experience of what they deemed problematic drug use. Each of them believed it had had a profound impact upon their attitude towards drugs and drug control. During interview, a senior officer disclosed that his son had become addicted to heroin some years ago, was caught shoplifting, and ended up in treatment—'it destroyed the family', he said.

From then on I've taken a hard-line approach to drugs, I want to try and stop it happening to other families. Lock up the dealers, arrest the users, and divert them into treatment—it's the only way.

Naturally, traumatic ordeals such as this are likely to influence or bias an officer's outlook and actions. In this case, the senior officer was very much in favour of an authoritarian and paternalistic style of policing drugs, hence his support for strict enforcement against suppliers and treatment initiatives that use the leverage of the criminal justice system. He accepted that treatment might be more effective for individuals who enter into it voluntarily but sided with the view that coercion is necessary when 'they're not thinking straight' and is ultimately 'for their own good'.

Alternatively, personal affliction might lead to a more jaundiced or acrimonious attitude. Having let slip that she used to date a 'cokehead', this detective went on to say:

I couldn't believe it! I didn't even notice for months! He'd work all week, then blow it all on drugs at the weekend. I couldn't put up with that. He knew what my job was! He must have tried hiding it from me. It's so disrespectful don't you think? At least, now I can say that I've seen the damage drugs can do to people firsthand.

The detective's ex-boyfriend had lost his job on account of his habit, racked up a sizeable gambling debt and still hadn't paid back the money that he owed her. When releasing her pent-up emotions she would say things like 'they're all the same' and 'once a druggy always a druggy'. It appeared as though she felt little but determined antipathy for anyone involved in the drug business. From what I observed, however, her feelings and views on the matter did not seem to have a negative impact on how she conducted herself when interacting with suspected drug offenders.

A chance encounter with an old friend was partly responsible for Jimmy's very different standpoint and approach to dealing with drugs:

This afternoon I was partnered up with Jimmy, a home-grown street-wise detective in his early thirties. He had a few tasks to finish in what remained of the day—check CCTV footage, get a warrant application signed, talk to a member of the source unit about an ongoing operation—but said he was happy to take me along for the ride. After a bit of small talk, he asked if I had any questions. Among other things, I asked him what his views on drugs were and whether he had any experiences he was happy to share. He told me about one particular incident: 'I was out getting lunch when I saw an old friend of mine shooting up in a phone box. I hadn't seen him in a year or two, so at first I didn't think it was him, but when I realized it was, I couldn't believe it; he looked like a junkie, like a completely different person! See, the last time I'd seen him, he was working in a gym, had a girlfriend, a flat... It actually made me angry, you know. He tried to explain, kept saying he'd lost everything and had nothing to live for. So what did I do, I walked away, I had to, I was shaking. You know, when you're so angry and upset at the same time. I wanted to smack some sense into him... I haven't seen him since.' Jimmy opened up, he said he felt guilty for how he acted on that day and wished he had been more supportive—not by taking his old friend into custody, but by helping him into treatment. Nowadays he says he is much more likely to lend a sympathetic ear and offer sound advice to those who need it most. (Fieldnotes, Metropolis)

As well as being influenced by structural, cultural, and personal factors, decisions and behaviours are also reactive to the dictates of the situation at hand. In fact, in understanding what officers actually do, the principal explanatory variables are often contextual (Fielding 1989; Skogan and Frydl 2004). This point is illustrated in the following extract, which documents an incident that took place when I was partnered up with Jimmy once again:

Today turned out to be another fascinating 'tour of the underbelly of society', during which I witnessed Jimmy exercise his discretion in quite a controversial manner. 'You'll usually find a few crack users in here,' he assured me before entering a multi-story parking lot. True to his word, on the second floor we heard the clicking of a lighter as we turned a corner and stumbled upon a middle-aged black man with a makeshift pipe fastened firmly to his lips. The man quickly pocketed the potentially incriminating evidence and looked sheepishly at the floor. For whatever reason, Jimmy decided not to act; we just walked past and continued our ascent. As we left the car park, he told me that the man was well-known to the police; he'd been in and out of prison and treatment many times over the years, but 'doesn't cause us much trouble anymore'. 'I know a lot of people wouldn't approve of how I handled it,' Jimmy explained, 'but in situations like that arrest and seize is not always the best policy.' In order to make sense of and justify his decision, he then proceeded to tell me about some of the futilities and harmful consequences of drug law enforcement. 'The way I see it is a night in the cells wouldn't solve anything, and a week or two in prison would solve even less. If I'd confiscated his drugs he'd only need more...Last I heard he was in treatment. I know it didn't look like it was going too well, but these things take time and I'm willing to give him a chance.' (Fieldnotes, Metropolis)

This episode left me with many questions swirling around inside my head. Would Jimmy have done the same if he had been partnered up with somebody else? What if he had been in uniform? What if there had been a public audience? What would another officer have done in the same situation? Fortunately, I ran into Jimmy the very next day and over a sandwich he satisfied a few of my curiosities. He guaranteed me that he would have stopped, searched and arrested the man—let's call him Bubbs—if members of the public had been present. Maintaining the impression that drug laws are rigidly enforced was believed to be of the upmost importance, not least because the police 'can't allow people to think they can get away with it'. As we chatted away it also came to light that Bubbs occasionally provided Jimmy with information and had done so ever since his patrol days with the town-centre team. 'Every now and again we have a little talk about this and that. He's more likely to keep talking if I go easy on him, you know, if he thinks he owes me a favour.' In light of this revelation, it became even more difficult to identify what truly determined how Jimmy acted on that occasion. A combination of factors contributed to his decision-making process, from his own values, belief systems and experiences of drugs, to his understandings of the role of the police and drug control in society and the practicalities of detective work.

Drug Dealers

Supplying drugs was generally considered to be a 'serious' or 'organized' crime and thereby much more socially problematic and morally reprehensible than using drugs. Paradoxically almost, when reflecting on people who supply drugs, the police image of the drug user was liable to shift from criminal or potential criminal to victim. Addicts, for example, went from being portrayed as parasites living off the state, or predators living off their criminal activities, to the prey of dealers who make their living by exploiting the vulnerabilities of the weak. Recreational users stopped being carefree and careless and became the innocent youth who are corrupted by drugs and in need of protection. Police officers were able to tailor their language and manipulate the light in which they cast drug offenders to serve the purpose at hand.

As with the problem drug user, assumptions and generalizations about drug dealers had created a powerful stereotype, which emphasized the worst-case scenario and played a significant role in shaping attitudes towards the policed and the policing of drugs. Take the following quotations for example:

Some of the dealers round here are the scum of the world. I've seen them get women addicted to crack, force them into prostitution, and then take all their money. They are bad people, and there's no changing that. (Patrol Officer, Metropolis)

Drug dealers feed off the misery of others; it's a cliché but it's true. (Detective, Metropolis)

Heroin dealers are the lowest of the low. (Detective, Smallville)

If the police 'can persuade themselves that those against whom coercive authority is exercised are contemptible,' Waddington (1999b: 301) notes, 'no moral dilemmas are experienced – the policed section of the population "deserve it"'. Almost without exception, dealers were depicted as deplorable and dangerous outlaws who were motivated by hedonistic materialism and had actively chosen to participate in the illegal drug business for financial gain. Moreover, seeing as they are one of the most despised groups in society, officers were easily able to make them the scapegoat for the drug problem and make the case for tough enforcement action on the tenuous grounds of 'no more dealers no more problems'. Drug dealers were held to account for being knowingly responsible for problematic drug use in a 'buck stops here' sense and as the root cause of the crime and disorder that is commonly associated with drug markets.

They know where their money comes from, they just don't care. Shoplifting, burglary, robbery—it doesn't matter. All that matters is that they get paid... If a regular punter's not got the money, they'll get them to run around for them until they've worked it off. (Detective, Smallville)

A lot of the key players are violent men with extensive criminal records. They've got a reputation, you know. People know who they are and they're scared of 'em.' (Detective, Metropolis)

Everyone who sells drugs or facilitates the distribution of drugs is part of the problem. They might think "no harm done" because they're only selling a bit to their mates, but the bottom line is they're propping up a system run by organizing criminals who hurt people. (Detective Sergeant, Smallville)

From a police perspective, there is no plausible justification for the intentional supply of a controlled drug because it is an illegal activity and there is always an accompanying risk of harm to individuals and communities. Even the most liberal-minded officers struggled to justify supply offences or think of any conditions in which they could be legitimately tolerated under blanket prohibition. They knew from experience that many of the dealers the police dealt with were from deprived neighbourhoods, unemployed, and struggling to make ends meet. In some of these neighbourhoods, deviance and informal economic activity was said to be a 'way of life'. They also knew that many were drug users themselves and sold drugs to fund their own use or sort out friends and acquaintances. The odd one or two were 'actually quite nice' people and lived ordinary lives but for their involvement in drugs. These were understandable reasons and extenuating circumstances but did not justify their actions or exempt them from policing or prosecution.

Having no money and no job is a sorry state to be in, but it's never an excuse to start selling drugs. There are always alternatives to crime. (Detective, Smallville)

The gang culture is what the kids from the estates grow up with. It's like their destiny, or something, like they were always going to fall in with the wrong crowd. They start wearing colours, dealing drugs, getting into fights, you know, then they end up with their picture on our board. (Detective, Metropolis)

Whilst all drug dealers were certainly 'in the wrong' they were by no means regarded as equally wrong within the police sense of crime hierarchy. 'Social suppliers', for instance, being private, peaceable, and not in it for the profit, were not seen as 'real' dealers, even though officers would emphasize the point that they are still technically drug dealers in a legal sense, since they are supplying controlled drugs.[3] For some, social suppliers were nothing more than recreational drug users who just happen to have a connection, whereas others earmarked them as the dealers of the future because 'that's how they all start out'. Yet, despite these mixed opinions, none saw them as serious criminals or categorized them as 'police property'. Police officers also tended to view the purveyors of recreational drugs as 'less bad' than those who deal in the death and destruction of problematic drugs, it being assumed that selling the latter requires a much more deviant and iniquitous type of person. There are, however, always exceptions to the rule:

You tend to get your worst dealers in heroin and crack markets, but this is not always the case. One of the most violent men I've ever known was a cannabis dealer. He was a proper Yardie... We never got him for murder but we know he's got a few bodies on him... People get shot over ecstasy. All I'm saying is, don't go making any wrong conclusions. (Detective, Metropolis)

Another important distinction was often made between dealers who are involved in other forms of criminality and those who are otherwise law-abiding:

If you discount the illegality of what they're selling, you find that a lot of dealers operate like legitimate businessmen. It's the ones who want to be gangsters that you've got to look out for. (Detective, Metropolis)

Obviously dealers were not thought of as legitimate in the sense that they operated within formal regulatory frameworks, advertised openly and made use of contracts. For the most part, the principal distinction between the 'legit' and the 'gangster' type of dealer seemed to rest upon whether they had ready access to firearms and were willing to use as much violence as necessary to protect their interests or to stake a claim to their perceived territories. The notion of a drug dealer acting legitimately related to the

[3] Legally speaking, there is little or no difference between social supply and other approaches to distributing drugs as drug laws are generally worded in terms of 'supply'. Factors such as profit and motivation are irrelevant to defining the offence although they may be relevant to sentencing.

business-like manner in which they organized and conducted their operations, the way in which they sought to create and maintain favourable market conditions, for example, or developed good business relationships, or divided labour and paid wages. It also took into account their personal life outside the drug trade: whether they were relatively 'normal' in the sense that they had a family, a mortgage, and a passion for conventional pastimes. Even though the police never viewed drugs as an acceptable alternative to legitimate work, it was widely believed that if dealers could run the drug trade like a legitimate business, things would be much better. Logically, however, this view makes little sense, less so when the idea moves from those individuals most able to operate as legitimate businesspersons to those whose cultural resources are best able to exploit the illegal status of the trade.

In their conversations and stories the detectives regularly portrayed the 'little-league players in the drug game' (Collison 1995: 12) in a harsher light than the bigger hitters. Street sellers and runners were 'nobodies', 'dross' who would 'never amount to anything', the 'low-hanging fruit' that was routinely harvested by the criminal justice system. International traffickers, wholesalers, and middle-market distributors, on the other hand, had 'made it'; they were condemned for their crimes but somewhat respected for their sophisticated criminality. Power, professionalism, and ingenuity in the face of adversity were personal attributes that the detectives valued and could relate to. Drug dealers who exhibited these traits were seen as a better class of criminal, worthwhile targets who presented a greater challenge.

Today I went out cruising for a few hours with Carver and Herc as they did a bit of reconnaissance for the drug warrants that are to be executed on Friday. As we entered one of the more affluent villages of Smallville, they took me on a slight detour to visit the house of a reputed drug dealer. 'We all know he's running things around here.' They parked up the unmarked car outside what can best be described as a gaudy fortress of a house and proceeded to tell me about 'Mr Big'; how he'd started out as a local hard-man, got into the drug game, and worked his way up the ladder—the classic rags to riches story. 'Now he's got a garage, a car wash, and a club in town, but he's still behind it all. I've got to hand it to him, he's bloody good at what he does.' It was a glorified account, one which glossed over the deplorable tales that could have been told. 'He likes to think he's untouchable. We've been trying to make a case against him for a couple of years now, and one day we'll get him.' (Fieldnotes, Smallville)

What is clear from the event described in this fieldnote is that the 'bigger dealers' were not always considered worthwhile targets because of the drugs they sold or the harms they caused to individuals or communities. From a cultural perspective, they were also worth targeting because a successful case against 'Mr Big' was the quintessence of 'real' detective work and represented what drug law enforcement is all about. These were the cases that became the substance of stories, that allowed officers to build a reputation for being an effective detective by demonstrating their skills in the art and craft of investigation, and by getting the 'good collars' and 'street cred' that were respected by their colleagues.

Drug Detective Work

Despite the complicated, contested, and counterproductive realties of drug control policy and practice, the detectives had a remarkably clear understanding of their role in the global prohibition regime. Above all else, they saw themselves as elite crime fighters and considered the detection, arrest, and conviction of those involved in the illegal drug business to be the core justification for the policing of drugs. Seizing their drugs and assets was 'the cherry on the cake'. This was the task to which the detectives had been assigned by the organization, their mission, the means through which they made a difference and helped 'keep the lid on' the local drug problem. They accepted the need for a multifaceted approach to drug control, appreciated that enforcement alone was never a silver bullet, and advocated the benefits of partnership initiatives in tackling both supply and demand, but for them it was essentially about disrupting markets by making cases against suspected drug dealers—ideally 'the biggest dealers in town':

It's about upholding the law and getting the dealers and drugs off the streets. (Detective, Metropolis)

Our job is to go after the biggest dealers in town. It's not our job to go after everyone who does drugs. (Detective, Smallville)

We play our part, but there's only so much we can do. We take a problem-solving approach to drug law enforcement, and work in partnership with local agencies to "tackle drugs together"—"protecting families and communities" is the new national strategy ambition. Only last week one of our neighbourhood teams was working with a housing association to close a crack house...We "test on arrest" and have drug workers carrying out assessments in custody suites. The idea is to get drug users into treatment and away from a life of crime. (Detective Sergeant, Metropolis)

Generally speaking, the detectives viewed community policing and multi-agency partnerships as 'soft' policing activities and low priorities in the drug control agenda of the police because they departed from 'proper' images of police work associated with masculine ideals of crime fighting (Fielding 1994; Holdaway 1983; Loftus 2009). Those officers with experience of such activities, however, so long as they proved to be pragmatic and beneficial, spoke highly of their colleagues in neighbourhood teams and partner agencies and worked with them wholeheartedly as and when required (McCarthy 2013, 2014; O'Neill and McCarthy 2014). 'You end up seeing the same people [drug users] from a different perspective,' said a trainee detective as she spoke about her community placement with the Drug Interventions Programme (DIP). 'It definitely opened my eyes and taught me a lot about the pros and cons of treatment and offender management.' Yet save for diverting drug-using offenders into treatment, a common feeling amongst police officers was that demand reduction is 'not our job' and has 'nothing to do with policing'. Opinions on drug treatment ranged from 'it's a complete waste of money' and is 'condoning criminal behaviour', through to 'there are some success stories, but most of them struggle to stay off drugs'. The fact that the police were repeatedly dealing with the same problem drug users served only to confirm these kinds of belief. And when they came across dealers in possession of prescription drugs, it could lead them to accuse the health service of being part of the problem. 'They're only giving them more drugs to sell,' said an irritated detective after discovering a dozen boxes of Subutex in a drawer in the kitchen of a suspected heroin dealer.

Police officers often have a heightened 'sense of mission' towards the role of the police in society. They view their 'thin blue line' of work as a vocation, a calling, or moral imperative, a unique and indispensible social function to preserve a valued way of life and protect the 'good' members of the public against the forces of 'evil' (Loftus 2009; Reiner 2010). The detectives I worked with knew that drugs are 'bad'. 'Drugs kill people', they said, they're 'behind everything these days', the breakdowns and broken families, for instance, the crime, disorder, and general deterioration of society.

The indisputable truth of such damaging effects left them with little doubt about their value and the righteousness of their actions. During fieldwork, an event that really brought this belief to the fore was when plans were put into motion to disband the Smallville drug squad. It provoked the detectives into questioning the motivations and competencies of their supervisors and chief officers. Signs of anger and frustration were regularly displayed as they told me about how management 'didn't have a clue' and would 'end up regretting their decision'. They were convinced that drug dealers would take advantage of their newfound freedom and in turn there would be more drugs on the streets and more drug-related crime and disorder. To be sure, the detectives truly believed in the importance of their work, so not only did the decision to disband the squad deprive them of their territory, it also challenged their sense of mission and made them feel devalued and dejected. From their perspective, the police no longer considered the control of drug supply to be a priority and this was a huge mistake. In Metropolis, the detectives said they remembered reacting similarly when the drug squad first became the firearms squad, but they soon accepted the decision and the need to concentrate on dealing with the most criminogenic aspects of the drug trade, as 'it's impossible to deal with them all'.

In terms of upholding the law, the drug detectives had the tremendously broad mandate of policing the illegal drug trade by investigating anyone suspected of producing, supplying, or being in possession of any drug controlled under the 1971 Misuse of Drugs Act. The Act provides the police with various powers and a list of prohibited drugs, drug offences, and penalties linked to offending. It does not, however, dictate what they actually do in practice. During fieldwork, it became apparent that the law was a discretionary power that could be enforced as a means to an end rather than an a rule that must be mechanistically followed in all drug control situations (Bacon 2013b; Dixon 1997; Waddington 1999a). This point is particularly salient in the following comments:

Without the law we wouldn't be able to police drugs. It gives us the power to arrest drug dealers and seize their drugs. It gives us the power to stop and search people who we suspect are in possession of drugs. It gives us the power to enter and search premises for drugs and evidence of drug dealing activity. (Detective, Metropolis)

The Misuse of Drugs Act empowers us to do what we do without dictating what we do. (Detective, Metropolis)

Observations revealed that the law required interpretation and could be manipulated or ignored when choosing between different courses of action or inaction. The detectives of Metropolis, for example, once decided to issue a formal warning to a person in possession of a bagged-up ounce of cannabis, instead of arresting for possession or possession with the intent to supply as I had witnessed them do for lesser quantities. They were looking for a handgun, which was thought to be in the possession of a fifteen-year-old suspected gang member who resided at the premises. No firearm was found, only the cannabis in a cupboard in the bedroom he shared with his older brother. The suspect's brother said it was his, for personal use. The detective who made the decision to caution told me that 'he was obviously taking the rap for his younger brother'. Having spoken with them both, he felt the older brother was a positive influence on the younger and that arresting him would have done nothing more than 'push him further into the gang way of life'. On the basis of his practical knowledge and understandings of how and why policing should and could be done in the given situation, the detective decided that enforcing the law would cause more harm than good. This indicates that morality and the unintended consequences of law enforcement are important for an understanding of the use of discretion. In contrast, the Smallville detectives once arrested a man for possession with the intent to supply on the grounds of a £10 bag of cannabis, some empty bags and a set of scales. The man was a suspected heroin dealer with a string of previous convictions and their recent intelligence suggested he was supplying local street dealers. As the suspect's house was being searched he kept taunting the police: 'You've got nowt on me! You're not going to find nowt here!' True to his word no heroin was found, but the disgruntled officers remained convinced that the community would be a better place without him—if only for a short while—so they gathered all the evidence they could and took him back to the station in handcuffs. What were the criteria here? Was it a moral judgement, a display of authority, or some other factor?

Whilst the detectives considered their basic function to be 'getting the dealers and drugs off the streets', in both police organizations they readily acknowledged that enforcement is a marginal activity with limited capacity and they certainly did not perceive their task as arresting *all* the dealers or eradicating *all* the markets in their service area. They were not at war with drugs in either a figurative or an operational sense. They were working within their limits to manage the drug trade, trying their best to 'make sure it doesn't get any worse' and 'keep the public happy'. A 'drug-free world' was simply 'not on the cards'. Even as an aspirational goal the slogan was ridiculed for being unattainable and criticized for creating unrealistic expectations. Drug war rhetoric was equally disparaged and noticeably absent from standard police vocabulary:

[The "war on drugs"] is a melodramatic way of saying drug law enforcement. You won't hear the police calling it that—it's the politicians and the press who call it that. (Detective, Smallville)

The "war on drugs" is nothing more than hot air coming out of politicians' mouths. (Senior Officer, Metropolis)

I don't like it; I never have. Don't get me wrong, I'm anti-drugs; I'm not saying legalize drugs and let everyone take them if they want to. Drugs should be illegal because they can do a lot of damage to people. But why can't we just call it what it is: we're not at war with drugs, we're policing drugs. (Detective, Metropolis)

Politicians are regarded by the police as 'remote and unrealistic ivory-tower idealists, corrupt self-seekers, secret subversives, or simply too weak to resist villainy' (Reiner 2010: 125). Being adherents of realism, pragmatic, 'down-to-earth' and 'anti-bullshit', the detectives said that in practice they targeted the drugs, dealers, and marketplaces that caused the greatest harm to local communities in terms of crime.

The fact of the matter is millions of people commit drug offences every year—what are we supposed to do about that? Apart from the ones that cause people harm, I'd say no one expects us to do anything. (Detective, Metropolis)

What you're calling "dance drugs" are just not a priority. Management aren't interested; they've got more serious problems to deal with… They've got targets to meet… The public aren't interested either; they don't kick up much of a fuss about people getting messed up on pills because it doesn't really affect them. (Detective Sergeant, Smallville)

As we can see from the previous quotations, the detectives sometimes inferred from the pervading presence of drugs throughout society that policing is only really necessary—or possible, given the limitless workload and limited resources of the police—when drug problems become 'serious problems' or cause harms that warrant calls for service from the public. This finding shows that they were implicitly applying harm reduction principles to the policing of drug markets. Furthermore, such a harm reduction approach to drug law enforcement was thought to reflect the norms, values, and beliefs of the communities they policed and be more responsive to their fears and perceptions of the problem. It might be implied, then, that drug problems that fall below this threshold for intervention are seen as falling within the remit of other drug control agencies. At a push, it might even be implied that some police officers think that recreational drug use is best dealt with through informal mechanisms of social control.

Whilst the detectives rarely questioned the authority of the law, believed they were making a positive difference, and remained motivated by operational successes on a case-by-case basis, their efforts were accompanied by a sense of futility and doubt. Many officers had a cynical outlook. They were defeatist, pessimistic about the future of policing drugs, and disheartened by their failure to stop things 'getting worse':

Drugs aren't going anywhere anytime soon. One thing you quickly come to realize in this job is that no matter how many dealers you put away there's always someone out there selling. (Detective, Smallville)

Sometimes I think we're like those [Japanese] soldiers in World War II, you know, those ones on the islands who just kept fighting because they didn't know the war was over. Only difference is we'd lost the war before we even started fighting. (Detective Sergeant, Metropolis)

We've thrown everything at it, even the kitchen sink, but drug problems just keep getting worse. In the end, the drugs are still on the streets no matter how many people we lock up. (Senior Officer, Smallville)

Yet, even though there was widespread acknowledgment that the current system is not exactly working as intended, the majority of police officers remained faithful supporters of the status quo and resistant to change. Prohibition was seen as the only morally legitimate and feasible policy option. The more authoritarian and closed-minded officers were of the opinion that the drug problems of today are the result of the failure to enforce fully and properly the external ordering imposed by the criminal law:

We've all gone soft on drugs, that's the problem. If the police decided to crack down harder on drugs we could make a massive difference. (Detective Sergeant, Smallville)

Arguments for reform, such as decriminalization or legal regulation, were generally viewed with scepticism or given zero weight when they appeared irrelevant or repugnant. The police were particularly dismissive of claims that enforcement was a waste of resources and actually exacerbated drug problems. 'Those people who want to do away with drug laws don't know what they're talking about,' I was told. 'They'd soon change their tune if they spent a day in our shoes'. Criticisms of police activities and attempts to correct them are often perceived as a direct threat to their integrity and authority, which, according to Crank (2004), reinforces rather than diminishes their cynicism and defensive solidarity.

After the morning's warrant the members of the firearms squad who had escaped the trip to the station to process and interview the arrestee promptly headed to a local café for breakfast. Over bacon sandwiches and coffee they decided to have a discussion about drug policy—for my benefit, no doubt. 'The truth is we're fighting a losing battle,' Joe said. 'Any cop with enough experience will tell you the same.' There were murmurs of agreement and nods of heads from some of the other detectives sat round the table. 'People want drugs, and nothing we can do will change that.' Another detective went on to tell the group how he thought enforcement was futile and treatment didn't work. 'Management wouldn't be happy if they knew I was saying this, but I think drugs should be legalized. You won't find many officers who'll say it on the record, but lots of us think it. I don't know how it would work, all I know is this shit isn't working. Can't you academics figure it out?' 'I think they should all be shot,' blurted out one of the other detectives. The officer to his right, who up until now had barely spoken, butted in to voice his disagreement. He said that heroin should be made legal, that way 'there'll be no crime, it's out of our hands and they end up killing themselves anyway'. 'Trust you idiots to come out with something like that,' Joe said in a jocular manner. 'You don't know your arseholes from your elbows.' (Fieldnotes, Metropolis)

A significant minority sat at the opposite end of the policy spectrum, however, said they would welcome fundamental change and were well aware of the unintended consequences of prohibition. Some of these officers believed that the criminalization of recreational users was overly punitive, for example, that 'a record can fuck you up for life', and that the disproportionate use of stop and search on young people of black and other minority ethnic origins had severely damaged police legitimacy and police-community relations. Then there were the agnostics, those who were open to change but remained on the fence because they were unaware of the evidence or uncertain about the practical application and likely outcomes of alternative policy options. 'Maybe we've just got to suck it and see.'

Conclusion

This chapter delved into the police worldview in order to explore and make sense of how officers perceive the drug world and their role in it. In other words, it analyses the police on drugs, their views on controlled substances, alcohol and 'legal highs', what they think about addicts, recreational users and those involved in the illegal drug business, the policing of drugs, and the drug policy debate.

Most police officers were resolutely anti-drugs and pro-prohibition. They sang from the same hymn sheet, the statute book, the unwritten rules, or the 'drugs are bad news' autocue, believed that the law must be upheld to preserve social order and protect the public, and viewed people who use or supply drugs as lawbreakers who are in need of policing and punishment. The legal status of a drug was of great significance to the police by virtue of their unique position in enforcing the law in a liberal democratic society. Drug-crime connections were taken for granted and as a simple matter of fact. 'Problem' drug users were criminals, 'lazy, unemployable scum' who were lacking in morals and social worth and warranted no sympathy for their self-inflicted afflictions. Supplying drugs was generally considered to be a 'serious' or 'organized' crime and thereby even more socially problematic and morally reprehensible than using drugs. Almost without exception dealers were depicted as deplorable and dangerous outlaws who were in it for the money and indifferent to the consequences of their actions. The drug detectives saw themselves as elite crime fighters and considered the detection, arrest and successful conviction of 'the biggest dealers in town' to be the core justification for the policing of drugs.

There were, however, subtle, not so subtle, and radical differences between the opinions and practices of the police officers under study. Drug laws were viewed and enforced with an ambivalent form of affirmation. Detectives who supported the status quo and tough enforcement worked alongside advocates for change and critics of police activity. Those with black-and-white mentalities had colourful colleagues who wore rose-tinted glasses. Some police officers recognized that contemptuous 'othering' was inhumane, stigmatizing and counterproductive. The majority recognized that the law does not reflect important distinctions between drugs, drug markets, and drug problems. Alcohol, for example, especially binge drinking and drunk and disorderly behaviour, was thought to present the police with an arduous task that by far surpassed the problems associated with recreational drug use in the night-time economy. The risky behaviour of 'every now and again' users was considered to be irresponsible, but their desire to have an ephemeral break from the norm was natural and permissible. Those who confessed to previous transgressions, or had socialized with such users in their private lives, tended to exhibit relatively liberal attitudes towards drug use and control and were more likely to take informal action. Indeed, when off-duty, officers tried to suspend judgement and said they would usually overlook what they considered to be 'tolerable' drug use. Furthermore, 'social suppliers', the purveyors of recreational drugs and those dealers who were otherwise law-abiding were almost capable of being tolerated. The 'normalization' of drug use, I would argue, the growing accommodation, acceptance, and tolerance of drugs throughout contemporary society (Aldridge et al. 2011; Parker et al. 1998), has created a seemingly irresolvable tension between the demands of the job and the realities of everyday life.

Police understandings about drugs, crime, and control were rooted in the everyday experiences, problems, and tensions of the job and transmitted across members through processes of socialization. Officers had sets of shared values and beliefs that underpinned how they viewed the drug world and held sway over their actions. They had a reservoir of norms and assumptions that transcended the contrasting terrains and provided them with frames of reference and coping mechanisms for how and why the policing of drugs could be done in any situation. The discourses and interactions described and analysed in this chapter expose the powerful influence of the 'core characteristics' of police culture revealed in a longstanding tradition of research (Loftus 2009; Reiner 2010). Many of the attitudes and behaviours of police officers might be explained by their sense of mission and preference for crime fighting, or their conservatism, pragmatism, solidarity, and informal working practices. However, the evidence presented here also emphasizes the agency of individuals in making up their own minds and structuring their understandings of police work and the wider policing landscape. Police officers are not institutionalized clones. New recruits do not automatically assimilate the values, beliefs, and assumptions of the occupational culture upon joining the police, nor do they passively and predictably acculturate as their career progresses. Disparities were readily apparent amongst rookies and seasoned veterans alike. 'The police' are a heterogeneous group of people who bring their own experiences, personalities, and outlooks to the table. They interpret the cultural paraphernalia that permeates the police service in nuanced ways and play an active role in 'developing, reinforcing, resisting or transforming cultural knowledge' (Chan 1997: 73). These differences illustrate the complexities of the police identity and reveal how officers can support and develop policing styles that exist in opposition to the dominant culture.

6

Intelligence-Led Investigation

'It's not what you were expecting?' said DS Freamon as we entered the intelligence unit. 'Most people are under the impression that these rooms are filled with hi-tech computer systems and gadgets like on CSI or something. I use a PC with Windows XP.' There were no exploding ballpoint pens or invisibility cloaks either. Aside from the secretive, sensitive, and film noir-esque nature of some of the work that goes on within the intelligence community, my initial observations were that police intelligence units are much like any other open-plan office. The people employed therein were checking emails, shuffling papers, making telephone calls, saying their 'good mornings' and generally getting themselves ready for another working day. 'So, what do you want to know?' This week I will mostly be learning about 'intelligence-led policing' by shadowing 'intelligence officers' and 'intelligence analysts'.

'Intelligence' is a malleable term that gets thrown around all over the policing world. Is it just hot air, a word applied by the police to describe or account for their actions to make them appear smarter? Or is intelligence a matter of substance that sums up what policing in the information age is all about? There have always been intelligent police officers who lead by example and intelligent policing strategies that lead the way in terms of efficacy and innovation. At the same time, intelligence does not lead policing in equal measure and there are those that have been weighed on the scales and found wanting.

(Fieldnotes, Smallville)

Over recent decades there has been widespread advocacy and adoption of 'proactive' styles of policing and a great many police organizations around the world now claim to be 'intelligence-led' (James 2013; Maguire 2000; Ratcliffe 2008). According to Maguire and John (2006: 82), in the face of the uncertainty, insecurity, and changing conditions characteristic of late modern

societies, it is unsurprising that there have been 'sudden swings between "philosophies", paradigms or "models" of how to respond
to crime and disorder'. Policing appears to have become 'smarter',
more streamlined, effective, and in some respects 'evidence-based'.
The police have explored and implemented a variety of innovative strategies in an attempt to rectify the shortcomings associated with their traditional reactive approaches to maintaining the
security of social order. Specific reform efforts that have emerged
include 'community policing', 'problem-oriented policing' and
'intelligence-led policing'. These models describe ways of conceiv-
ing and doing policing. They aim at very broad institutional reform
and give precedence to proactive ideologies, strategic planning and
the systematic prioritisation of issues on the basis of analysis at the
organizational level. What's more, over the same time period, information technology and new management techniques have been
combined to produce tighter control of resources and the enhancement of targeted deployments against local concerns and prolific
and progressively sophisticated offenders.

What is rather unclear at present is how these changes to the
field of policing have been incorporated into the inner workings of
police organizations and affected the everyday realities of police
work. This chapter aims to fill part of this knowledge gap by
examining the impact of intelligence-led policing on proactive detective work and the initiation of drug law enforcement operations. Taking a step back, it begins with a concise review of the
academic and policy literature so as to consider the political and
economic context in which these reform agendas emerged, their
values, objectives, and norms, and the ways in which they have
been interpreted and implemented in practice to date. Particular
attention is paid to the establishment of the National Intelligence
Model (NIM) in England and Wales. The focus then shifts to the
meaning of 'proactivity' and the complex mix of competing but
ultimately complementary styles of policing that coexist within
the contemporary police service. Zeroing in on proactive investigation and the policing of drugs, the chapter moves on to provide
an in-depth analysis of the interactive relationship between the
drug detectives and the organizational frameworks within which
their formative intelligence and investigative practices were constructed and performed. In so doing, it explores how the NIM has
been received and the policy of 'compliance'; the significance of
drug strategies, official priorities, and performance management;

what constituted 'intelligence', how it entered the police intelligence system and the routine activities of intelligence work; and the setting of operational targets.

The Rise of Intelligence-Led Policing

The shift to proactive policing in Britain and other Western democracies came about because of a combination of driving forces that have shaped the policing landscape. As the work of Weatheritt (1986: 99) clearly illustrates, 'innovations and change do not just happen. They take place within a political and economic climate in which particular changes come to be seen as more or less inevitable or desirable, and others as unnecessary or impracticable'.[1] Crime rates rocketed in the 1980s without corresponding increases in resources, detection rates fell and there was a swelling sense that the police were failing to reduce crime or bring offenders to justice. The need to adapt to emerging crime trends and complex new forms of threat in the national and transnational arenas further bolstered enthusiasm for innovative change (Garland 2001; Gill 2000; Maguire 2000). At the same time, the new consensus of neo-liberalism accentuated the deep socio-economic causes of crime and promoted 'tough' law and order policies and 'new public management' reforms. These managerialist interventions exacerbated concerns about the 'demand gap' by introducing a range of business-like terminologies, principles, and mechanisms into the running and regulation of the police service in order to deliver greater economy, efficiency, and effectiveness (McLaughlin 2007; Savage 2007).

Police work became more heavily influenced by national objectives and performance indicators and was increasingly subject to external bureaucratic oversight. In seeking to address the matter

[1] In her book on innovations in policing, Weatheritt (1986) critically reviews a number of operational and management initiatives in the areas of patrol and crime prevention. Interestingly, she found that the initiatives under scrutiny were 'sold both by drawing on time-honoured justifications and assumptions about policing, and by reconstructing a past in which, in the attempt to bring about a desired future state of affairs, evidence about what was the case easily becomes distorted' (p5). The implications of this finding are that police researchers should be wary of overstating the degree of change when assessing police innovations and be sure to scrutinize the accompanying rhetoric and other techniques of impression management.

of police effectiveness and efficiency, the hugely influential reports of the Audit Commission (1993) and HMIC (1997) made a strong case for greater proactivity and management of resources in the fight against crime. Crucially, taking into account the growing realization that a significant amount of volume crime is committed by a small number of prolific and serious offenders, the fundamental objective of proactive policing was identified as targeting the core criminal contingent by positioning intelligence at the hub of operational policing and making better use of informants and surveillance. Another key feature of this new managerialism is that organizational actors are governed through internal controls embedded in systems of reporting and auditing that require them to account for their decisions in highly specific ways. Furthermore, in addition to transforming accountability through communication formats, technological changes in computerized intelligence databases, software packages, and surveillance equipment have also restructured the daily routines of policing and allowed for advancements in proactive forms of investigation to be developed and supported (Chan 2001; Ericson and Haggerty 1997; Manning 2008b).

Proactive ideologies and intelligence work are by no means new policing innovations. Nevertheless, the principles and practices of proactivity only really began to enter the mainstream with the emergence and development of 'intelligence-led policing' in the last decade of the twentieth century. The precise meaning of intelligence-led policing is not as straightforward as meets the eye. It is an evolving concept, almost chameleonic in nature, one which has been inconsistently interpreted across the world and is confusingly applied to a variety of crime-control processes that rely on the efforts of analysts and intelligence specialists engaged in problem-solving and capacity-building initiatives (James 2013; Ratcliffe 2008). 'Intelligence' in this context is generally understood to be information that has been subject to some form of analysis with the intention of informing police decision-making processes. In basic terms, intelligence-led policing is most accurately used to refer to the expansion of intelligence work beyond the remit of specialist detective units in order to direct the policing styles of police organizations (John and Maguire 2007, Maguire and John 2006). Dorn et al. (1992) observed the early stages of this shift in the late 1980s when studying drug law enforcement. With amazing foresight, the authors concluded that intelligence 'is becoming the tail that wags the dog. The tendency for operational matters to be strongly influenced by and, to some extent, actually *directed* by intelligence priorities, is emerging and likely to grow in the 1990s' (p148). Today, intelligence-led policing typically involves effectively sourcing, amassing, and analysing intelligence about criminals and their activities so as to disrupt organized crime networks and incapacitate prolific offenders through targeting enforcement and patrol where it can be expected to yield the best results. More broadly, it is also conceived as a management philosophy that places emphasis on information sharing and collaborative, strategic solutions to policing problems.

The first genuine attempt to introduce intelligence-led policing in a systematic manner to routine police work occurred in the Kent Police Service, under the pioneering leadership of Chief Constable David Phillips. This attempt entailed a major reorganization of existing roles and functions to produce a tactical capacity that would enable intelligence to be worked through effectively, the idea being that everyone on the staff would contribute in some way to the achievement of a clear set of strategic goals. Greater intelligence gathering was promoted throughout the force, the intelligence unit was assigned a pivotal role in analysing information and identifying targets, and resources were moved from reactive criminal investigation departments to specialized proactive units. No 'gold standard' evaluation was carried out but the initiative was widely hailed as a success nonetheless (Amey et al. 1996; James 2013).

Although many other forces went on to preach the same intelligence-led policing mantra, very few carried through the structural changes that were necessary to produce a significant shift from reactive to proactive patterns of working. Maguire and John (1995) conducted an examination of the value of criminal intelligence systems, surveillance, and informants across eight police forces and considered what organizational and cultural changes were needed for a shift to occur. They concluded that without 'holistic, structured systems in which officers are given clearly defined and protected roles, initiatives are frustrated by constant abstractions to cope with reactive demand, and by blockages and hiatuses in what should be a steady flow of information and actions' (p54). Furthermore, they suggest that major organizational reform can only succeed if there is wholehearted commitment from senior officers and that the possible negative influence of the occupational culture of the lower ranks should not be underestimated.

A common vision amongst the governing elite of integrating an intelligence-led approach within all police forces led to the development of the NIM. On the back of the putative success of his own constabulary, Chief Constable Phillips acted as the key policy entrepreneur championing the model and succeeded in gaining the support of ACPO and the Home Office (James 2013). With the passing of the Police Reform Act 2002, the government made compliance with the NIM a statutory obligation and by April 2004 all forces were required to have implemented it to the national minimum standards (ACPO 2005). According to its architects, the NIM 'represents the collected wisdom and best practice in intelligence-led policing and law enforcement' (NCIS 2000: 7). By taking a broad view of intelligence-led policing, however, the scope of the NIM is much more ambitious in that it aims to provide a model for policing that brings together disparate strands of policy and can be adopted by other agencies engaged in crime control or community safety work (Bullock 2013; Maguire and John 2006; John and Maguire 2007). A fundamental principle of the model is that contemporary policing is a complex mix of competing but ultimately complementary styles that might be integrated and managed through the same framework. According to Chief Constable Sara Thornton (ACPO 2007: 3), within the framework of the NIM, the concept of intelligence-led policing now 'underpins all aspects of policing, from neighbourhood policing and partnership work to the investigation of serious and organised crime and terrorism'. This 'revisionist approach' appears to have superseded the original formulation of the model as an enforcement strategy that emphasizes the use of criminal intelligence when planning investigations against prolific and serious offenders (Hale et al. 2004; Oakensen et al. 2002).

In principle, the NIM provides the police service with a 'business model' for conducting proactive policing, which, if rolled out and put into practice as designed, should enable police managers and their counterparts in partner agencies to systematically preside over key decision-making processes, prioritize issues of concern and allocate resources accordingly for both strategic and tactical purposes. It functions at three distinguishable but interconnecting 'levels of policing': (1) local crime and disorder problems; (2) force, inter-force, and regional criminal activity; and (3) serious and organized crime at a national or international level. This straightforwardly reflects the organization of policing and the politically defined territories of the police. The idea is to replicate the business process at each level in the hope that this will improve the flow of information and facilitate cooperative and coordinated activities.

At the heart of the NIM lies a set of basic assets, structures and procedures that are intended to underpin police activities and their attempts to identify, understand and address problems and trends. Analysis is central to these arrangements. The effectiveness of the process is heavily dependent on the generation of standardised 'analytical products' through specialist techniques that make sense of the large amount of information collected by the police and make recommendations for action. Analytical techniques include crime pattern analysis, demographic analysis, market profile analysis, target profile analysis, network analysis, and results analysis. Force and local intelligence units staffed by intelligence officers, civilian analysts and researchers are responsible for producing such products and monitoring the collection, review, and interpretation of information entering organizational databases.[2] Analyses and other data should be presented as 'intelligence products' and fed into the 'tasking and coordination group' meeting cycle. The key purpose of strategic meetings is for police managers and partner agencies to discuss the 'strategic assessment' and decide on crime prevention, intelligence and enforcement priorities. These priorities form the basis of the 'control strategy' and the 'intelligence requirement'. Regular tactical meetings are driven by short-term issues identified in 'tactical assessments'. They are conducted in accordance with control strategy priorities and thereby ensure that plans made at strategic meetings are carried through and communicated to everyone on the staff via briefings and daily management meetings. The final stage of the NIM business process is the operational review. Evaluations of police operations are fed back into the 'organizational memory' so as to inform future strategies and tactics in an iterative and progressive fashion.

Political science literature on policy change recognises that few policies are implemented as their architects anticipate (Hill 2009; Kingdon 2003). Policymakers must be willing to reach

---

[2] The force intelligence unit is usually known as the Force Intelligence Bureau (FIB) and has a dual role to provide an intelligence-led response to crime and disorder at force level and to assist Basic Command Unit (BCU) intelligence units. BCU intelligence units are primarily responsible for gathering, developing, analysing and disseminating information about local crime and disorder issues.

compromises and accept that reform efforts are often renegotiated or transformed to reflect 'real world' demands as they are put into practice. Commissioned by the Home Office, John and Maguire (2003, 2004) carried out an early evaluation of the NIM and found that the police forces under study were making progress but there remained a number of significant failings: the commitment of some local managers was judged to be inadequate; there was a lack of appropriate training and technology and limited partnership involvement; and widespread cultural resistance was further fuelled by ignorance and dislike of the overly 'academic' structure and language. In the first comprehensive analysis of the NIM, James (2013) identifies partial impacts in some places and specialisms. He demonstrates, however, that it has not affected organizational practice in any meaningful way on account of deficiencies in the pre-existing intelligence architecture, the role of police 'fiefdoms' and the hold of orthodox cultural attitudes and ways of working. His work also shows that the simultaneous implementation of intelligence-led policing and the neighbourhood policing programme resulted in competing demands and disjointed operational strategies.

What is 'Proactive Policing'?

During fieldwork, the terms 'proactive', 'intelligence-led' and 'problem-solving' were used somewhat interchangeably in documentary sources and when police personnel spoke about their work and styles of policing. For many members of the rank-and-file they were overused and had become little more than management jargon or 'bullshit bingo'. Practically any operational activity that involved intelligence analysis, strategic planning or crime prevention was hailed as proactive. Yet, despite its breadth of application, the proactive approach to detective work dominated conceptions of proactivity.

[The drug squad] work proactively because we're intelligence-led. You've been working with us for months now so you've seen proactive police work at its best! (Detective, Smallville)

Most proactive work is carried out by specialist units against prolific and priority offenders and organized crime groups. (Detective Sergeant, Smallville)

Proactive policing is just another way of saying intelligence-led policing. It's what we do. (Detective, Metropolis)

Being proactive is part of the job because we're an intelligence-led organization. All police officers work proactively in one way or another... [The uniform branch] are still largely reactive though. Only specialist units are driven by intelligence instead of incidents and calls for service. (Police Sergeant, Metropolis)

In the police forces under study, proactive work was traditionally conceived in narrow terms as being what specialist detective units do, a relatively rare and reserved aspect of the police investigative function that was undertaken by only a select few officers at any one time. Proactive units were distinguished from 'general office' CID in name, assignment and physical location. There was even a noticeable difference in how they dressed, with proactive detectives usually opting for a casual and inconspicuous trainers, jeans and t-shirt look over the more formal suited and booted attire of their reactive counterparts. 'Working proactive' gave detectives a sense of identity, status and purpose. They viewed themselves as members of a professional elite within the police service and their role in crime control as the epitome of intelligence-led policing. 'We're the crème de la crème of the detective ranks,' remarked one such officer.

Although the drug detectives wanted to protect the public by ridding the streets of dangerous drugs and tackling drug-related criminality, this was not what motivated them to specialize in drug law enforcement. The nature of the job not the mission was their foremost rationale: the greater autonomy, kudos, and respect that was attached to the position; the potential to use covert policing strategies and the craftsmanlike possibilities of police work; and the aspiration of making 'good collars' and working challenging cases with flair. Additional motivations for specialization included the enhanced prospect of overtime and promotion.

This is what I signed up for; it's what being a detective is all about. (Detective, Metropolis)

I enjoy this kind of police work, you know; I really get off on it. It's not all about the stats. You're not always having to deal with victims or take witness statements. It's about finding your targets and then taking them out. (Detective, Smallville)

When you're working proactive you have so much more freedom; you actually start investigations, you don't just respond to whatever job gets dropped on you like in reactive... I enjoy building up cases, getting my teeth into them and figuring out how to get the evidence to put the harder-to-catch criminals away. (Trainee Detective, Metropolis)

Whilst notions of proactivity were most strongly associated with the work of specialist detective units, it should be stressed that officers generally understood that it had broader application and were cognisant of various other types and techniques of proactive police work. Indeed, when discussing examples of 'best practice' from their own back catalogues, detectives frequently referred to operations that took a holistic approach to intelligence-led policing and incorporated aspects of community policing and partnership engagement. The work of neighbourhood police officers and partner agencies was perceived as proactive in that it generated community intelligence and involved interaction, consultation, and cooperation between the police and the public to reduce crime and disorder problems through coproduced initiatives. Detectives also viewed the work of civilian analysts as proactive because their analytical products informed their investigations and were underpinned by the principles of problem-oriented policing. Training programmes, policy documents, and management meetings inundated officers with information containing the same intelligence-led policing mantra. Furthermore, the fact that assignments are only ever temporary meant that most officers had experienced a range of policing functions and proactive ideologies during the course of their careers. Collaborative operations, routine interactions, and off-duty socializing also played a crucial part in circulating basic understandings about the crossovers, complementarities, and conflicts of interest between different occupational roles and policing strategies.

Still, as can happen with specialization, the division of labour and a hierarchical bureaucratic structure, few officers could fully comprehend how distinct approaches to proactive policing coexist at an organizational level and might operate in unison within the framework of the NIM. Within police organizations, different specialist units take the lead on different activities conforming more or less to policing according to the values, objectives and norms of different proactive strategies (Tilley 2008). They tend not to look beyond their specific roles and interpret rules in ways that resonate with the themes of their occupational culture. There was a tendency, then, for the drug detectives to see their investigative work as a type rather than an element of proactive policing that had little connection with neighbourhood policing programmes. For them, intelligence-led policing was principally an enforcement strategy that emphasised the use of criminal intelligence when planning investigations against prolific and serious offenders. Diverse and multi-pronged approaches to tackling drug problems were viewed first and foremost as optional operational 'bolt-ons' that were designed to further their crime control agenda. Only police managers thought of proactivity as an integrated approach to all aspects of operational policing. However, they too were of the opinion that a centralized model was at odds with the philosophy of neighbourhood policing and sent out 'mixed messages' to the rank-and-file.

A lot of police officers do what you might call proactive work; it's not just the detectives you're studying. Working with partner agencies is proactive; working with communities is proactive. Doing research and analysis is proactive... What [police managers] have to try and do is make sure they're working together, or at least make sure they're not working at cross-purposes. (Senior Officer, Metropolis)

From a management perspective, if the police are to be truly intelligence-led, officers must operate in accordance with the strategic agenda of the organization as opposed to alongside or against it. They must learn to see the 'bigger picture' of policing and work as a proactive collective. This is precisely what the NIM business process set out to achieve.

The 'NIM-Lite Approach'

When I first entered the field, most research participants claimed that the police were fully NIM-compliant and that the codified business process near enough dictated the management of intelligence work and operational policing. 'We live by policy and procedure,' were the words of one senior officer. On the whole my initial observations supported these claims. The prescribed structures, procedures and personnel were in place and functioning in accordance with their role profiles and specifications. I sat in on strategic, tactical and daily management meetings, listened to briefings and witnessed the undertaking of research, intelligence development and tactical resolutions. I watched officers submit intelligence reports and shadowed intelligence officers and civilian analysts as they worked on intelligence and analytical products. I saw control strategies on walls, professional practice publications on desks and heard the language of the NIM being spoken fluently in conversations. But I knew better than to be taken in by first impressions.

Yeah, I know it's codified in the Police Reform Act; the government made their point loud and clear. But don't think that means we're legally bound to the letter like with PACE or RIPA though. Our hands are tied, but we've got a bit of wriggle room. (Senior Officer, Metropolis)

The 'wriggle room' this officer was referring to was the degree of flexibility written into the NIM code of practice, as well as the working rules, tacit understandings and underlying assumptions of policymakers and police managers, which allowed police organizations to take into account local demands and resources when implementing the model. He described the approach taken by Metropolis as the 'NIM-lite approach', whereby the minimum standards were complied with, the HMIC inspections were satisfactorily passed and the framework was tailored to suit the specific needs of the force. He explained, for example, that owing to the geographical size of the borough, its large population and the scale of crime and disorder problems, the decision had been made to keep in place one pan-borough intelligence unit and two substations rather than merge them into the recommended single unit. He also confessed that even though the senior command team supported the spirit of the NIM and strove to demonstrate compliance they were relatively unconcerned about sanctions for breaching the code of practice. '[The regulations are] all bark and no bite.' Another senior officer said he encouraged his inspectors and sergeants to be 'on your feet cops', by which he meant for them to acknowledge and comply with relevant rules whilst exercising discretion or bending them if necessary for getting the job done. For him, the NIM almost always functioned in a smooth and advantageous manner and was a welcome development in both intelligence-led policing and performance management. However, he firmly believed that simply 'going through the motions' was no guarantee of achieving beneficial results. 'Cops are "can do" people and sometimes it's better to just let them get on with it.' The police managers of Smallville took a similar approach:

It's not perfect, but as you can see we've got NIM up and running just like it's supposed to be. You probably know by now that's not to say everything runs as smoothly as it could, but it's enough to tick all the boxes. (Senior Officer, Smallville)

When I asked in what ways the NIM did not run 'as smoothly as it could', he said it remained difficult for management to impose absolute conformity upon the rank-and-file and implement an integrated approach to intelligence-led policing throughout the organization. Having worked his way up the ranks, the officer in question was well aware that certain 'personalities' would never report all of the information in their possession or routinely listen to the recommendations of civilian analysts and use analytical products to proactively plan their operations. He recognized the hold of orthodox cultural attitudes and ways of working and how they were capable of undermining efforts to reform the police.

Notwithstanding the cultural resistance to change, it was widely believed that policing had become much more intelligence-led, systematic and accountable since the onset of the NIM management regime. As I sat waiting for a daily management meeting to commence, a seasoned detective with nearly thirty years' service told me that:

In the old days it was like *Life on Mars*... We were out on the streets doing "real" police work, busting heads and making up the rules as we went along. Nowadays we just follow management's orders and jump through all their hoops.

Clearly his points were slightly exaggerated and overemphasize the differences between now and then. This was a common trait of the self-professed 'dinosaurs' and their stories about the wheeling and dealing of how things were and the bureaucratic managerialism of how things are. DS Daniels nicely summed up how the NIM had impacted upon his day-to-day activities and the operations of the drug squad:

I have to attend a lot more meetings—if I don't have a good enough reason not to. There are more forms to fill out and reports to write; that's why we try and have a designated office day every week, to catch up on all the paperwork... We spend too much time in the office if you ask me... But it's not as though any of this is completely new; we've always had meetings and paperwork. I'd say the real difference for units like us is that most of our intelligence is now in the hands of the intelligence and source units

What is evident in both these quotations is that the detectives resented the erosion of their autonomy by the managerialist agenda and the somewhat tedious micromanagement of the NIM business process. Yet, despite widespread feelings of resentment, officers said they complied with procedure, or at least paid it lip service, because they were 'professionals' and did not want their reputations to be compromised. It was their job to follow orders and abide by the chain of command. Most officers assured me that there were disciplinary mechanisms in place to ensure that compliance was maintained. They had stories about getting 'a right bollocking' from their supervisors, and colleagues who had been reviewed or even reassigned for persistently disobeying orders, missing meetings and messing up paperwork. However, the concept of police professionalism meant different things to different people. Some understood it to be upholding bureaucratic standards of conduct, whereas others interpreted professional status as having integrity, accumulating expertise in a particular area, exercising discretion in accordance with internalized norms, and self-regulation through the ongoing interrogation of the types of responsibilities that were owed to others (Sklansky 2014).

The police are a very professional service if you ask me. It comes with the territory: the chain of command, the training, the discipline and all that. I was in the army before this so it's something I'm used to... We're doing an important job and we need to do it to a high standard. (Detective, Smallville)

"Professional" police officers play by the rules, but when they're making decisions they rely on their experience and specialist knowledge... As a sergeant it's part of my role to make sure they're up to speed with the law and organizational procedures. I'm also responsible for their training needs, and passing on my wisdom—such as it is! [laughs]... Once they've settled in and have a few years under their belt it becomes second nature. (Detective Sergeant, Metropolis)

'Compliance' was an equally malleable concept, and non-compliant behaviour was neither consistently challenged nor brought to book through formal disciplinary mechanisms. There were a range of accepted justifications for not following policy and procedure and circumstances in which compliance was deemed situationally inappropriate for the exigencies of police work. For example, it was found that in practice the Smallville drug squad operated largely outside the tasking and coordination process. DS Daniels would begrudgingly attend the bi-weekly meetings or send a deputy, though seldom graced the weekly intelligence meetings or daily management meetings with his presence. When present he rarely contributed to discussions, provided detailed updates in respect of ongoing operations, or received recommendations for tactical resolutions. 'We're a covert unit,' he explained. 'We don't want everyone knowing our business.' This 'need to know' mentality sat alongside a shared opinion within the squad that 'meetings don't get the job done'. From what was observed, the detectives had good relationships with their line manager and members of the district command team. There appeared to be a tacit 'nod and a wink' understanding that, so long as the squad got results and complied with procedure in at least a superficial manner, they could continue to have a relatively free rein over their priorities and operational matters.

The detectives of Metropolis, on the other hand, were subject to a much greater level of governance through tasking and co-ordination and came across as being more committed to the NIM ideal. The leadership within the squad was central to garnering and sustaining this commitment. Inspector Rawls and her three sergeants were strong advocates of intelligence-led policing and made conscious efforts to impress the value of the NIM business process upon the officers under their command and explain the intricacies of organizational strategies and management philosophies. Line managers and supervisors are hugely influential figures and have the capacity to establish professional boundaries within an occupational group, acknowledge and encourage positive contributions, and challenge undesirable behaviours and attitudes. Sergeants, in particular, play a key role in this respect, as they interpret the operational meaning of organizational policies, are directly involved in delivering policing on the ground and supervise what the rank-and-file do on a day-to-day basis (Chatterton 1979, 1992; Engel and Peterson 2014; Van Maanen 1983, 1984).

Organizational Priorities

At the organizational level, police managers exercised discretion when deciding how to prioritize the deployment of limited resources to enforce the law and perform other policing tasks. Within this constraint further decisions about the appropriate use of policing interventions and the suspect populations against which they should be targeted were made. In both Metropolis and Smallville, tackling the illegal drug business was a control strategy priority and had been ever since the inception of the NIM. 'Drugs have always been and will always be a priority,' the police frequently assured me. Having considered the nature and extent of the local drug problem, strategic assessments repeatedly identified entrenched drug markets and related criminality as significant issues affecting the police services areas and recommended enforcement and multi-agency initiatives as tactical resolutions. These documents provided an overview of trends, performance, strategic issues, public perception, future issues and intelligence gaps. Apart from slight variations in language and layout the priorities outlined in control strategy documents were substantively very similar and subject to only subtle revisions during the fieldwork period. For the supply reduction strand of drug control efforts, the primary objective was to focus on disrupting Class A drug markets—especially heroin and cocaine—and the measurable outcomes included arrests, seizures, prosecutions, and assets recovered. There were also crossovers between drug-specific priorities and priorities aimed at addressing drug-related crimes, such as disrupting organized crime groups and reducing serious violent crime, street robbery, and domestic burglary. Where drugs are not a priority for a force or borough there may not be the same level of coordinated activity and additional resources are unlikely to be made available.

A more comprehensive statement of the role of the police in drug control was set out in force-level drug strategies. These documents were produced in consultation with partner agencies on the part of the senior command team and designed for internal and external dissemination with the intention of guiding police personnel and informing audiences about their aspirations and activities. Moreover, they were political documents, intentional expressions made by police administrators to present an 'organizational front' and maintain control over the symbolic meanings of policing that are oriented towards legitimating existing practices publicly (Jermier et al. 1991; Manning 1997). For the most part, whilst proclaiming to be 'evidence-based' in-house products that were designed to tackle local demands, the respective strategies of the two forces under study were virtually identical in substance and contained much the same terminology and rhetoric. This was not because the forces were policing exactly the same drug problems or enlisting the services of the same ghostwriter. Rather, it was down to the fact that the strategy makers were obliged to incorporate the relevant elements of the National Policing Plan, the National Community Safety Strategy and successive national drug strategies (Home Office 1998, 2002, 2008). At the time of the empirical research, police service areas across the country were broadly focused on 'reducing the harm caused by drugs' by means of the following key activities: tackling Class A drug supply; disrupting open markets; closing crack houses; disrupting cannabis cultivation; arresting and diverting prolific and priority offender drug users; supporting communities by working together in partnership; and seizing assets and disrupting funding. The government has been much more active in setting the strategic direction of drug control since the mid-1990s through the development and implementation of national drug policies that are aimed at shaping the actions of state actors assigned to the task of dealing with drug problems. This method of imposing objectives and performance indicators can obscure the fact that it is politicians and policymakers in Westminster who govern the local police agenda:

> We don't get much of a say about what our aims are anymore; drug policies are designed by central government and then we just roll them out locally and try and make them work (Senior Officer, Metropolis).

Most of the detectives knew there was a drug strategy, though few had taken the time to go through it with a fine-tooth comb. Those who had were of the opinion that it was largely irrelevant to their everyday work, and where it was it simply documented what they were already doing and would continue to do regardless. 'I understand why it's important for the police to have a drug strategy, but there's nothing in there I don't already know,' said the longest serving member of the Smallville drug squad. He proceeded to skim through the document. 'Okay, there might be a couple of things I need to brush up on, but there's nothing in there that's going to help me do my job.' Line managers and supervisors were well acquainted with force strategies, kept their teams abreast of significant developments, and would refer officers to the literature if they demonstrated a lack of strategic awareness or business acumen. One of the Metropolis sergeants instructed all the 'newbies' to 'sit down with a cup of tea and read the papers' on their first day in the office so that 'we all know what we're playing at'. However, they too believed that policy documents are generally 'fully of politics', out of touch with local crime and disorder problems and lacking in practical relevance. Even senior officers conceded that drug strategies did not 'carry much weight' and barely influenced or constrained the work of detectives on the ground, a finding which indicates the accepted limitations of centralized control over the investigation of drug offenders. The only occasions when I observed detectives making reference to strategy documents was when they were copying out or paraphrasing prescribed justifications for policing drugs in order to construct an administratively accountable record of their operations.

Albeit an explicit priority in strategy documents and official mission statements, during fieldwork it was found that drug law enforcement had been unofficially deprioritized and was regularly downplayed when there were deemed to be more serious and pressing issues to deal with. It was more of a symbolic priority in that it represented police values and their sense of mission as opposed to their true objectives and practices. Observations revealed that drugs were a peripheral and sporadic feature of tactical tasking and coordination processes, which were more or less restricted to dealing with volume crimes such as burglary, street robbery, vehicle theft, and incidents of extreme violence. According to the senior officer who made the decision to refocus the Metropolis drug squad on firearms offences:

If all other crimes somehow go down, if we can get rid of all the serious crime, all the shootings and stabbings, the terrorist threat, then maybe drugs will become a priority again.

On a separate occasion, the same officer also informed me that the district was hitting its targets for drug detection rates through routine searches and arrests and so there was no longer a need for a dedicated response. He said that investigating street gangs committing robberies and firearms offences and arresting burglars and shoplifters almost certainly uncovers drug offences and leads to incidental seizures which in turn swell arrest numbers for possession and supply.

A consequence of this re-specialization was evident in a drug case that barely made it off the shelf. The investigating officer had reliable intelligence suggesting that a couple of men were involved in wholesale cocaine distribution and were using a café they owned as a legitimate front to launder the proceeds of crime. After a bit of pre-surveillance surveillance to develop the case it became clear that the suspects were very risk averse. Covert surveillance was needed to move forward with the operation and so an application was made for authorization. But management decided not to allocate the requested resources, chiefly because there was no firearms threat and the suspects were not known to be affiliated with any of the local gangs.

Police officers still considered drugs to be a serious problem, but, in their daily activities, responding to drug-related crime and disorder took priority over proactively policing drug markets. In effect, drug control per se had been largely replaced with drug-related crime and disorder control. As has been highlighted in previous research (Lister et al. 2008; Lupton et al. 2002; Parker 2006), the police were essentially attempting to 'manage' the market by keeping it from growing or causing too many problems locally. Furthermore, since the overwhelming majority of drug offences are victimless crimes in the sense that there is ordinarily no party to the act who has an interest in being the plaintiff, police managers frequently asserted that they struggled to justify using their limited resources to rigorously enforce drug laws when there were 'statistically significant' victims of crime in need of police services. Upon reflection, however, they recognized the paradox that many victims of crime were the direct victims of drug-related crimes and thereby the indirect victims of the production, supply, and use of controlled drugs. When I asked about where the investigation of markets for recreational drugs such as amphetamines, ecstasy, and ketamine fit within the business processes of the police, a senior officer responded by saying:

The short answer to your question is it doesn't really fit within them at all. Apart from the occasional proactive operation, most of our arrests and seizures come from routine stops and responding to calls for assistance from licensed premises... It's not a perfect system, I'll give you that much, but the fact of the matter is no one upstairs or downstairs cares enough to do anything more about it.

This 'management' approach to policing drugs had been shaped by the exercise of discretion, the everyday demands made upon the police to respond to calls for service and the strategic direction of the government. Indeed, by the early 2000s, policymakers were making a clear distinction between recreational and problematic drug markets as a way of managing the drug problem. Although no directives from the Home Office to police managers accompanied the *Updated Drug Strategy* (2002), it suggested that greater priority should be attached to policing Class A drugs over those defined as less harmful. In addition, police managers told me that, since the government had removed drug offences from national indicators designed to assess the performance of individual forces, it had become easier for them to selectively target interventions at meaningful local issues on the basis of intelligence instead of the meaningless targets of the 'numbers game'. Be that as it may, a few detectives pointed out that the removal of targets had also resulted in a loss of incentive and bemoaned the continuing pressure to meet volume crime targets as a causal factor in the deprioritization of drug law enforcement and the reallocation of resources. Take this interview excerpt, for example, in which the officer really highlights the selective nature of drug law enforcement:

We could choose to ignore drugs if we wanted to, because it's victimless and isn't performance managed anymore...In the police there's a saying: "you only have a drug problem if you look for it". The more we police drugs the more problems we find, and management don't want us to go out and find any more problems—just look outside, we've got enough work on. (Detective Inspector, Metropolis)

The DI's comment is not to be taken literally of course. The officer in question certainly did not believe that it was no longer necessary to enforce drug laws or that drug problems should or could be overlooked. It is perhaps best conceived as a somewhat flippant statement that was intended to express the scope of police discretion and the vagaries of measuring performance by means of numerical targets in the field of drug control. Similar views are expressed in following fieldnote about a shift in operational focus for the Smallville drug squad:

Today I was able to uncover a little more about the hidden politics of policing drugs in Smallville. The squad were carrying out a surveillance operation on a couple of suspected dealers, waiting for a pattern to emerge —or 'Lady Luck'. Bunk, Dozerman and myself were in an unmarked car, parked up across the street from the property being monitored. We watched nothing happen for five hours so had plenty of time to chat. Last week, the 'warrant a day' tactic had been stopped. Instead, the 'top three' warrants of the week were now to be executed on the same day. Bunk told me that the Chief Superintendent had spoken with DS Daniels and asked him to go after the bigger dealers. 'If you can bring me one a month I'll be happy,' he'd said. The reasons for this shift in focus, the detectives suspected, were performance and politics. 'We've been getting some good results from warrants over the past year, getting more arrests and seizures than any other district—that's the problem'. I asked Bunk what he meant. 'If you hammer it day in and day out, it looks like you've got a massive drug problem; leave it alone and the drugs seem to go away. They're still there of course —just not on paper.' (Fieldnotes, Smallville)

At best, the numbers are an easily manipulated administrative record of what the police decided to do and how they decided to document the outcomes of their actions. They tell us very little about the nature and scale of the drug problem and should not be used as an indication of the effectiveness of policing interventions (Loveday 2000; Maguire 2012).

Intelligence Work

Intelligence-led policing relies on a steady stream, and a bountiful reservoir, of information. To this end, an essential part of dealing with a drug problem is to properly identify and understand the problem, which is only possible if the police officers tasked with tactical resolutions have access to the appropriate information sources and analytical resources.

Given that drugs had been identified as a priority in the control strategies of both Metropolis and Smallville, to be in keeping with the NIM business process, the police should deliver a coordinated strategic and tactical response to drug problems in their service area. A full analysis of local drug markets should be carried out so that relevant action plans can be developed. The market analysis should then be used as a basis for creating specific problem and target profiles. Intelligence units should include drugs in their tactical assessments and police managers should use these assessments to make decisions about tactical resolutions to address the issues identified therein. Intelligence requirements should drive the issues and be widely communicated to police staff. Drug detectives should work closely with intelligence analysts to commission analytical work to support their operations and help them make sound tactical decisions. They should also submit intelligence reports that relate to their investigations so that tactical assessments can be kept up-to-date, and collaborate in the production of results analyses in order to evaluate the effectiveness of their enforcement activities.

Information enters police organizations from wide and varied sources.[3] It can be tasked, collected as part of routine policing

[3] Sources of information that are available to the police for drug investigations may include the following: alarm/security companies; Automatic Number Plate Recognition (ANPR); chemists/drug registers; CCTV; community schemes (e.g. Neighbourhood Watch, Shopwatch and Pubwatch); Controlled Drug Liaison Officers; Covert Human Intelligence Sources (CHISs); Crimestoppers; Forensic Science Services; Force Drugs Coordinators; HM Prison Service (HMP); housing associations/departments; Human Intelligence Sources (e.g. victims, witnesses, neighbours, suspects, colleagues in partner agencies, community sources, local

activities, or volunteered to the police by members of the public. Not all information is immediately identifiable as being of intelligence value. Nevertheless, any information obtained by the police that might be of value should be recorded and submitted to the intelligence unit by way of an intelligence report. The fixed-choice '5x5x5 Information Intelligence Report' format is designed to embed the form and flow of information in police intelligence systems. Standardized devices such as these prospectively guide communicative action and act as retrospective audits to guarantee accountable data.

The nature and quality of the information submitted very much depends on the motivations of the individual police officer and their understanding of what is required of them in terms of intelligence gathering. Far from being a neutral channel of communication, existing research indicates that the processes involved in the construction of intelligence are rooted in notions of crime control and so officers typically value 'real time' information about known offenders that they believe will be useful for facilitating the enforcement of the criminal law. Valid knowledge is contextual and grounded in experiential understandings generated from what officers observe on the streets. Research also reminds us that intelligence reports cannot precisely capture all of the information that resides in the memories of the authors. They are filtered versions of events that necessarily involve a degree of simplification and a reduction of the symbolic complexities that are experienced in social reality. In other words, the police intelligence picture can only ever provide a partial insight into the policed milieu and the wider policing landscape (Bullock 2013; Cope 2004; Innes et al. 2005; Manning and Hawkins 1989).

councillors, local school teachers, religious leaders, youth leaders and other members of the community); other law enforcement agencies (e.g. Europol, HM Revenue & Customs (HMRC), Interpol, National Crime Agency (NCA); Serious Organised Crime Agency (SOCA) (2006–2013); UK Border Agency (UKBA)); Licensing Officers; news media; partner agencies and stakeholders (e.g. Ambulance Service, Crime and Disorder Reduction Partnerships (CDRPs), Drug Action Teams (DATs), Environmental Health, Local Education Authorities, Primary Care Trusts (PCTs), Probation Service); physical evidence gained from the scene (e.g. drugs paraphernalia); police databases (e.g. computerized incident handling systems, crime recording systems, ELMER database for suspicious activity reports, force and local intelligence systems, HOLME2, Police National Computer (PNC)); Safer Neighbourhood Teams (SNTs); Youth Offending Teams.

When filling out intelligence reports, the submitting officer is required to make an interpretive judgement about the reliability of both the source and the information. This adds another layer of subjectivity to the outwardly objective intelligence process. The intelligence unit then assess the value of the reports, apply a handling code and enter the information onto the intelligence system (see Tables 6.1, 6.2, and 6.3). Information contained within police intelligence systems constitutes the core source of data for intelligence-led policing. The grading system used for evaluating and disseminating information is of considerable significance as the assigned grade impacts upon the subsequent information pathway and how intelligence is perceived by those required to act on it.

Around one hundred intelligence reports were entering the police intelligence system of Smallville on a daily basis. There could be as many as one thousand in Metropolis—a situation that can aptly be described as 'information overload' (Sheptycki 2004). After

Table 6.1　Source Evaluation

A. Always reliable	There is no doubt of the authenticity, trustworthiness and competence of the source. Information has been supplied in the past and has proven to be reliable in all instances. *Example: information received from technical products, such as DNA and fingerprints.*
B. Mostly reliable	Information has been received from this source in the past and in the majority of instances has proven to be reliable. *Example: information received from police officers, registered sources and partner agencies.*
C. Sometimes reliable	Information received from this source has proved to be both reliable and unreliable. Any information with this grading should not be acted upon without corroboration.
D. Unreliable	Information under this grading will refer to individuals who have provided information in the past which has routinely proven unreliable. There may be some doubt regarding the authenticity, trustworthiness, competency or motive of the source. Any information with this grading should not be acted on without corroboration.
E. Untested source	This grading refers to information received from a source that has not previously provided information to the person recording. Corroboration of this information should be sought. *Example: this grading will usually apply to members of the public and the majority of information received from Crimestoppers.*

information entered the intelligence unit, trained officers, analysts and researchers got to work on filtering out the 'noise', developing 'action packages' to provide reliable intelligence in a practical format, and conducting analyses to generate knowledge about

Table 6.2 Information/Intelligence Evaluation

1. Known to be true without reservation	This grading refers to first-hand information. This could be information generated from a technical deployment or an event which was witnessed by a law enforcement officer or prosecuting agency. *Example: an officer witnessed an incident or refers to live evidence.*
2. The information is known personally by the source but not to the person reporting	*Example: a registered source provides information which they know of first-hand to the person recording the information.*
3. The information is not known personally to the source but can be corroborated by other information	Information given may have been received by a source from a third party; its reliability has been corroborated by other information, such as CCTV or other force systems.
4. The information cannot be judged	The reliability of this information cannot be judged or corroborated. Information with this grading must be treated with caution. *Example: anonymous information received from members of the public that a crime has occurred but it is not possible to corroborate.*
5. Suspected to be false	*Example: a registered source who is engaged in criminal activity and provides exaggerated information against others in order to deflect attention from themselves or to prepare a defence of working for the police should they be arrested.*

Table 6.3 Handling Code

1   Permits dissemination within the UK police service and to other law enforcement agencies as specified

2   Permits dissemination to UK non-prosecuting parties

3   Permits dissemination to (non-EU) foreign law enforcement agencies

4   Permits dissemination within originating force/agency only: specify reasons and internal recipient(s)

5   Permits dissemination but receiving agency to observe conditions as specified

patterns in crime and disorder and the wider policing landscape. Much intelligence work was desk-based and involved the compilation, cross-referencing, and comprehension of information from various sources. The police were inundated with information, tip-offs, and rumours about drug market activity. 'Drugs are a constant,' explained an intelligence officer. 'They were here yesterday, they're here today and they'll be here tomorrow. The challenge for us is not a lack of information; it's figuring out what to do with the plenitude of information we have.' Here is a random selection of anonymized drug-related intelligence reports with the assigned grade in brackets:

X, street name 'Y', deals heroin and cocaine on the Metropolis Town Estate. He is a close friend of Z. Z lives at ADDRESS and X stores his drugs there (B24).

X is reported to be selling cannabis from his home ADDRESS. He is also reported to smoke cannabis in his back garden with unknown people of a similar age (E41).

X, DOB, Male IC3 PNCID, a senior North Metropolis gang member, is closely associated with senior members of the ABC street gang from South Metropolis. Some members of the ABC gang known to have close connections with X are Y and Z (B11).

Information from 2008 continues to state that X, DOB, aka 'Y', is involved in the movement of large quantities of controlled drugs (primarily cocaine) in Smallville. Information also states that X is associated and involved in drug dealing with Y and Z (B24).

On DATE police were called to attend Metropolis Road, where an anonymous caller claimed she had seen a black jeep moving up and down and a woman screaming for help. On police arrival, the street was quiet and there was a Black Porsche Cayenne REGISTRATION parked behind the Metropolis Town Estate. There were four occupants who had just been smoking cannabis so a search was conducted of the occupants and the vehicle. Negative result. X was one of the occupants, who is believed to supply drugs and regularly carry a firearm (B11).

X is involved in the supply of heroin. X owns property at ADDRESS. It is believed that he provided false details to obtain the mortgage and subsequent re-mortgages of that property. It is believed that X is not currently receiving any 'employment' income (B24).

If the information received was assessed as 'live', 'high risk', 'now or never' and needing to be acted upon immediately, intelligence officers would follow a 'fast-track' procedure and pass the information on to the applicable unit without delay for tactical resolution. 'When we receive reliable intelligence about a deal that's going down or a threat to life the policy is "act now, think later," ' an intelligence officer said during interview. 'There isn't always time for research and development when the circumstances demand a hair-trigger response.' As well as emphasizing the centrality of rapid response to the police role, this quotation points to the fact that all operational policing is fundamentally reactive in the sense that it is always a reaction to a trigger, whether it be proactively generated intelligence, the occurrence of a criminal event, or a call for service from the public. It also illustrates that the police use the term 'intelligence' when referring both to raw information that is believed to have factual status and that which has been systematically analysed to determine its meaning and relevance. Indeed, a number of intelligence specialists confirmed that in practice a lot of the 'intelligence' which prompts and supports police operations is actually little more than loosely assembled pieces of information that are subject to only a cursory form of analysis. In such instances 'analysis' normally meant 'corroboration', in that the separate pieces of information about a particular crime or criminal corroborated each other.

For urgent intelligence about drug supply offences, the drug detectives were usually the first port of call. Specialist squads are in place to deal with specific forms of criminality on a more or less exclusive basis and so automatically take the lead on intelligence that falls within their field of activity. 'It's kind of a no-brainer that drug intelligence goes to the drug unit. They're the experts after all.' If the 'right people' were unable to take on the job, however, it would be reassigned to reactive CID officers or the local SNT. This happened much more frequently in Metropolis because deployment of the firearms squad was generally reserved for drug dealers who were also implicated in firearms offences and gang-related criminality.

Alternatively, when viable intelligence needed to be developed further before action could be taken, intelligence officers would devise a 'collection plan', carry out 'field research', and liaise with members of police staff and partner agencies to gather the required information. A 'flagging' system would also be set up for identifying specific targets that were subject to operational tasking or intelligence collection. In the police forces under study, at district level, field intelligence officers were organized into 'intelligence development teams'. All of the officers were certified detectives and had completed the national research and development course. Their 'research' in relation to the illegal drug business basically consisted of making enquiries, utilizing a range of surveillance techniques to monitor suspected dealers, and working with the drug detectives and other specialists to determine appropriate recommendations for intelligence products about the resources that might be employed. If you strip away the terminology, field research performed an investigative support function and was largely synonymous with the proactive approach to detective work—only without the climactic conclusion.

To tell you the truth, there isn't all that much difference between what I'm doing now and what I was doing when I was working drugs before I transferred to the intelligence unit. The intelligence side of things is more sophisticated here, especially when you factor in the training, software packages, and analytical products, but the tactics and objectives are the same as they always were. The main difference is we don't make the arrests. (Intelligence Officer, Metropolis)

We're the guys in the background. The idea is we build up the case to the point of execution and then pass it on. It's great work, but I do miss the action. (Intelligence Officer, Smallville)

When an intelligence case was being developed for a drug investigation, the drug detectives were almost always kept informed from the outset and actively involved in the production process. This close working relationship often amounted to a collaborative endeavour that allowed the detectives to shape the intelligence collection and enforcement plans. 'If we pool our skills and knowledge, the end result is bound to be better,' reasoned one intelligence officer. The detectives agreed. They also preferred to be in control of their intelligence and to 'know what's coming next' in terms of their caseload. The optimal output of the research and development stage was sometimes described as 'current, accurate, and ongoing' intelligence that could be used to initiate a covert investigation or justify a quick enforcement intervention.

After an intelligence case had been developed into an action package it was effectively a pending operation awaiting the allocation of a 'plan owner' to organize a response to the identified problem. The operations that were allocated to the drug detectives, either directly from the intelligence unit or following decisions made in tactical tasking and coordination group meetings, typically took the form of 'target profiles'. The content of these target profiles varied depending on the nature of the subject, the available resources of the intelligence capability, and the requirements of the commissioning officers. For the most part, they simply contained the reasons for targeting an individual or group of suspected offenders and an overview of their personal details, criminal record, recent activities and known associates.

[Police managers] don't want us spending all day on a target profile. They just want the basics, something that can be turned around in a couple of hours tops so the operation can get underway as soon as possible. (Analyst, Metropolis)

On a handful of occasions the detectives also received 'problem profiles' on open drug markets containing a detailed picture of the intelligence assembled on the problem and a crime pattern analysis of the 'hot spot' geographical areas.

In theory, intelligence action packages should be able to be operationalized without the need for any further development. By and large, this held true in practice. 'When we get a quality intelligence package we can hit the ground running.' However, a number of detectives argued that on the occasions when they were not involved in the production process, more intelligence work was required before the script could be enacted on the streets.

You'll hear people saying we're intelligence-led but in my opinion we've still got a long way to go. We're supposed to get the intelligence and then just do a warrant or start up surveillance, but that's not what happens. Don't get me wrong, the intelligence unit are good at what they do. All I'm saying is we have some intelligence work to do before we have a case-worthy job. (Detective, Metropolis)

Although a few 'gaps' were filled and updates made, the additional research and development undertaken by the detectives was essentially a 'dot the i's and cross the t's' exercise that rarely contributed anything substantially new to the intelligence picture. Observations revealed that the main reason for this duplication of effort was to allow the detectives to familiarize themselves with the suspects and take ownership of the case.

On top of the jobs coming from the intelligence unit, the drug detectives were constantly on the lookout for 'dynamite' information, developing intelligence for action against future targets, and playing the system in order to initiate their own operations. They searched police intelligence systems on a daily basis and regularly enquired about recent goings-on in the drug world during conversations with their colleagues and non-police contacts. They believed it was necessary to 'stay on top of our game' and make sure they picked up on cases that might 'slip through the cracks' of the intelligence architecture. For the detectives, the most valid 'current, accurate, and ongoing' intelligence was that which was grounded in experiential understandings learnt in the course of the investigatory process. Drug investigations were said to generate a wealth of information.

We learn more in the field than in any meeting or from any piece of paper. (Detective, Metropolis)

When we're out on a job we're working real time. You know? We see drug deals as they happen. We find out who's doing what and when they're at it. You get to know what they're about... When we bring suspects in they'll give us something on their mates or some other dealer because they're trying to save their skin. A lot of it's bullshit like, but there's usually something in it... If we work it right one case practically follows on from the other. (Detective, Smallville)

A great deal of the information gathered during drug investigations was stored in the personal memory banks of the detectives or the informal repository of the squad room. Detectives have what Collison (1995) refers to as a 'squirrel instinct', which compels them to store information in their heads in case it proves useful for some future investigation rather than input it into the system. However, when they were in possession of high-grade intelligence of potentially case-worthy value, an intelligence report would be submitted. Information that fell short was perhaps remembered but not recorded. On the whole, the reports were not submitted because the detectives felt a pressing need to keep tactical assessments up-to-date or to contribute to police knowledge about patterns in crime and disorder. Their motivations were much more parochial and concerned with self-interest and gratification. Reports were submitted so that the information would be entered into the police intelligence system and the wheels set in motion that would in turn enable them to set their own operational targets. The ability to generate intelligence and then use it to initiate and make cases was perceived as central to the craft of the effective detective. Furthermore, their sense of elitism and territorial instincts made them much more inclined to trust, prioritize, and act upon intelligence that was under their control. These snowballing tactics are problematic as they are open to manipulation, limit the scope of enforcement activities, and provide only a partial insight into the drug world. As Cope (2004: 199) contends, if information is not passed on and analysed it can undermine the intelligence process and lead to 'policing-led intelligence', whereby the information that officers value, generate, and record coalesces around 'the usual suspects' and does not consider the nature of crime and criminals more broadly.

Drug detective work was viewed as a case-focused enterprise in that efforts were organized and framed by the present and prospective caseload. For the detectives of Metropolis and Smallville, information valued as relevant was that which was needed to make a case against a suspect for a specific crime. They worked in a tactically focused environment and would usually discount intelligence concerned with enhancing deeper understanding of crime and disorder issues and the wider policing landscape as having little relevance for operational policing. Police studies have repeatedly found that officers are very pragmatic and are concerned with concrete realities or actual instances, rather than abstract concepts, long-term trends and theoretical reflections (Reiner 2010: 131–2). It is hardly surprising, then, that intelligence analysts and their analytical products were notably absent from the intelligence work underpinning drug investigations. Analysts, working alongside researchers, focused their efforts on analysing information to inform strategic planning, assist in the composition of intelligence products, and identify intelligence requirements. They were all civilian members of staff and had attended a variety of training courses to learn the basic tools of their trade. Most were female and university graduates. Generally speaking, intelligence analysis constitutes a 'new' type of knowledge that does not sit well with traditional understandings of knowledge as being something that is gained through experience of police work on the streets. Research has revealed that the cultural challenge of integrating analysis into routine policing and the symbolic boundaries between police officers and 'civvies' has created frictions and a sense of division in the workplace (Atkinson 2013; Cope 2004).

The detectives who participated in this study tended to view analytical work with scepticism as being overly 'academic', 'all about performance management', 'pointless descriptions of what we already know' and the concoction of 'university-educated types who need to take a reality check'. This was especially true of the drug market analyses that were produced on an annual basis. These lengthy documents provided an overview of performance and were aimed at enhancing understanding of trends in drug use and supply and the impact of social, economic, and political factors on drug-related crime. As with the force drug strategies, few detectives had taken the time to read them and those who had were of the opinion that they were largely irrelevant to their everyday work and simply documented what they were already doing and would continue to do regardless.

Some [analytical products] make for interesting reading, but if I'm honest it's all a bit highbrow for me. I'd rather sit down with a brew and read the paper when I get a minute. (Detective, Metropolis)

The way I see it is [analysts] are doing their job and we're doing ours. (Detective, Smallville)

With few exceptions, despite being essential to the organizational effectiveness of the NIM ideal, the detectives rarely collaborated with analysts on knowledge production or integrated analysis into their operational endeavours. In Smallville, the detectives had very limited contact with the analysts, hardly ever kept them informed about their activities for tactical assessment purposes, and never commissioned them to produce analytical products. The only products they held in high regard were target profiles that brought together intelligence on a suspect and their activities, because they could be used to initiate operations and provide further support for established investigative practice. Besides their scepticism about the role of analysis in intelligence-led policing, a particular source of contention for the detectives was the idea that civilian analysts should be consulted on tactical resolutions. They considered themselves to be the unrivalled experts on drug law enforcement and did not think analysts possessed the necessary knowledge and expertise to inform them about operational matters. 'It's like a spectator giving advice to a professional athlete.' The advice of intelligence officers was taken on board, but when analysts made recommendations they were habitually disregarded and passive-aggressively disparaged. Furthermore, the fact that analytical products were being channelled towards management in an effort to guide decision making on resource deployment and enforcement strategies was perceived as a challenge to their authority and cultural capital. During interviews, analysts regularly expressed feelings of frustration and job dissatisfaction when talking about their occupational experiences:

Even though we're supposed to be of an equivalent rank [police officers] don't see us as equals. If I were a cop I'd be taken much more seriously. (Analyst, Smallville)

We spend hours working on products for detectives that they don't even look at. It can be very frustrating to be ignored on a daily basis. (Analyst, Smallville)

The situation was somewhat different in Metropolis because Inspector Rawls and her three sergeants had made some headway by making a conscious effort to explain the value of analytical products to the officers under their command. A greater understanding of intelligence analysis within the firearms team was also facilitated by the fact that several members were trained intelligence officers who had previously worked in the intelligence unit. Although analytical work remained a sporadic and relatively peripheral feature of their everyday practice, the detectives did occasionally commission analysts to produce a range of products to support their operations and help them make sound tactical decisions. These included crime pattern analyses, network analyses, risk analyses, and criminal business profiles. Once officers had experienced the pragmatic benefits of these analytical products they tended to embrace them and in turn developed greater respect for the analysts who produced them.

[Civilian analyst's name] is brilliant at her job. That gang profile she put together was a top quality piece of work. You've seen it, right? She even set up a fake Facebook account and was accepted as a friend by some of the gang members. Genius! Social media is an untapped goldmine for intelligence work. She came back with a list of people as long as my arm for us to look into – photos and everything. It really helped us make the case. (Detective Sergeant, Metropolis)

To the best of my knowledge, no operational reviews or results analyses were carried out in either police force during the fieldwork period to evaluate the effectiveness of drug investigations. The detectives judged arrests, seizures, and prosecutions to be sufficient evidence of success and had little interest in commissioning analysts to carry out systematic research in order to measure their efficiency or impact of their efforts on local drug problems. 'We just don't have the time,' said one detective. 'As soon as we've finished one operation we're onto the next one.' According to Manning (2004: 223), the focus on flair, style, and quantifiable results 'means that formal modes of evaluation based on written files or paperwork, abstract goals, or hypothetical achievements are weak and avoided'. The problem here is that arrests and seizures are measures of activity and output rather than impact and outcomes. Whilst they may sometimes be associated with an over-all reduction in drug problems, this will not necessarily always be the case (UKDPC 2009).

Operational Targets

According to the police intelligence picture, absolute drug law en-forcement was an insurmountable task, for at any one time there were seemingly infinite numbers of suspected dealers whom the detectives could be targeting. During fieldwork, the detectives always seemed to have a burgeoning pile of intelligence reports and action packages to be working through. Not all of the intel-ligence was acted on as they simply did not have the resources or the incentive to do so. In consequence, they had considerable discretion when setting their operational targets and were often able to 'cherry-pick' from a number of the potential jobs using what Collison (1995: 40) referred to as 'more idiosyncratic crite-ria'. These criteria typically aligned with their recipe knowledge of drug offenders and cultural sense of mission and crime hierar-chy. Moreover, given that the detectives preferred to own the case from start to finish, they were much more likely to prioritize intel-ligence that they themselves had generated and helped develop. This practice led to occasional tensions between the detectives and the intelligence unit, when they decided to postpone or not act on reports or action packages that intelligence officers and analysts had laboured over and considered case-worthy. 'It's frustrating when [detectives] take it upon themselves to shelve our products, or take it on and then just sit on it until its dated. That's not how intelligence-led policing should work.'[4]

The detectives considered their basic function to be 'getting the dealers and the drugs off the streets', but in both forces they readily acknowledged that enforcement was a marginal activ-ity of limited capacity and dwindling resources. Drugs were not

---

[4] That being said, I found that the detectives of Metropolis had less autonomy than their counterparts in Smallville because they were required to act on intel-ligence suggesting that someone had committed a gun-enabled crime or was in possession of a firearm, especially if there was a threat to life. 'We have to be able to show that we've done everything in our power to prevent people getting shot,' said one detective. If a person committed murder and it was later discovered that the firearms squad had not acted on intelligence, they assured me that they would 'be in the shit'.

policed simply because they are illegal, nor drug dealers for committing a criminal offence. In practice, drug laws were selectively enforced with the aim of reducing the crimes caused by and associated with drug distribution. Proactive investigations were thus heavily concentrated on only a small segment of the drug trade. Dealers who traded in heroin and crack became the targets of operations, chiefly because of the perceived link between the use of these drugs and acquisitive crime, as did dealers who had a history of violence and access to firearms, dealers who were part of organized crime networks or streets gangs, dealers who operated openly in public places, and 'Mr Bigs' who dealt in large quantities and made large profits. For the most part, therefore, the drug detectives targeted the drugs, dealers, and marketplaces that emerged from the intelligence picture as being the most 'harmful' in terms of crime and disorder. Their role was to police the consequences of prohibition.

Suspects who were 'known' to the detectives always seemed to find their way to the top of the pile. Indeed, being 'known' is all that is sometimes needed to make someone an official suspect. When the detectives said they 'knew' a dealer, what they meant was they had personally encountered them in the past, in that they had a little or a lot of intelligence on them but had never built up a case or secured a conviction, or that they had 'put them away' and they were out of prison and back in the game. 'It makes it a bit easier when you know the suspect,' explained one detective. 'You start the case with a good idea of what they're about–what they're into, who they're connected to, that kind of thing'. The obvious problem here is that pre-existing knowledge can quickly become preconceived notions and in turn operational responses remain too narrowly focused on simply arresting a small set of known individuals rather than identifying previously unknown offenders or addressing underlying problems. 'If this process does not encourage "negative feedback" to modify initial targeting decisions', Gill (2000: 131) contends, 'it may become a circular system of "rounding up the usual suspects"'. As a result, the police reproduce the disadvantage of that group by policing them at a rate disproportionate to other members of the public. It was a personal vendetta for some detectives, what Maguire and Norris (1992: 15) described as 'a continuing "battle" with fairly bounded groups of persistent offenders'. Others saw the usual suspects in a more cynical light, which highlighted the failings of the criminal justice system and reinforced the view that the police were fighting a losing war on drugs.

In effect, the detectives were attempting to maintain a sense of order by regulating the drug trade in accordance with what I came to think of as the *Drug Trade Code of Practice*. What I mean by regulation here is that the detectives were attempting to shape and control the trade in their respective territories through enforcement interventions. They were, in other words, performing an 'order maintenance' function, which differs from traditional understandings in that order was maintained through legitimate coercion rather than by means other than formal law enforcement (Reiner 2010: 144). This finding sits well with the work of Lister et al. (2008: 27) on the street policing of problematic drug users, in which the authors suggest that 'policing objectives such as law enforcement are now much less pursued purely as ends in themselves. Instead, contemporary policing is more concerned with the surveillance and control of territories and populations'. The unwritten rules of the *Code* essentially required dealers not to trade in crime-related drugs or operate in a criminal manner. The underlying rationale was that interventions would punish priority offenders and criminal groups in the first instance and alter the market in the long term by deterring other actors from engaging in the designated harmful behaviours. There were plenty of dealers who broke the *Code*, more than enough to keep the detectives of Metropolis and Smallville constantly busy. Those who abided by it were more or less abandoned to go about their ordinary business, either because they were off the police radar or at the bottom of the 'to do' list of actionable priorities.

Conclusion

Policing appears to have become 'smarter' over recent decades as police organizations around the world have developed innovative strategies to respond more effectively to the challenges of contemporary crime and disorder problems. 'Intelligence' may well be a malleable term that gets misused and overused in police discourse but there is substance behind the rhetoric. Since its emergence in Britain as a discrete policing strategy, James (2013: 1) notes that intelligence-led policing 'has been advanced as a panacea for the most pressing of policing's ills'. Advocates have presented it as a paradigm change that will rectify the shortcomings associated with traditional reactive methods of policing by giving precedence to proactive ideologies, strategic planning, and the systematic prioritization of issues on the basis of analysis at the organizational level. This chapter has examined the impact of intelligence-led policing on drug law enforcement, the processes involved in the initiation of drug investigations up to the point of them becoming operational, and the interactive relationship between drug detectives and the organizational frameworks within which their formative intelligence and investigative practices were constructed and performed.

In one form or another, intelligence has always been the driving force behind drug investigations. Without intelligence, drug detectives would be blind; they would not be able to see the illegal drug business, identify their targets, or the opportunities for enforcement intervention. Traditionally, detectives have tended to regard intelligence as a personal resource, a kind of property that is not easily shared with others, especially outside the squad room. It provides them with a form of currency that can be used to buy power and respect. With the rise of intelligence-led policing, however, intelligence has become an organizational resource, as reformers have attempted to expand intelligence work beyond the remit of specialist detective units so that it can direct the policing styles of police organizations. The findings discussed in this chapter describe how, following the implementation of the NIM, much of the autonomy detectives previously had to develop information into actionable intelligence and set their own operational targets has been eroded by the centrality of the intelligence unit to the police intelligence function. Furthermore, they show how police managers were, in varying degrees, able to preside over key decision-making processes, prioritize crime and disorder problems, and allocate resources accordingly for both strategic and tactical purposes. When I first entered the field, most research participants claimed that the police were fully NIM-compliant and that the codified business process near enough dictated the management of intelligence work and operational policing. Some officers were resolutely committed to the NIM ideal and believed that it facilitated smarter policing and the targeting of resources where they could be expected to yield the best results. Others resented the erosion of their autonomy by the managerialist agenda but they complied nonetheless and there was little overt resistance.

What the findings also reveal is that there were discrepancies between the formal ways in which the organization presented itself and the informal ways in which police officers actually operated. Senior officers did not appear to be wholeheartedly committed to implementing the model to the letter. They took a 'NIM-lite approach', encouraged the rank-and-file to comply with the rules whilst exercising discretion, and accepted that certain 'personalities' would never report all of the information in their possession or routinely listen to the recommendations of civilian analysts and use analytical products to proactively plan their operations. James (2013) criticizes the policy of compliance as being largely presentational, outweighing any meaningful consideration of outcomes, and failing to significantly affect conventional practice. There were a range of justifications for not following policy and procedure, and circumstances in which the detectives could work the system, or compliance was deemed situationally inappropriate for the exigencies of police work. Freedom from organizational control was bolstered in both forces by the fact that drug law enforcement had been unofficially deprioritized and was regularly downplayed by management owing to the pressure to meet volume crime targets.

The ability to generate intelligence and make cases remained central to the craft of the effective detective and their sense of elitism and territorial instincts made them much more inclined to trust, prioritize and act upon intelligence that was under their control. Accordingly, although most of their jobs came from the intelligence unit, the detectives were constantly on the lookout for 'case-worthy' information, would submit intelligence reports in order to set the wheels in motion that would, in turn, enable them to set their own operational targets, and then work closely with intelligence officers to shape the intelligence collection and enforcement plans. The information the detectives valued, generated, and recorded coalesced around the marginal and powerless groups in society and known offenders in particular. With few exceptions, despite being essential to the effectiveness of the NIM business process, the detectives rarely collaborated with analysts on knowledge production or integrated analysis into their investigative work. They worked in a tactically focused environment and would usually discount intelligence concerned with enhancing a deeper understanding of crime and disorder issues as having little relevance to operational policing. When they did use analytical products it was generally to initiate operations and provide further support for established investigative practice. In consequence, the police were not utilizing the potential of intelligence analysts, who could make significant contributions to reducing drug-related harms by producing analytical products to inform tactical resolutions and by evaluating the impact of enforcement interventions. Given the size of the drug problem and the fact that there is always another operation waiting, it can be hard for the police to find the resources needed to review, monitor, and evaluate impact, but this is essential if they are to learn what works under what circumstances and effectively address the harms of the illegal drug business and the unintended consequences of drug control policy.

7

Licensing Criminals

I saw Herc approaching through the glass of the security door, his tree-trunk-like arms still clearly pumped from an early morning gym session. He was the officer usually tasked with battering the door open during 'no-knock' forced entry warrants, so he had to keep his strength up. A relatively new member of the squad but by no means a 'rookie' detective, Herc was friendly enough, had a good sense of humour, and a predilection for t-shirts with retro prints. 'Morning mate, come on in... Lovely weather isn't it?' It was raining.

I followed him through the rabbit warren of a station: down a few corridors, up a few flights of stairs. 'You've missed a few good jobs since you were last here.' As we neared the squad's base of operations, Herc stopped, knocked on the closed door of the 'Source Unit', and hurriedly went in to arrange to come back after the morning meeting for a mid-morning meeting. 'It's about the surveillance job we're working on; what we're seeing isn't what we're hearing, so we have to see a man about a dog.' The idiom wasn't used here in its traditional sense to mean an excuse for leaving without giving the real reason. Such excuses were reserved for ducking needless meetings or needy colleagues. On this occasion, the usage was much more literal: the 'man' was a source handler and the 'dog' was a registered informer. I asked Herc if I could attend the meeting and both he and the handler agreed.

The drug squad were acting on, as yet, uncorroborated 'intelligence' suggesting that their target had recently established himself as a heroin wholesaler in East Smallville. He was a 'known' dealer, had a previous conviction for possession with intent to supply, and was suspected of having ties with a Grandville 'organized crime group', which gave them reasonable grounds for carrying out the surveillance operation. According to the source, the suspect was supplying 'serious weight' to another unspecified wholesaler and anything between a 'henry' and a 'half' to local retailers. He was supposed to be active most days and transactions generally took place in the stairwell of a specified block of flats. The source was said be to an 'on and off' heroin user, who had been working with the police for the past three months. 'We've been on it four days and we're not seeing any evidence of dealing,' said Herc. 'Our guy showed up on Tuesday and stayed for a couple of hours. There was a bit of curtain twitching going off in one of the flats so we think he was waiting for someone.' For the next ten minutes, the detectives engaged in a speculative conversation. Maybe the source was wrong. 'He's been reliable so far,' said the handler. Maybe the suspect was suspicious of police activity and had changed his business pattern. 'It's always possible.' Maybe the source was working for the suspect and playing the handler. 'I doubt it.' No conclusions were reached. The handler promised to touch base with the source and see if there was any further information. 'Let's just see how it plays out for now.'

(Fieldnotes, Smallville)

The use of what are varyingly known as 'informants', 'informers', or 'covert human intelligence sources' has been persistent and pervasive throughout the history of policing because police organizations are to some extent dependent upon information from those connected to the activities over which control is being sought (Billingsley et al. 2001; Billingsley 2009; Fijnaut and Marx 1995). Much more so than other police functions, criminal investigation can be viewed as an 'information game' in that it is ultimately about piecing together a body of evidence in order to determine 'what happened' and 'who did it' in the eyes of the law. Despite being described as '*the* dirty secret of policing' (Reuter 1983b: 22) and the ' "unlovely" face of police work' (Billingsley 2009), the literature on detective work emphasizes that informants are and always have been an essential component of police intelligence systems. Westley (1970: 70) refers to the informant as 'the lifeblood of the good detective'; the observations carried out by Ericson (1981) demonstrate how without informants it would be nigh on impossible to make cases; and Brodeur and Dupont (2006: 14) suggest that the 'handling of informants is as much a part of criminal investigation as investigation'. The shift towards proactive intelligence-led approaches to policing in recent decades has led to an unprecedented growth in the use of informants and other surveillance techniques for offender targeting and the investigation of crime (Dunnighan and Norris 1999; Innes 2000; Maguire 2000; Maguire and John 1995).

That informants are vital for the proactive investigation of drugs and other consensual crimes is almost a truism. Skolnick (2011: 108) argues that without a network of informants 'narcotics police cannot operate'; part of the traditional oral lore of the drug units Manning (2004: 147) studied was that 'informants were the sine qua non of drug law enforcement'; and Dorn et al. (1992: 135) found informants to be 'very much the "bread and butter" of drug policing' and the 'mainstay of a number of operations'. For many types of crime, the police learn about and respond to violations of the criminal law when an aggrieved citizen reports an offence and requests legal action. This is rarely the case for drug offences because they typically take place in secret between consenting individuals and so there is no party to the act who has an interest in being the plaintiff. In terms of the provision of a police response, what this means is that unless drug offenders or their acquaintances talk to the police they are relatively unaware of the offences they are supposed to be policing. Drug detectives need to know who is dealing drugs if they are to police them, as well as where, when, and how dealers operate, information that can only 'be found deep within the interior of the drug culture itself' (Collison 1995: 133).

This chapter considers the role of informants in drug investigations and examines how drug detectives perceived and operated within the regulatory constraints of the police informer system. It should be noted that the police did not allow me to observe the routine activities of the source units, interview registered sources, or analyse the associated paperwork for 'security reasons'. They were somewhat reluctant to reveal the covert world of informer handling or divulge the secrets of the craft. Moreover, they were unwilling to jeopardize the safety of those working within the informer business. Research on source units was limited to interviews with the handlers and controllers employed therein and observations of their interactions with the drug detectives.

The Police Informer System

Before moving on to discuss the routine employment and regulation of informers in the context of drug investigations, it is necessary to first clean up what has become something of a terminological mess. Broadly speaking, an 'informant' is a person who provides information to the authorities about the private and potentially criminal activities of their fellow citizens. They come from all walks of life and provide the police with an extensive array of tit-bits for a variety of reasons. Unsurprisingly, then, it has proven difficult to construct a complete and coherent definition of what constitutes an informant (Innes 2000: 359–62).

A distinction is often made in the literature between an 'informant' as a general source of information and the 'informer' sub-group. Informers covertly provide information to the police on a regular basis in exchange for remuneration and are normally either actively involved in crime or closely associated with the criminal milieu. Yet, albeit a useful starting point, this dichotomy is too simplistic as it confuses a number of established informant roles and neglects the importance of relationships. Greer (1995) sug-gests that it is essential to analyse both the relationship between the informant and the person(s) about whom they are informing and their relationship with the policing agency concerned. Based on these variables, he develops a typology which distinguishes be-tween insiders and outsiders and between single and multiple event informants: 'the casual observer' is an outsider who observes a single event and then brings the relevant information to the atten-tion of the police; 'the snoop' is an outsider who observes multiple events; 'the one-off accomplice witness' is an insider who shifts from being a suspect to a witness and provides the police with information about a single event; and 'the informer', 'agent provo-cateur', or 'supergrass' is an insider who enters into a regular rela-tionship with the police and informs them about multiple events. It is this latter type of informant that is more commonly known as a 'grass', 'nark', 'snitch', 'snout', or other such pejorative slang. Clayman and Skinns (2012) add the 'one-off acquaintance wit-ness' to this typology in order to capture those individuals who inform the police about a single event which they observe by dint of being acquainted with the victim and/or the suspect.

The close relationship between detectives and their informers is portrayed in much of the literature as a devious and risky business that generates a profound sense of moral ambiguity. Billingsley et al. (2001: 5) describe it as a 'murky world of half-truth, decep-tion, innuendo and betrayal'. Much of the discussion has to do with the 'necessary evil' character of this policing strategy within dem-ocratic societies. In short, the use of informers is widely accepted as an indispensable aspect of crime control, but at the same time it inevitably involves 'the invasion of privacy, the exploitation of trust, danger to third parties and the risk of police corruption and a compromised judicial system' (Fijnaut and Marx 1995: 1).

Detectives have to make difficult judgments as to the status of the information they receive and become adept at managing the risks associated with protecting the identity of their informers and working with active criminals who are inherently untrustworthy. Traditionally, they have made use of informal and often unsanctioned strategies for dealing with risks arising from the practice of recruiting and 'handling' or 'running' informers. Although legal precedent and administrative codes of practice have existed for many years, Maguire and John (1995: 27) note that, in practice, the manner in which informers are handled has been left largely to the personal preferences of individual officers. The lack of training in the area meant that they either learned from more experienced colleagues or simply devised their own methods. Research has shown that, in order to have informers maintain their position in the criminal milieu, officers have no choice but to turn a blind eye to their criminality, 'license' them to commit crimes, or perhaps even have some involvement in facilitating the crimes they commit (Collison 1995; Dunnighan and Norris 1996; Ericson 1981; Hobbs 1988; Reuter 1983b). Dunnighan and Norris (1996) found that officers frequently bypassed the formal supervisory mechanisms aimed at controlling the use of informers, failed to obtain the required authorization, and were reluctant to disclose to courts the contribution made by informers in the arrest and prosecution of suspected offenders.

Furthermore, detectives are prone to regard informers and case knowledge as a personal rather than an organizational resource. The individualistic nature of their work and culture engenders what Collison (1995) refers to as a 'squirrel' instinct. They are highly secretive, have reservations about sharing information, and jealously guard the informers they have cultivated because of the opportunities for career and reputational enhancement offered by exclusive access and control (Billingsley 2004; Dunnighan and Norris 1996; Maguire and John 1995; Maguire and Norris 1992). A consequence of these practices is the problem of unrealized potential in the sense that detectives can be selective in the information they handle, which is often not reported, collated with intelligence from other sources, or acted upon.

These moral conundrums and practical problems have prompted many to call into question the efficiency and integrity of the police use of informers and advocate the need for better safeguards and scrutiny. Attempts to reform internal regulatory mechanisms occurred during the 1990s, which coincided with concerted efforts to increase the proactive employment of informers (Innes 2000; Maguire and John 1995). These changes saw the implementation of formal bureaucratic systems of registration, monitoring, and control in a number of police forces and a growing trend towards the employment of trained 'handlers' and 'controllers': handlers are responsible for the day-to-day running of informers; controllers provide general oversight and ensure that the risk assessment process is up-to-date and proper records are being kept. According to Innes (2000: 371), the principal aims of this process of 'professionalization' were to regulate the activities of informers and police officers, minimize unethical conduct and the risk of corruption, improve the overall quality of information received from informers, and use it in a more systematic manner. Yet, although some advances were made, the empirical evidence indicates variable results across forces and gives prominence to the cultural resistance that these reforms encountered. Officers still made use of unregistered informers and were reluctant to follow official guidelines and administrative procedures (Billingsley 2004; Dunnighan and Norris 1996; Maguire and John 1995).

Statutory regulation of informers is a relatively recent development. It came about primarily in response to the need to ensure that the covert operations of public authorities have a clear legal basis and are compliant with human rights law. Left with little choice but to find a formal legal instrument to underpin the use of informers and other covert investigative techniques, the Regulation of Investigatory Powers Act 2000 (RIPA) was drafted and hastened through parliament just in time to beat the coming into force of the Human Rights Act 1998. To a lesser extent, the new regime also reflects a growing concern within government and the police service about the ethics of covert policing.

With the passing of the Act, the term informer was replaced with 'covert human intelligence sources' (CHIS). A 'CHIS' includes informers and undercover police officers and is defined as a person who establishes or maintains a relationship for the purpose of obtaining and then disclosing information to the authorities. As a consequence of RIPA, there now exists a prescribed framework and associated codes of practice that set out the conditions under which covert and deceptive methods are justifiable, the kinds of limits that should be imposed, and the most effective ways of preventing their abuse. Informers can only be deployed as a method of investigation for a legitimate purpose that is both necessary and proportionate in a democratic society. According to Harfield (2009: 46), this precludes speculative 'fishing trips' because such deployment is not pursuant to proper tasking and coordination and so there is no foundation on which to base assessments of necessity and proportionality. The use of a source must be the subject of prior authorization by a senior officer, and specified individuals have statutory obligations in respect of source management. With regard to detective work at the operational level of policing, perhaps the most significant change brought in by the new regime is that sources are now dealt with exclusively by handlers and controllers employed in 'dedicated sources units'. Such units are 'deliberately intended to divorce informers from front-line investigators who traditionally have managed their own informers' (Harfield 2009: 50). In addition to these internal regulatory mechanisms, the whole process is also subject to the external controls of the Office of Surveillance Commissioners, HMIC, and the Audit Commission.

The effectiveness of these developments is as yet empirically unknown. Anecdotal evidence suggests that most practitioners agree that the system is much more accountable and corrupt practices have diminished as a result (Billingsley 2009). However, strict adherence to the rules is likely to stifle techniques that have long been considered part and parcel of detective work and drug law enforcement in particular. If history has taught us anything, it is that such dramatic changes to the old regime are likely to encounter cultural resistance and implementation challenges.

The Role of Informers in Drug Investigations

The perceived and actual centrality of informers to drug investigations—especially those who were actively involved in or on the periphery of the drug world—was affirmed time and again during fieldwork, as these two interview excerpts illustrate:

I'd guess that around ninety per cent of drug investigations are started because of information coming from a source. That's how it worked when I was working as a controller two years ago, and that's how it worked when I was in the drug squad twenty years ago... Drug law enforcement is an uphill struggle at the best of times, but without sources we wouldn't stand a chance. (Detective Sergeant, Metropolis)

All of our best jobs are triggered by intelligence coming from a CHIS. (Detective, Smallville)

What these detectives are referring to is the part played by informers in initiating drug investigations by providing the police with a 'tip-off' or detailed 'insider information' that they could not otherwise obtain. The drug trade is predominantly a closed and consensual market, subterranean, hidden from view, and inaccessible to outsiders. Apart from being witness to open markets at the retail level, or drug offences committed by members of their social networks, it was believed that law-abiding citizens are rarely privy to the detailed information about the activities of criminals that can make or break a 'good pinch' or a 'big case' (Skolnick 2011). Every detective who had had experience of proactive investigation shared similar sentiments on the matter. As these two experienced officers explain:

The police have access to so many different sources of information, it's hard to say which one is the most useful... For drug investigations, I'd say the most useful source is what I like to call the "insider informer"... "A good detective is only as good as his information", you know that saying? Well, when you're working drugs, good information and good informers are one and the same. (Senior Officer, Metropolis)

A source can get us the kind of information that no one else can get. It's not very hard for us to find out who's dealing on the streets; the difficult thing is to find out the "who, what, why, where, and when" that makes for a successful operation. (Detective Sergeant, Smallville)

Observations revealed that the information coming from informers was diverse and variable in its specificity and usefulness. It ranged from rumours and information that was suspected to be false to that which needed only a little development to become actionable intelligence.[1] Informers gave the police an insight into the local drug scene, the products, prices, and purities, provided them

---

[1] Hobbs (2013) argues that rumour and gossip plays an instrumental role in illegal markets by assisting individuals in gaining a sense of order and structure from an environment that is chaotic, disordered, and largely unpredictable. For example, 'stories of threats, beating, and rather more vague allusions to killings are relayed across generations as traditional forms of order maintenance, and these folktales survive as long as they engender significant cultural values, central of which is the acceptance of violent authority as an everyday reality' (p180).

with knowledge about the 'key players', their backgrounds, 'street names', risk management strategies, last known whereabouts, and routine activities. In many instances, the information acted upon was what the police called 'single source, single strand', which was essentially uncorroborated information provided by an informer to their handler about who was dealing, what they dealt, and how they carried out their dealings. Take the following fieldnote, for example, which recounts a story about an unexpected result for the reactive CID detectives of Metropolis:

Upon arrival at the police station the detectives were hurriedly preparing for the drug warrant I had arranged to observe—sifting through paper-work, discussed the plan of action, and donning their protective attire. The inspector in charge talked me through the job and then walked me through the office, introducing me to his 'troops' as we passed them by on our way to the briefing room. Intelligence had been received suggest-ing that the owner of a Moroccan café was selling hash under the counter and so a warrant had been obtained to enter the premises to search for evidence of the suspected offence. After the briefing, a detective I knew beckoned me over to join her group. They were talking about an 'unex-pected result' from the month before. A member of the source unit had brought them the phone number of a suspected drug dealer and assured them he was selling heroin and crack in the town centre. Dealers were usually quite wary, they said, and would hang up if they did not know the caller, but according to the source this dealer wasn't very risk averse. 'Just call and arrange a meet.' The only precautions he was known to employ were the code words 'brown' and 'white'. So, the detective with the most felicitous accent made the call, said something like 'a friend told me you might be able to sort me out'. Silence. 'Can you sort me out with some brown?' The man on the other end of the phone said nothing besides a time and place. The officers quickly got a team together and set out to the specified location. Buy-bust. Easy. 'But this bloke had a bullet proof vest on, something just didn't sit right.' A couple of the officers took him into custody as the others went to search his home address. They found over a kilo of crack, a bundle of cash and an automatic weapon. When the forensics came back it turned out to be the firearm that had been used in a recent gang-related shooting. And so an easy buy-bust resulted in the solving of an attempted murder. 'Sometimes you get lucky like that.' (Fieldnotes, Metropolis)

Occasionally the detectives were gifted reliable and precise in-telligence, suggesting that someone was dealing and storing his drugs in the ventilation system of a factory where he worked, for instance, or that someone was stashing his product in a broken jukebox in his ex-girlfriend's spare room, or in the guttering of his mother's house. Information about future intentions was also highly prized, such as when and where exchanges were set to take place. If it checked out, the word of an informer could be all that was needed to set the target for drug law enforcement and identify opportunities for evidence-gathering. In the following case, not only would the detectives of Smallville have been completely unaware of the drug offence that had taken place, but without the informer's timely clarification they would have also failed to find the drugs.

We've been told it's a sure thing, at least a couple of kilos.' I quickly read over the paperwork and spoke with the detectives about the job. From what I could piece together, two days ago a source had informed his handler about a deal that had taken place the night before. The suspect had gotten himself into a bit of debt, and to pay it off he'd decided to buy four or five kilos of amphetamine from a known wholesaler to sell on to some local retailers. Shortly before heading out, the source handler came into the office. 'Are we still on?' asked DS Daniels. 'I've just had the source on the phone, he says your man's in the house and the drugs are being stored in the garage.

Their earlier optimism soon faded when nothing was found in the garage. And when nothing was found in the house either the detectives became outwardly disappointed and disgruntled. The suspect was adamant that he was innocent, nothing but 'legit', and kept claiming that some local dealers were obviously 'feeding [the police] shit' because of an unsettled gambling debt. Outside, DS Daniels was on the phone to the source unit. 'Get in touch with the source, find out what's going on and ring me back.' He hung up. Ten uncomfortable minutes passed. He went outside to take a call. Moments later he came back in, looking somewhat relieved. 'Is that your car parked up down the street?' he asked the suspect. 'Is that your garage it's parked in front of?' The source had told his handler that the suspect's daughter lived down the street and that the suspect regularly used her garage for storing and fixing cars. The detectives didn't have a warrant to search the daughter's property, but the suspect didn't know that and so, after a bit of 'why'd you wanna look in there' toing and froing, he begrudgingly handed over the keys. It didn't take them long to find the drugs. (Fieldnotes, Smallville)

Whilst the drug detectives put the insider informer on a pedestal, those officers with little or no experience of proactive investigation tended to view sources of good information in quite a different light. The following quotations certainly underscore the centrality of informants to policing, the competing perceptions of 'intelligence' in the context of proactive policing, and the conflict of interests between the CID and the uniform branch. They also highlight the sense of self-worth that officers often express and their tendency to portray their particular role and style as the quintessence of policing.

Detectives think their way is the only way, all that spying and gadgetry. If you ask me it's bullshit, a complete waste of time and money...I've been with the police for over ten years now and I know for a fact that the best information comes from the community. If you have a good relationship with the people, you can find out almost anything you need to know. (Police Constable, Smallville)

In many respects, however, the views of this police officer are not so very different to those of the drug detectives. Informers are part of the community and the only real difference is that the detectives are more particular about whom they build relationships with.

You know how it is round here. It'd be an understatement to say the locals aren't the biggest fans of the police. You've seen how some of them stare at us. It's like they think we're the cause of all their problems...But let me tell you, things are much better than they were when I first started. Since the guvnor's been pushing forward neighbourhood policing and all that, community relations have improved no end. When I'm out on the beat people talk to me, sometimes just to chat, sometimes to tell me about something they think I might want to know...The people have all the information, what we need to do is find ways to tap into it, get them to trust us and work with us...I'd trust a member of the public over a grass any day of the week. (Police Constable, Metropolis)

The 'casual observers' and 'snoops' (Greer 1995) of the community certainly saw and heard many things, so much so in fact that the bulk of the drug-related information received by the intelligence units of Metropolis and Smallville was from members of the public and anonymous informants through Crimestoppers. Such information can lead to valuable information and successful operational results.[2] Be that as it may, in and of itself such information was routinely disregarded or devalued by the drug detectives.

---

[2] Fielding (1995), for example, cites evidence that more detailed, actionable information was received from informants garnered by community constables than the conventional tip-off from an informer. In 2013/14, Crimestoppers received 10,103 pieces of useful information about crime from the public, 6,242 criminals were arrested and charged, and £18.5 million worth of illegal drugs were seized (Crimestoppers 2014; see also Griffiths and Murphy 2001).

This was largely because they considered it to be irrelevant to their work. Furthermore, since citizens did not view the world through a police lens, it was thought that they were unable to see 'the bigger picture' or 'read' the signs of criminal behaviour. Both Collison (1995) and Manning (2004) also found that citizen tips tended not to be accepted without question and were shaped by investigators to suit their purposes. As Herc explained as we made our way to see the sergeant of neighbourhood team in south Smallville:

When you get say two or three people complaining about drug dealing chances are they're right, there's probably dealing going on – but it's going on everywhere. From my experience it's hardly ever about anyone we'd be interested in.

A few local residents had called the police about the 'druggies' on their street, a PCSO had been for a walk past the house in question and confirmed that 'something did look a bit dodgy', and so the team were set to execute a drug warrant the next day.[3] The sergeant had notified the drug squad and requested some advice about gathering evidence at the crime scene. 'Looks like you'll get a result, let us know how it goes.' We continued talking on the way back to the station:

A couple of teenagers with no previous convictions: looks like it's just low-level cannabis dealing to me. If it'd been Class As or someone we knew I'd have gone along, but when we've got a surveillance job on we don't have the time to be doing warrants like that; we let the SNTs take care of them.

In the main, the attitude towards informants was much the same in both police forces, although what certain sections of the community had to say carried more weight with the detectives of Metropolis.

We don't have nearly enough registered sources from our ethnic minority communities; it's always been a problem in this borough. If we want to know what's going on we need to engage with the community. (Senior Officer, Metropolis)

---

[3] When members of the public made a drug-related complaint to the police they rarely received an immediate response. Such complaints were simply not priorities. If the police decided to respond, a patrol car was sometimes deployed during a 'quiet period', but more often than not a neighbourhood police officer or PCSO made a visit as and when they were able.

Like this senior officer, the Metropolis detectives recognized the importance of information coming from the community—in the absence of the coveted insider informer this was perhaps more out of necessity than choice. An accepted practice was to proactively identify and approach members of the community who might be willing to act as informants, particularly those who were geographically or socially well situated for policing purposes. This was done in the hope of enhancing the community intelligence 'feed'. The work of Fielding (1995) shows that one of the instrumental motivations for the implementation of community policing strategies was to try to obtain better access to information held by the public about crime.

Whenever [the police] get the chance we try to speak with the "pillars of the community", the people who seem to know everything about everyone in their neighbourhood and hold some sway...The local businessmen, the religious leaders, the people involved in the local clubs, groups, and organizations—even some of the gang members. (Detective, Metropolis)
   People who live or work in areas where there's a lot of dealing going on can provide us with valuable information, if we can get them to talk. (Detective, Metropolis)

The detectives presumed that reputable members of society wanted to rid their community of drugs and drug-related problems. Even so, I was told several stories to illustrate that this was not always the case; stories about how the police had been unwittingly played by outwardly public-spirited informants. 'You end up losing faith, when you find out people you trusted and respected are criminals just like the rest of them.' The man this detective was referring to was an 'elder' who had come over from Jamaica when he was young. He was a businessman, a family man, and a churchgoing man. He was an active member of the community, well connected, and influential. For years he had been informing the police about the local gangs. 'Turned out he was bankrolling some of the dealers and taxing others for protection.' In this case it was for personal gain; in others, the storytellers blamed it on dealers coercing 'innocents' into misinforming the police, feelings of hostility towards them, or deliberate attempts to make them 'look stupid' by acting on false information.

   Getting citizens to talk was the hard part. Despite their efforts, the detectives had only managed to identify, cultivate, and maintain a small number of 'confidential contacts' in their police service areas—people who regularly acted as a source of information for the police. When asked why people might not want to talk, the detectives said that there was a general lack of trust and cooperation between the public and the police; that potential informants or witnesses were probably frightened of retribution; and that some communities had a strong culture of 'self-help' and preferred to sort out their disputes themselves. These findings are supported by the work of Clayman and Skinns (2012) on why young people do not 'snitch' and Westmarland (2013) on US homicide detectives. Drawing on in-depth qualitative interviews and two focus groups with teachers, police officers, and youth workers in one London borough, Clayman and Skinns (2012) argue that the decision to cooperate may be affected by young people's relationship with the police and whether or not the police are regarded as legitimate. Furthermore, they argue that young people learn not to cooperate with the police within the context of peer groups. Abiding by a 'code of silence' was accepted practice within certain groups or subcultures with negative repercussions if the code were violated.

'Licensing Criminals'

In both Metropolis and Smallville, the officers who worked with informers, or had done so in the past, seemed to labour the point that police informers come from 'every walk of life'. They wanted me to know that 'ordinary decent citizens' provide information to the police on a voluntary basis just as much as offenders who are coerced into doing so through interrogation or the threat of legal sanction. Nevertheless, when I spoke with investigators and analysed the nature of the 'B24' grade information in intelligence reports and action packages it was often self-evident that the source was close to both the crime and the person(s) about whom they were informing.[4] Detectives openly admitted that:

Most of our [drug-related] sources are users; they act as our eyes and ears on the streets...It might seem strange to you, that we get people

---

[4] Dunnighan (1992) provides one of the few insights into the type of people who become informers. In a survey of detectives and their informers in one police service area, he found the typical informer to be male, under the age of thirty, unemployed, and with previous convictions (also incidentally the typical criminal). He also noted that around thirty per cent of all informers were known drug users. A more detailed study by Billingsley (2001a) largely confirms these findings.

who break the law to tell us about other people who break the law so that we can enforce the law, but that's the way it is. (Source Controller, Metropolis)

The local punters are our best friends. They always know who's dealing because they need to. They'll never give you their regular supplier, but you can usually get something out of them, especially if you catch them in possession. (Detective, Smallville)

For the police, the main sources of 'actionable' or 'quality' information on local drug markets were the drug users who sustained them. The amount of faith officers seemed to have in the word of people whom they otherwise perceived as unreliable and unscrupulous criminals was undeniably contradictory. '[Addicts] are the kind of people who'll steal from their own mothers and turn on their friends,' said a detective as we covertly monitored drug transactions taking place during a surveillance operation. The operation had been triggered by a tip-off from a heroin user who had been caught in possession the previous week and informally cautioned in exchange for their 'cooperation'. When I alluded to the apparent inconsistency in his views, the detective said: 'It's not that we trust them. They're scared of us; they don't mess us around because they know we could put them away if we wanted to.' To put it another way, it was an accepted practice for the police to exploit both their unequal bargaining power and the vulnerabilities of 'police property' for information and results in operational policing. Police officers might disregard the drug use of an actual or potential informer but would not hesitate to employ any knowledge of a user's offences to a police advantage. The relationship between the police and informers is thus riddled with what contractual lawyers refer to as 'undue influence', because the threat of legal sanction substantially undermines their autonomy of decision-making (Lucy 1989; Madoff 1997; Smith 1997).

Quite disconcertingly, only a minority of officers acknowledged that their dependence on dependent drug users to police drugs was somewhat hypocritical and counterproductive in terms of harm reduction. 'It's bad isn't it,' Joe opined, 'that we need them to keep using. If they're clean they're no use to us anymore.' He went on to tell me about a source who had died from an overdose after injecting the product being distributed by a dealing network under police surveillance:

My first thought was "there goes another good informer". That's the kind of mentality you have when you're working a case. It's sort of like tunnel vision. I know there are a lot of "ifs" and "buts", but when I think about it now I can't help think there's a good chance he'd still be alive if he'd not been working with the police. We tasked him to gather information and keep making buys.

Drug detectives acknowledged that their dependence on informers from inside heroin and crack markets restricted the intelligence picture and in turn the scope of their drug control efforts. There was, for example, a significant lack of sources from within recreational drug markets. The detectives had a range of explanations for why this was the case. They said recreational drugs like cannabis, ecstasy and ketamine were not police priorities and so the NIM business process was not geared up to deal with them. Not being priorities meant that source units were not proactively attempting to recruit such informers or tasking registered informers to gather information about this aspect of the drug world. They said that most people who supply and use recreational drugs commit no criminality other than their dealings with prohibited substances and so rarely came into contact with the police. This makes it harder for them to recruit informers. It is people who have entered the police domain as suspects, particularly those held in police custody, who provide officers with the pool of potential recruits. Arrested recreational users would often provide information on a one-off basis under interrogation, but seldom agreed to enter into a regular relationship with the police. Finally, they said the recreational drug scene is characterized by social supply networks, friendship groups, and social bonding—something enhanced by the drug using experience itself—which makes it less likely for members to inform the police and more difficult for test-purchase or undercover officers to infiltrate the markets.

The risk management strategies deployed by dealers, and their attempts to maintain a structural form that allows them to divide labour and disseminate information on a need-to-know basis, meant that drug users were flawed informers because of their level of access to the drug supply chain.

The main problem with users is they can only get you in at the bottom. They might be able to help you identify who the street dealers are, but they've no idea who they're getting it off... The ones that do a bit of grafting for the dealers can usually tell you a bit more—maybe who their associates are, when they drop off to their runners, that kind of stuff—but they'll never land you the bigger dealers. (Source Controller, Smallville)

To get at the 'bigger dealers', those who operate above the street markets through closed distribution networks, some degree of organizational penetration *is* necessary. The detectives believed that the best way to achieve this was to persuade someone close to them to talk. 'You'd be surprised how well some dealers conceal their business from their nearest and dearest. When they find out what's been going on it doesn't take much effort on our part to get them to spill the beans.' This could be their legitimate business partner, for example, a family member, friend, neighbour, or social acquaintance. Handlers often tasked informers to get close or closer, by frequenting the bars and clubs frequented by dealers and observing their activities, eavesdropping, or striking up a leading conversation. 'One of the tricks of the trade is to know who's fucking who,' a source handler said during interview. 'There's nothing more dangerous to a dealer than a woman scorned.' Yet, from the range of potential sources, the most useful information generally came from people who were actively involved in the drug trade.

Most officers took a pragmatic approach, which recognized the irony of allowing criminals to benefit from police deals and the betrayal of family, friends, and associates.

As much as it pains me to say it, we wouldn't know half as much as we do about what's going on out there if we didn't talk to the criminals. It doesn't take an academic to see the irony in that, now does it? (Senior Officer, Metropolis)

Such 'necessary evil' sentiments were shared by almost every detective who had experience of proactive investigation. There were, however, a number of vocal critics, and some members of the uniform branch were very much averse to the practice of 'working with the enemy'. This is an example of the tensions and conflicts within police organizations that are documented by Norris and Dunnighan (2000) in their essay on the unintended consequences of the police use of informers.

I just don't like the idea of us going easy on the scum we're supposed to be putting away, it makes a mockery of what we stand for. (Police Constable, Smallville)

In light of the dubious characteristics of their sources, the source units assured me that risk assessments and the management of informer motivations and behaviours was of paramount importance. During interviews, they explained that there are a wide range of reasons for informing. Some informers were motivated by a sense of public duty, the financial reward, or the thrill of having a covert relationship with the police. 'Insiders' did it for leniency and future good will, in the hope that they might not be charged with an offence, for example, or, if facing trial, that they might receive a sentence discount. Revenge was another motivation, as was fear and the need for police protection, the desire to learn about police activity, criminal career advancement and taking out the competition.[5] Source handlers and controllers were alert to the deceptive techniques used by informers. They recognized the risk of them 'taking liberties', or 'playing' the police for personal gain, but argued that the rigorous regulations now in place helped counteract such behaviours. Moreover, the detectives felt that they were smarter than their informers and not easily duped. 'They haven't got the nounce to pull the wool over our eyes.' Risk assessments aside, I was regularly told that even treacherous or underhand motives would not always prevent police action if the information provided was 'current, accurate, and ongoing'.

I mean yeah, you've gotta think about why they're telling you what they're telling you. But if they're telling you the truth what does it matter? Like, if they tell you Joe Blogs is dealing just to get him out of the picture that doesn't change the fact that he's dealing, does it? What, just because they have an ulterior motive we should just leave it? I don't think so. If they keep it up it'll be their turn next anyways. In the end someone'll grass on them too. (Detective, Metropolis)

In effect, then, the police informer system informally permitted lawbreakers to continue engaging in certain forms of criminality without significant interference in exchange for the provision of information. With this in mind, like Reuter (1983b), I would argue that most 'insider informers' are actually nothing more than 'licensed criminals'. There is limited evidence of such licences in the research literature and the police tend to deny their existence outright. On several occasions Hobbs (1988: 203) observed detectives 'turn a blind eye' to criminal activity 'in anticipation of receiving information of a higher status at some future date'. The detectives Collison (1995: 42) worked with entered into '[u]nwritten and unenforceable contracts' with drug users and petty dealers which

---

[5] For further discussion on informer motivations see Billingsley (2001b), Collison (1995), and Dunnighan and Norris (1996).

promised 'some benefit to both sides of the deal'. Dunnighan and Norris (1996: 13) found that informers were allowed to remain at large even though they were wanted on warrant, keep some of the proceeds of their criminal activities, and keep test purchases which had been paid for by money provided by the officer. The officers who participated in their study actively encouraged informers to participate in crime so that the information provided was more accurate and timely. Bean and Billingsley (2001) came across dealers who claimed to have a 'licence to deal'. These so-called 'licences' were said to be given to dealers who, in return for information, enjoyed a favoured relationship with the police. It was believed that certain clubs were never raided, or that certain houses were allowed to sell with impunity. The police denied they issued licenses but the term was used so often as to lead the authors to suspect that something of this nature was occurring.

The police are not officially permitted to incite or allow informers to commit crimes, or act as *agents provocateurs*. It is vitally important for them to ensure, as far as possible, that informers do not create an offence that would not have otherwise been committed. When I broached the subject of licensing criminals, I was told that no registered sources are given a licence to commit crime and that they are informed from the outset that they have no immunity from prosecution. Criminally active informers were only authorized to be on what was referred to by one controller as the 'fringes of criminality':

I know it's a murky way of putting it, but you're asking me about a very murky area that we don't like to talk about...I wouldn't call it a "licence" if I were you; it makes it sound like we meet with criminals, draw up contracts, and get them to sign on the dotted line. It's more like an understanding; the sources know there's a line they can't cross. (Source Controller, Metropolis)

Participation in criminality may be at different points on the spectrum of 'activeness'. From what I could fathom, registered sources that were known to use drugs were expected to commit the victimless crimes that were an aspect of their normal behaviour and corollaries of the information they provided. In other words, when users provide information about dealers they do not cross the line if they continued to buy, possess, and use drugs. The responses I got when asking about informers who were suspected of being involved in the illegal drug business were much more cryptic and nebulous. Their role, it seems, must only be of a relatively minor nature in comparison to the offence being investigated. For example, being present at a transaction was said to be on the right side of the line if the informer played an entirely passive role and was not directly involved, though research participants were reluctant to clarify what exactly constituted 'direct involvement'. Still, a small number of officers alluded to the practice of 'turning a blind eye'. According to one source handler, 'if they stay under the radar we can continue to ignore what we think we know.' From this admission it might be inferred that some handlers are willing to leave informers to their own devices until they trigger a police response by being arrested or implicated in an intelligence report. As Skolnick (2011: 112) points out, however, to 'assert that police ignore the infractions of persons who have acted as informers in order to maintain their "good will" is to overlook that informers have no specific affection for police and are themselves often coercively persuaded to play their roles by threat of legal sanction'. The reality is often one of limited choice, a lack of real options, and a weak bargaining position on the part of the informer.

Condoning certain crimes in this way might be considered ethically reprehensible and undemocratic, not to mention that it raises obvious questions about police legitimacy. If, however, the information gained is worth more than the costs of the collateral criminality is it not for the greater good? This remains a moot point and there are equally convincing arguments on both sides of the debate. Bean and Billingsley (2001: 28) propose that gains obtained through informers 'must be offset by the offences committed by them'. For them, the advantages of criminal licensing are outweighed by the consequential increases in drug use and drug-related criminality. Yet, whilst there is a simple logic behind this argument, it inevitably falls short because it is near enough impossible to quantify the value of information, and the crimes committed by informers will always be a 'dark figure'. At best such calculations can only be made speculatively on a case-by-case basis. Conversely, Reuter (1983b: 11) is of the opinion that 'we place demands on the police which can only be satisfied if the police enter into long-term cooperative relationships with a number of criminals'. Certain classes of criminal, he suggests, can only be policed with the assistance of informers who participate in crime, and so either 'we must accept the tensions created by the ill-monitored licensing or we must lower our demands upon the police' (p3). This, again, is an uneasy balancing act, but at least it holds true to the realities of police work.

The Everyday Regulation of Informers and Some Unintended Consequences

Unlike previous systems of regulation, RIPA has imposed a statutory obligation upon the police in relation to the use and management of informers. By the time I entered the field, the framework as set out in the statute and associated codes of practice had been incorporated into police organizational structures and procedures. 'It wasn't easy,' I was told, implementing, functionalizing, and maintaining compliance with a prescribed regulatory system that markedly departs from time-honoured detective practice and goes against the grain of their occupational culture. However, there was something of an acceptance that 'the law is the law'.

Have you actually sat down and read RIPA? The logic behind it makes a bit of sense, but what a load of gobbledegook! It's always the same, [the government] passes laws and hands out guidelines telling us what to do and then it's down to us to make it work. (Source Handler, Smallville)

The changes brought about by RIPA were said to have had a dramatic impact on the criminal investigation process and how detectives perceived and carried out their work. For the most part, this was because informers had been removed from frontline officers and were now dealt with exclusively by the specially trained handlers and controllers working in dedicated source units. All of the handlers and controllers were trained detectives. In Metropolis, the source unit had actually been in place since late-1994, when the organization first attempted to reform its internal regulatory mechanisms and increase the proactive employment of informers, whereas in Smallville it had been established as a response to RIPA. From the point of view of the drug detectives, the fact that they were no longer able to directly handle their own informers had detrimentally affected their ability to effectively police drugs and had stifled the enlightening and at times questionable techniques that have long been considered part and parcel of drug law enforcement. They were no longer 'out and about' trawling the streets for intelligence, mingling with shady characters, bargaining for a tip-off, or racking up sizable phone bills talking to their drug world connections.

Aside from the glorified stories of how things used to be, the post-RIPA detectives had known nothing else. It was common for them to view the current system as being much more accountable and less open to corruption, although they could see the appeal of the old ways and means and the disadvantages of strict adherence to formal rules and authorization procedures for operational policing. 'You need a bit of leeway to do this job,' said one early career detective. 'There's more to it than just following orders.' Those who had worked in the pre-RIPA era invariably expressed feelings of conflict, as they longed for the wheeling and dealing of the past whilst at the same time recognizing the problems that came with it and accepting the need for a more 'professional' approach to using and managing informers.

Being a detective was much better back then. For me, having your own snitches was one of the main attractions of the job. I knew a lot more about what was going on that's for sure. I knew where to find out what I needed to know and how to get it... It's lost a lot of its appeal... I'm not saying things didn't need to change; all I'm saying is, Did they need to change so much? (Detective, Smallville)

One thing I still can't understand is why we couldn't have kept our own sources; it makes no sense to only have handlers in the source unit. (Detective Sergeant, Metropolis)

Being able to identify, cultivate, and handle informers has traditionally been considered a requisite quality of an effective detective. As Norris and Dunnighan (2000: 392) note, the 'ability to run informers is seen by many senior officers as an important, if not essential criterion for selection to the CID and to ensure a permanent posting'. During a lengthy discussion with members of the Metropolis CID, the inspector in charge told me that before the source units were established the only way for a detective to make the drug squad was to have a good network of informers. In his opinion, drug law enforcement is a 'contact sport' and informers are a 'form of currency'. He turned to the officers in the room and said in a jocular manner: 'Detectives don't know how to recruit informers anymore; the older ones are out of practice and the younger ones have never learned'. 'What're you trying to say guv?' replied a cocky young detective. 'We ain't got the minerals?' The group let out a chuckle. 'I encourage the detectives under my watch to recruit whenever possible, but we're still not getting half as many as we did before RIPA came into play. Most of them have the mentality that sources are now the sole responsibility of the source unit.'

As can happen with occupational specialization and the division of labour, officers tended to view the police as a highly segmented organization. They had a narrow focus on their specific role and seemed not to have the motivation to work above and beyond their demarcated tasks. 'We're happy to do some of the legwork, but we've got our own job to be getting on with.' The source unit were proactively searching for potential sources, by monitoring custody records, for example, identifying and approaching people who might know something of value and be willing to talk. The drug detectives, on the other hand, were no longer actively seeking to recruit informers as a matter of course. When officers came into contact with a potential source, procedure dictated that they refer them to the source unit, or do the preliminary groundwork and then pass them on. Instead, the accepted practice was for the detectives to extract as much information as possible on a one-off basis before notifying the source unit. Suspected drug offenders and their associates were routinely subjected to a barrage of questions about their business practices and criminal networks whilst under police control. This informal questioning generally took place at the scene of forced entry warrants, at the point of arrest, in police vehicles as suspects were being transported back to the station, 'off the record' at the booking-in desk and in the cells. And then again during the formal interrogation process itself. 'You've got to get all you can out of them before they slip through the net.' Evidence of unofficial interviewing practices has been found by a number of other policing scholars (Choongh 1997; McConville et al. 1991). Unless the source unit had flagged persons of interest on local computer systems, the notification procedure would only be followed if the detectives believed that the potential source was likely to provide them with case-worthy information for future operations.

Although I struggled, and failed, to get hold of the precise annual figures, there was little doubt within the police organizations under study that the number of informers had fallen post-RIPA. Even if this assumption was factually inaccurate, the widespread belief that the police intelligence capacity had been depleted as a consequence of RIPA is significant as it indicates a lack of faith in the system and raises the risk of noncompliance. In Metropolis, I was told by a detective who had acted as a source controller during the late-1990s that there were around sixty registered sources when he left his position. During fieldwork, the current controller said there were forty. However, this figure was challenged by one of the handlers, who confided that it was more like twenty-five and that the controller was exaggerating in an attempt to present the unit in a more favourable light. In Smallville, a detective who had been working drugs for over ten years said that prior to RIPA there were at least twenty drug-related informers on the books. He thought there were probably only six on the day that I spoke with him. The source unit said they had twelve registered sources in total. Of course this drop in numbers was due to numerous factors, not only to the lack of recruitment on the part of the detectives. The other reasons mentioned were that potential sources were often unwilling to formalize their relationship with the police; that they were willing to talk to individual officers, but not act as an organizational resource; that the mandatory risk assessments made the registration process far more restrictive; and that registered sources were subject to legal sanctions much more frequently when they 'overstepped the line' in terms of their criminal activities.

Under RIPA, only registered sources are supposed to be 'tasked' by the police, and the necessary authorization must be properly obtained beforehand. Tasking refers to the strategic deployment of informers to obtain specific information or provide access to information that is in line with organizational intelligence priorities. The 'task' can be in general terms so specific activities need not be identified on the record. Amongst other things, the use of authorized assignments is designed to restrict the autonomy of both the handler and the informer by preventing them from manipulating the system for their own agendas. Although a few officers categorically denied the existence of unregistered sources, most admitted that 'off the books' informers or 'confidential contacts' still played a central part in detective work and the accumulation of knowledge about drug markets. These contacts included drug users, staff from drug treatment services, and people who worked in the licensed premises of the night-time economy. Many of the source unit officers were of the opinion that detectives remained overly parochial and were therefore reluctant to let go of their most valuable sources. The detectives, however, accounted for their use of unregistered sources by saying that some informers 'didn't sit well' with the bureaucratic procedures and that the provision of information was dependent on the close personal relationship they had nurtured. Yet, whilst it was generally accepted in both police forces that some officers were still in contact with unregistered sources, it was persistently affirmed that such sources were not formally tasked. 'I'm sure it still happens,' said one detective, 'but I can't think of when I last came across it.' Be that as it may, there was a degree of ambiguity surrounding what exactly constituted tasking, especially in the grey area between setting assignments and asking questions in the hope of receiving a subsequent response.

When you're talking with informants they sometimes volunteer information. Like, the other week, I ran into one of the local sex workers and she told me about this quality gear that was doing the rounds. It's only natural to ask questions isn't it? So I asked her where it was coming from. She said she didn't know. But then the next time she came back with a name. That doesn't mean I tasked her. She took it on herself. (Detective, Metropolis)

Aside from the official police standpoint and anecdotal evidence, the only data I have to speak of on this matter relates to an occasion when I witnessed a confidential contact being mildly tasked.

This afternoon, Bunk and I were driving through Smallville when he received a phone call. After a couple of minutes of catch-up talk the topic of conversation turned to police business. From what I could make out, the caller was informing Bunk about a pair of 'known dealers' who had moved into a house across the street from where he lived. My ears pricked up. 'We're on a job this week, can you keep an eye out and I'll come round and see you first thing on Monday... Note down any names, descriptions of the people, any vehicles that are coming and going, and the times you think they're dealing.' 'Looks like another promising job Matt.' It turned out the person on the other end of the phone was a retired police officer and a regular though not registered informer, who let the 'right people' know about the usual suspects and suspicious activities as and when he happened to stumble across them. 'I wouldn't have asked just anybody to do that, but we worked together and I know he can be trusted.' (Fieldnotes, Smallville)

What the detectives resented the most about the post-RIPA regime was the loss or lack of personal control over drug-related informers and in consequence the intelligence that informed their operational activities. They were possessively territorial and sensitive to unwanted incursions into their domain. Furthermore, not only had the detectives lost the ability to handle informers, but a so-called 'sterile corridor' had been put in place to safeguard the confidentiality of sources and ensure that covertly obtained information could not be shared or disseminated without prior sanitization and appropriate authorization.

The detectives had developed a number of informal practices to circumvent these regulatory controls. 'What I always say is it's a sterile *corridor*,' said one of the more wily detectives, 'and corridors are designed for us to walk through.' Owing to the closely intertwined nature of their respective roles, the drug detectives worked closely with members of the source units through daily emails, phone calls and meetings. Although a few handlers and controllers were resolutely by the book, most were willing to bend the rules—if only slightly. It very much depended on the individuals concerned and the closeness of their relationship. Identities were never explicitly revealed during observations, but little was left to the imagination about who the source might be. Details were discussed informally and 'accidental' security breaches did happen. For example, on one occasion a detective and I were parked up in a supermarket car park eating lunch when he pointed out an unmarked police vehicle at the other side of the lot. 'Now there's a coincidence.' It was possible to make out a handler talking with a man in the passenger seat who was wearing his hood in a way that obscured his face with shadow. We sat and waited until the obscure man vacated the car and started to walk towards the entrance of the supermarket. 'I knew that was our guy!' When we returned to the station, the detective informed the rest of the team about his discovery and then went to quiz the handler for more information. On the subject of tasking, the source units assured me that they operated in strict accordance with tasking and coordination processes, never failed to obtain the necessary authorization, and had the audit trail to prove it. They also said that it was a perfectly legitimate practice to elicit additional information from informers about other matters to those which had been specifically tasked. This meant that the drug detectives were able to gather intelligence vicariously through handlers by getting them to ask informers questions on their behalf.

When commenting on operational matters, the detectives consistently complained that the police informer function was much slower under RIPA. They said that mandatory risk assessments and authorization procedures caused unnecessary delays in the transmission of intelligence and that this could result in missed opportunities and wasted resources. It was thought that drug-related intelligence had a very limited shelf life and so had to be acted upon posthaste. An example of this problem was when the Smallville drug squad spent a shift carrying out surveillance on a warehouse because an informer had informed their handler that a 'drop' was set to take place there. The following day, the handler in question paid a visit to the detectives to inform them that the source had attempted to contact him the previous afternoon but he had been unable to call him back owing to other work commitments. Having just spoken with the source, it turned out that the location had been changed at the last minute. The retarding knock-on effects of RIPA were felt throughout much of the investigatory process. When applying for warrants on the basis of single source intelligence, for instance, magistrates tended to ask about the reliability of the source, but all the detectives could do was tell them the intelligence report grading. On several occasions this was considered inadequate and the source handler had to be called in. Another complaint was that requests for information from the source unit were not always dealt with in a timely fashion. In the event of slow response times, it was not unheard of for accusations of deliberate stalling to be bandied around the squad rooms. 'They like to make us wait so we know who's boss.' Such accusations may well have been baseless, but they nevertheless stoked intra-organizational tensions. Source unit officers argued that detectives failed to appreciate that they were an organizational resource and therefore unable to attend to each and every request. 'Some of [the detectives] call on us like we're their own personal service,' asserted a source handler during interview. 'It's not that we don't want to help. We're not ignoring them or anything like that, but we've got our own priorities and are already stretched to capacity.' There were differences between the two forces in this respect, however, inasmuch as the detectives of Metropolis were notably more understanding of the complex and competing demands of the source unit function and vice-versa. This was largely because several members of the firearms team were trained handlers or controllers and had previously worked in the source unit. None of the Smallville detectives had received such training or work experience. 'I see myself a generalist,' said one of the Metropolis sergeants, 'a "jack-of-all-trades" detective.' He explained that undertaking a wide range of assignments enhances career prospects and provides officers with a better appreciation of the various tasks performed by their organizational colleagues. 'We're all just cogs in the machine.' Such attitudes and understandings were passed on to other team members through socialization and on-the-job training sessions.

It was common for the drug detectives to hold the source unit responsible for unsuccessful operations and results that were not as good as expected. If a warrant was executed but no evidence of drugs or drug-related activity was found it was because 'the source unit aren't doing their job properly'. If a surveillance operation was going nowhere it was because there were no registered sources with access to pertinent and reliable information, or the handlers weren't tasking their sources effectively enough. 'It's easy to blame someone else, but sometimes we're literally searching for scraps of cannabis when we came in expecting bags of heroin.' Again, however, this mentality was far more pronounced in Smallville, where the detectives firmly believed that if they could still handle their own sources 'the right doors would be kicked in'. For them, drug-related sources are best handled by drug law enforcement specialists.

> The problem with the source unit is they're not dealing with drugs day in and day out like us; they don't know what's going on like we do...It's not just what your source tells you, it's how they tell it and why they're telling you. Sometimes it's what they're not telling you. Only one of our handlers has worked drugs before so he's pretty switched on. But the others don't seem to know the first thing about the local market; they don't know how to read between the lines, and this can lead to mistakes. (Detective Sergeant, Smallville)

On top of such sentiments, the uneasy relationship and rivalry between the two units certainly did not help matters. The source unit valued the level of control they had over the police informer system and repeatedly claimed to have the best local knowledge. Some of the drug detectives did not take kindly to this attitude, saying that the handlers had 'an inflated sense of self-worth' and 'like to think their role is the most important and secretive' aspect of the investigative process. Norris and Dunnighan (2000: 393) similarly observed that the 'quest for status can lead to intense competition and outright conflict'. The drug squad suspected that the source unit falsely reported that suspects were dealing Class A drugs, even when intelligence suggested otherwise, because they knew the detectives were less likely to act upon intelligence about a dealer of a different class. 'They're after the numbers and we're after the quality busts.' Handlers confirmed that they had a vested career interest in the number of detections generated by their informers. It was also suspected that the source unit doctored risk assessments so that the drug squad had to postpone or even cancel their operations to protect the identity of the source. This, they explained, was partly to do with the fact that the source controller fancied taking over from DS Daniels when he changed assignments and so was making a conscious effort to overshadow their enforcement efforts in order to advance his own career prospects.

Conclusion

The use of informers is a mainstay of criminal investigation because police organizations are dependent upon information from those who are actively involved in crime or closely associated with the criminal milieu. Despite the unprecedented level of surveillance that is now achievable through various technological methods, Hewitt (2010: 147) clearly demonstrates that 'informing by humans remains a crucial type of intelligence-gathering for modern state security agencies'. For the drug detectives of Metropolis and Smallville, informers played a central part in their everyday work by providing tip-offs and detailed 'insider information' about the local drug scene that they could not otherwise obtain. Their belief that law-abiding citizens are rarely privy to the kind of information that could make or break cases against closed market dealers meant that intelligence coming from members of the community was routinely disregarded and devalued. This might be interpreted as a clash of policing philosophies. It also confirms the earlier finding of Collison (1995: 25, 35) that drug law enforcement is perceived 'as a *closed* match between thief-takers and villains'— 'a process from which the public are largely excluded'. Instead, the main sources of 'actionable' or 'quality' information were the criminal networks of the illegal drug business and the drug users who sustained them. In the context of policing drugs, the informer system relies on the ability of the police to coerce drug offenders into providing information through interrogation or the threat of legal sanction. To work effectively, it requires them to informally license certain criminals to continue engaging in certain forms of criminality without significant interference in exchange for their cooperation.

The close relationship between detectives and their informers is portrayed in much of the existing literature as a devious and risky business that generates a profound sense of moral ambiguity. Traditionally, detectives have made use of informal and often unsanctioned strategies for dealing with risks that arise from recruiting and handling informers. The findings presenting in this chapter indicate that reform efforts have made significant advances in changing these practices by restructuring the organization of the police informer system. Informers have been divorced from detectives and are now dealt with exclusively by the specially trained handlers and controllers working in dedicated source units. Moreover, as a consequence of RIPA, there now exists a prescribed framework for covert policing and an obligation for sound business practice through tasking and coordination in order to meet the legitimacy, necessity and proportionality criteria of human rights law. The police who participated in this study agreed that the current system is much more accountable and corrupt practices have diminished as a result. However, the changes were poorly received by detectives engaged in proactive investigation on the frontline and were thought to have had a negative effect on operational efficiency.

From the point of view of the drug detectives, especially the older generation, the fact that they were no longer able to directly handle their own informers had stifled the craft of drug law enforcement and detrimentally affected their ability to effectively police drugs. The number of registered informers had fallen, detectives were no longer recruiting informers as a matter of course, and mandatory authorization procedures caused delays in the transmission of intelligence. Unsurprisingly, then, there were occasional tensions between the drug squads and the source units, when the detectives acted upon intelligence that did not yield the expected results or when intelligence was not received or delivered in a timely fashion. What the detectives resented the most about the post-RIPA regime was the loss or lack of personal control over drug-related informers and in consequence the intelligence that informed their operations. In response to the strains of the job, they had developed a number of informal practices to circumvent the constraints of their regulatory controls. An accepted practice was for detectives to extract as much information as possible from potential sources on a one-off basis before notifying the source unit. They still made use of unregistered sources, pushed the boundaries of what officially constituted tasking, and gathered intelligence vicariously through handlers by getting them to ask informers questions on their behalf. A consequence of these practices is that the problem of unrealized potential remains, in the sense that detectives were selective in the information they handled and it was not always reported, collated with intelligence from other sources, or acted upon.

8

Making Cases

Intelligence suggested that the three suspects under surveillance were picking up from a known heroin wholesaler in Grandville every other week and supplying some of the retailers who operated in and around the local marketplace. The detectives had given the reputed leader the nickname 'Hopalong' on account of his limp. Years of intravenous drug use had left him with a severe case of deep vein thrombosis. Today, the operational plan was to carry out static surveillance of the council flat where Hopalong lived with his girlfriend and mobile surveillance of their movements when they were out and about. 'He's on the move,' said a voice over the radio. The three vehicles that were parked in the vicinity leapt into action.

'We've got to keep a visual on them at all times,' said Bunk as we drove towards the town centre. 'Looks like they're coming this way.' After a few minutes the targets came into view walking towards a fast-food outlet, and went inside. When they emerged half an hour later they headed for the train station. 'There's a 12:36 train to Grandville,' came another voice over the radio. 'They might be going to meet their supplier.' We watched and waited. Dozerman leapt from a vehicle that was parked in the station car park and made his way onto the platform. When the targets got on the train he got on the train. 'Get to the next stop.' The detectives put the pedal to the metal and followed the train as it journeyed towards its final destination. Several traffic violations later we crossed the district line and arrived at the station as the train was pulling in. 'They're getting on the tram.' And so the journey continued. When they got off the tram, Dozerman got off the tram and then got back into the passenger side of the unmarked police vehicle.

'What are you up to Hopalong?' The targets entered a convenience store and came out with a bunch of flowers. Meanwhile, the detectives continued to speculate about the events that were unfolding before their eyes. 'They're going to a funeral!' The targets entered a churchyard and joined a small crowd that was congregating around a freshly dug grave. The detectives parked up outside the church and continued their observations. It reminded me of the scene from *The Sopranos* where the FBI were taking advantage of Jackie Aprile's funeral to indulge in some Godfather-style anti-mob surveillance. The targets left the churchyard. Surveillance continued. They took a tram back to the train station. They took a train back to Smallville. They walked back to their flat. Surveillance continued until the end of the shift.

(Fieldnotes, Smallville)

The craft of detective work lies in the ability of detectives to penetrate the criminal milieu and translate an opaque 'social reality' into a transparent 'legal reality' that can be neatly categorized and dealt with by prosecutors and courts. This chapter provides an account of the everyday realities of the war on drugs by examining the dynamics and dilemmas of how drug investigations are planned, authorized, and carried out after a case becomes operational. The events described are typical in that they present key features in patterns of local drug law enforcement and in processes of making cases against suspected drug dealers. Attention is given to drug warrants, covert surveillance, and test purchase operations, the tactical resolutions that were used time and again for taking care of business. It focuses on the occupational perspective and practices of detectives, how they interpreted, made sense of, and manipulated the rules of the drug game, and the ways in which they used intelligence, gathered evidence, exercised power, and defined success.

Drug detectives generally mixed working on their own or in pairs with working as a team. At the outset of each case, the line manager or a supervising officer assigned squad members various administrative duties to perform. Decisions about who should do what were based principally on experience, competence, and the current workload allocation. There was also an element of 'turn taking' and making sure that everyone 'pulls their weight'. The 'officer in case' was the primary investigating officer who 'calls the shots' and completed the bulk of the paperwork. Following the completion of an investigation, investigating officers submitted a closing report detailing the outcomes, the intelligence obtained, and the financial costs. If the suspect was charged with an offence, they were accountable for managing the case up to and beyond the conduct of the trial. Investigating officers were assigned a 'deputy' to assist them in the aforementioned tasks. The 'disclosure officer' monitored the sensitive and non-sensitive material, prepared 'schedules' and arranged for the disclosure of material that might be considered capable of undermining the prosecution or assisted the defence. Finally, the 'exhibits officer' was responsible for the recovery, handling, storage and submission of all relevant exhibits. Yet, whilst individual officers were expected to perform their designated functions in the construction of a case, from fieldwork it became clear that drug squad work was very much a team enterprise. Most tactical resolutions required a team of officers and the whole squad had a vested interest in the cases they investigated and worked together to achieve a successful prosecution. It was a collective effort, teamwork in the Goffman (1959: 88) sense of the word in that detectives 'related to one another by bonds of reciprocal dependence' and cooperated 'to maintain a given definition of the situation before their audience'.

Drug Warrants

When the detectives were in possession of intelligence suggesting that an individual was actively involved in the illegal drug business, the 'go-to' tactical resolution was to obtain a warrant to enter the premises where the suspect resided, operated from, or stored their merchandise in order to search the specified location and any persons found therein for evidence of the alleged offence. If evidence of an offence was found, the suspect would be arrested and the evidence would be seized. This tactic is more generally known as a 'raid'. Multiple warrants would be carried out simultaneously against targets who occupied or controlled a number of premises or when targeting a drug dealing network because to do otherwise could frustrate the purpose of the operation.[1]

---

[1] The warrants were ordinarily obtained under Section 23 of the Misuse of Drugs Act 1971. Section 8 of the Police and Criminal Evidence Act 1984 was used when applying for a warrant to search for evidence of any indictable offence. In general, powers of entry allow search of premises but not of people on those premises unless either the premises are those to which the public has access or the relevant people have already been arrested. The Misuse of Drugs Act, however, does permit the police to search people as long as the warrant specifies this.

We'll do a warrant if it's half decent intelligence and looks like there's a good chance of a result. When they're dealing regularly from home, it's likely there'll be a bit of evidence knocking about. (Detective, Smallville)

Even when we're planning an operation that's likely to last several months, it's good practice to get a warrant asap. We can't always predict what's going to happen when we're on a surveillance job. Sometimes we get a break and need to act right there and then. (Detective Sergeant, Metropolis)

A single piece of information from a reliable informer was some-times considered sufficient grounds for a warrant in and of itself, especially if it needed to be acted upon immediately and indicated that the target and evidence linking them to a drug offence would be present at the time of execution. In most instances, however, the detectives only considered violating privacy laws if they had at least three pieces of corroborating information. More often than not this was the word of an informer backed up with intelligence generated through police observations and citizen complaints. Even if the 'who, what and why' were believed to be true, three pieces of information from members of the public was usually deemed insufficient grounds for immediate action as it lacked the precise 'where and when' that made for a successful enforcement intervention. 'We don't like doing a forced entry warrant if there's a big risk we'll be coming out empty handed,' said one detective as he explained the value of community intelligence. 'People think if they tell us someone's dealing we can just go in and arrest them. They don't understand the process or what we need in terms of evidence.' Whilst it was widely accepted that no intelligence is foolproof, the detectives had learnt through experience that com-munity intelligence almost always required further research and development to make it actionable.[2]

---

[2] A noteworthy exception to this working rule on community intelligence occurred during National Tackling Drugs Week (8–12th June 2009), a govern-ment information and publicity initiative intended to build public confidence in the national drug strategy and provide drug control agencies with a platform on which to raise awareness of the work being done locally to respond to local drug priorities (Gilling 2012). The detectives of the Smallville drug squad used this platform to orchestrate a series of highly publicized drug raids in response to public concerns about drug market activity. They worked closely with tactical support and neighbourhood police officers to execute three warrants per day on the basis of community intelligence and they invited local media to accompany them. Much the same approach was taken in Metropolis. These interventions were deliberately manufactured to showcase police activity and send a message to the public that the force was tackling the problem.

Applications for drug warrants were made to a magistrate after being authorized by an officer of at least the rank of inspector. In both forces, the police used a standardized warrant application form. It basically required officers to specify the grounds on which the warrant was sought and explain why it was necessary and proportionate to the criminal activity under investigation. They also had to set out a risk management strategy. 'With these types of thing the trick is to be as vague as possible and give no hostages to fortune.' Most experienced detectives had an almost completed copy of an application form saved on their computers and simply changed the specifics on a case-by-case basis. The formulaic grounds and justifications were practically identical because they had been copied or paraphrased from drug policy documents and professional practice publications. 'They're a pain, but all you need to do is write down what [authorizing officers and magistrates] want to hear and you're golden.' Copies of such forms were bequeathed to new recruits during their apprenticeship period, along with helpful advice about how best to 'guarantee success' and 'cut down on the paperwork side of things'. Detectives who botched the paperwork were rebuked by their supervisors and disparaged by their peers for being unprofessional and compromising the reputation of the team. Once or twice, the Smallville drug squad only noticed that the information on the form was incorrect during the pre-warrant briefing or whilst on route to the premises to be searched. 'It's 23B not 23A you fucking numpty,' DS Daniels shouted into the radio as he called off the raid. 'Fuck up like this again and I'll have you reassigned.' Although it did not happen during fieldwork, the detectives had stories about accidentally going through the wrong door and said that such occurrences were not only embarrassing for the police but also costly as they had to resolve complaints and pay for damages.

The detectives never failed to obtain authorization for a warrant. Indeed, the application process was often described as being 'just a formality'. Magistrates tended to 'rubber stamp' requests and rarely asked probing questions or challenged what officers said under oath. All they wanted to know was that the police were confident the information was accurate and there were reasonable grounds for suspecting that there would be evidence relating to the alleged offence on the premises or in the possession of the persons to be searched. Observations revealed that detectives were on first-name terms with the magistrates who signed off on their applications and had built up a good working relationship. On the handful of occasions when magistrates were initially unconvinced, detectives usually managed to turn them around through the art of persuasion. They would personally attest to the infallibility of the intelligence upon which the application was based, make reference to their specialist experiential knowledge, and threaten to call in the authorizing officer or source handler—a threat which they were rarely forced to follow through on. In their review of the research literature, Sanders et al. (2010: 354) argue that 'this virtual police self-certification is a classic crime control provision' and that magistrates are hampered in their ability to genuinely regulate the police as they do not have access to the relevant information.

The police can enter and search premises at any time within one month of the date of the warrant but tended to act swiftly on account of the limited shelf life of intelligence and the risk of their target finding out about the planned intervention. Prior to the raid, detectives would 'do a recce' in order to ascertain the most inconspicuous way for their vehicles to approach the location and identify possible methods of entry and escape routes. 'If they see us coming they'll either flush the drugs or fly the coop.' Any information known about the address and its occupants was considered when deciding on the operational strategy. This included the building layout, whether the premises had been searched before, and whether there were any security devices in place. 'The smarter dealers invest in fortified steel doors,' explained a trained 'method of entry' officer. 'There's no way we're getting through one of them in a hurry.' Some even set up booby traps in the form of hidden spikes under fake windowsills and electrified door and window handles. The police also wanted to know who was likely to be present at the scene, whether they were linked to information about firearms or other weapons, and whether there was a risk of violence, dangerous dogs, or children in distress. Raids can be dangerous and volatile encounters so rules of thumb were to 'suspect the worst', 'be on guard', and consider how any young or vulnerable persons will be managed if all adults at the address are arrested.

If you're going to break in on a group of Yardies all high on crack with their weapons on the table, you need to know about it. Chances are they'll blow your head off thinking you're a rival gang there to rob them. (Detective, Metropolis)

This one time I went through the door and this Rottweiler comes running straight at me. Took a right bite of my wrist before we managed to get it out to the back garden. I'm lucky it didn't have rabies or something! (Detective, Smallville)

I feel for the kids when they get caught up in it. As you might expect, they get upset; they don't understand what's going on when these strange people come into their home and detain their mum and dad. You've got to be sensitive in those situations. Get the situation calmed down and make sure they're alright. There's no need to traumatize the kids... We usually speak to social services in advance so that they're prepped and ready to intervene if they have to. (Detective, Smallville)

The overwhelming majority of raids carried out during the field-work period were of houses in deprived neighbourhoods with longstanding and serious drug problems. Other premises that were entered and searched included bars, bookmakers, cafes, factories, fast-food restaurants, nightclubs and warehouses. Most took place in the early hours of the morning, when the unsuspecting target was likely to be asleep and thus unable to dispose of any contraband or incriminating items. A convoy of unmarked police cars and a tactical support van would make their way through the quiet streets and park up outside the marked address or at a predesignated spot. Officers dressed in protective gear would then quietly assume their positions and wait from the bang of the battering ram. 'POLICE! POLICE! POLICE!' Upon entry, the primary objective was to secure the property and detain all of the occupants in one room. Handcuffs would only be used on individuals who were violent or otherwise noncompliant. Once the commotion had died down, an officer would explain the situation in simple terms as the others set about gathering intelligence and searching for evidence. There was a standard procedure for executing warrants, but the way in which events unfolded on the ground was largely unpredictable. The following two fieldnotes indicate that the demeanour of the occupants and their socioeconomic status and criminal background had a significant impact on how the police treated them. Being in 'contempt of cop' was likely to be met with force whereas deference was repaid in kind (Waddington 1999a: 153-5). They also provide more examples of inaccuracies in the police intelligence picture and show how evidence could be used as leverage.

'Fuck you you fucking pigs!' roared a young man out of an upstairs window of a poorly maintained council house. He gave us the finger and persisted with his onslaught of insults and threats as the detectives made their way to the front door. 'I'll fucking kill you!' A short scuffle ensued on the stairs, after which he found himself lying face down in handcuffs and slightly the worse for wear. His mum and dad were sitting in the kitchen with a look of stunned bemusement, smoking over their cornflakes. 'Where's the heroin, Preston?' asked DS Daniels in a cool yet forceful manner. He was a member of the perpetually unemployed and had previous convictions for possession and common assault. 'What's the matter, cat got your tongue?' A reliable informer had told their handler that Preston had recently started retailing heroin for his cousin, a known wholesaler with reputed links to a regional organized crime group. 'Tell us what your cousin's up to.' The detectives kept up their aggressive questioning throughout the duration of the search but only got the odd 'fuck you' or 'don't know what you're talking about' in response. Mum and dad kept suspiciously silent. They found a '9 bar' of cannabis resin and just over £500 hidden in a box in a cupboard. 'Never seen it before.' After a quick chat out of earshot the detectives decided to offer Preston a deal: either he confessed to possession with the intent to supply or they would take him and his parents into custody. After a few minutes of protestation they had a promise of confession. (Fieldnotes, Smallville)

'Oh my god! What are you doing? What's going on?' screamed a smartly dressed black woman as the police occupied her house and told her to move back into the living room. She sat down, put her head in her hands and started to cry. She would be late for work. The detectives escorted her teenage sons from their bedroom and sat them down on the couch. They were here because intelligence suggested that Little Kevin was a runner for a local street gang and was taking his turn at holding on to a firearm for one of the more senior members. Little Kevin looked scared. It was his first time. 'What've they done officers? What've they done?' The investigating officer responded to her questions in a gentle and courteous manner. She said that she understood the disconcerting nature of the situation but that they had to search the premises because they had received information that controlled drugs and an illegal firearm were being stored here. The mother looked mortified at the idea and started to cry again. The search yielded only a pay as you go phone with some known names in the contacts list and a blunt wrap. No one was arrested and nothing was seized. 'Have a word with your boys,' said Inspector Rawls as the detectives readied to leave. 'Our information is hardly ever wrong. If you need anything or notice anything suspicious call us.' (Fieldnotes, Metropolis)

Police searches are highly disruptive intrusions into the private lives of citizens; officers have wide powers to seize almost anything that they have reasonable grounds for believing is evidence of a crime, or has been obtained as a result of a crime. 'We don't like to leave until we've completely ransacked the place.' For the detectives, the two main aims of drug warrants were to recover evidence of a drug offence and gather intelligence about drug market activity. The optimal outcome of a raid was to catch the target in possession of a substantial quantity of controlled drugs and uncover evidence of conspiracy to supply or possession with intent to supply. Recovering assets from offenders was pursued as a matter of course. Evidence included drug paraphernalia, mobile phone handsets and money suspected to have been gained through unlawful conduct. Small re-sealable plastic bags, weighing scales and cocaine and pill press machines were clear signs of drug deal-ing activity. Phonebook lists showed associations between dealers and electronic messages provided evidence of 'drug texts'. Bank statements, diaries, notebooks, phone bills, receipts, and pieces of paper documenting names and numbers were also viewed as potentially valuable evidentiary sources that might help construct the case for the prosecution. In a case against a suspected cannabis cultivator and wholesaler, a 'lynchpin' piece of evidence was a ten-ancy agreement covered in fingerprints, which provided proof of a previously denied association between the suspect and the tenant who had been arrested and charged for cultivating cannabis at the property in question.

Search times varied from a couple of hours to the best part of a shift. The amount of time spent in latex gloves was very much dependent on the size of the premises and the available resources. Sniffer dogs certainly speeded up proceedings but were few and far between. 'Our job would be a hell of a lot easier if we had a des-ignated dog handler.' Add to this the sophistication of the hiding place and whether or not the evidence was even present at all.

Sometimes the drugs are out in plain view or in their pockets. Then it's just bish, bash, bosh. When they're hidden away, they're usually in a drawer or a cupboard, or under the bed. It's commonsense really. The one's who are a bit more precautious can be quite clever in their hiding places though. I've come across secret panels in walls and compartments under floor-boards. Another good one is to bury a safe out in the back garden; they're hard to find. This one guy had hundreds of DVDs in his spare room; it was like Blockbusters or something I'm serious. I opened up near enough all of them before I found a bag in a 24 box set. (Detective, Smallville)

It's maddening when you're sure they're guilty and you have to walk away with nothing. They'll be looking at you with this smirk on their face. It's like a little victory for them. (Detective, Metropolis)

When we think they've got drugs concealed in their body orifices, we'll do an intimate search. It's not exactly a part of the job I enjoy; the last thing I want to see first thing in the morning is a shitty arse! But we've got to make sure we find the drugs. (Detective, Smallville)

A lack of evidence did not exonerate a suspect if the detectives had a hunch that they were 'dirty' and the intelligence case against them was still strong. 'You can tell when someone's guilty,' claimed a seasoned detective. 'They've got it written all over their face.' Failure simply added fuel to the fire and the investigation would continue largely unabated until the time was right for another enforcement intervention.

An additional aim of the drug warrant tactic was to let the dealers know the police were 'on to them' and to reassure the public that they were tackling local drug problems and community concerns. Raids are a highly visible display of power that demonstrate the capacity and will of the police to manage contraventions of the law and social order and send messages to a number of audiences about who belongs within society and what behaviours will or will not be tolerated (Innes 2014b; Loader and Mulcahy 2003; Manning 1997). Furthermore, if the address in question was also connected to disorder or serious nuisance to the public, the raid would often be followed up with a 'crack house closure' order to reinforce the 'not welcome' message and stop anyone from entering or residing at the property.[3] From a 'control signal' perspective (Innes 2014b), detectives opined that forced entry warrants are designed to increase the perception and actual risk of detection for those offenders still at large and hence deter them from engaging in drug market activity. The impression of 'the always imminent raid', Collison (1995: 172) notes, 'serves to sustain a symbolic influence for the squad when the lack of intelligence or resources precludes a real presence'. Some detectives wanted to be feared, recognized as a force to be reckoned

---

[3] The Anti-Social Behaviour Act 2003 introduced powers allowing the police and local authorities to close properties where an officer not below the rank of superintendent has reasonable grounds for believing that the address has been used for the use, production, or supply of a Class A drug and is causing disorder or serious nuisance to members of the public. Under s 1(8) it is not necessary for any occupant of the premises to have been convicted of a drug offence. Initially, the police will serve a closure notice on the occupiers of the property. The notice must then be effectively converted to a closure order by the court within 48 hours of service. Upon the granting of the order the occupants lose any right to remain there and the property is often sealed up within the day.

with, and they aspired to be the reason why the inhabitants of the drug world had to sleep with one eye open. Others had more modest ambitions, were sceptical about the deterrent effect, and questioned whether 'the message' was actually being received as intended.

[Drug warrants] get the other dealers all rattled up. They're sat at home wondering if they'll be next, or if the guy we've taken in is going to grass them up. The market usually goes quiet for a while because people are laying low trying to figure out what's going on. (Detective, Smallville)

If I'm honest, I don't think the dealers are even half as worried about us catching up with them as we'd like to believe. We're an occupational hazard. Most of them are used to living with a heavy police presence so they're well practised at avoiding the law. Chances are they'll be a tad more cautious for a short time after a raid, but it's soon back to business as usual. (Detective, Metropolis)

News about dramatic enforcement interventions was said to 'spread like wildfire'. The scene of a raid was guaranteed to attract a crowd of onlookers and endless passers-by and their interpretive accounts would be passed on through the grapevine and soon become common knowledge. These accounts then entered into the collective memory, where they 'interact and intermingle with a range of other influences upon public experiences, perceptions, and judgements about safety and security' (Innes 2014b: 130). Detectives or tactical support officers were stationed at the entrance of the property being searched to maintain order and prevent members of the public from crossing the threshold. This vantage point enabled them to communicate with local residents and gauge their initial reactions. Subsequent reactions were occasionally fed back via informants and neighbourhood police officers, but no real effort was made to monitor the fallout. Here is a selection of quotations that capture the various ways in which detectives perceived public reactions to drug raids:

If it's a real scumbag you can hear the community breathe a sigh of relief when we take them away. (Detective, Metropolis)

People can be genuinely shocked to find out they've been living next door to a drug dealer. It makes them all worried about what else is going on under their nose. (Detective, Smallville)

In the worst affected areas the residents have mixed feelings towards drug enforcement operations. I mean, they're pleased to see that the police are doing something, but at the same time they know that arresting one or two dealers is not going to make a difference in the grand scheme of things. They've seen it all before. They know the dealers will be right back at it as soon as we're gone. (Detective, Metropolis)

You'll get a few who'll come over asking questions cos they're after a bit of gossip, but most people keep their distance and let us get on with it... When we're in the rougher areas we might get a bit of lip, people telling us to stop harassing them and leave them be like. Their family and friends come down and start eyeballing us and giving us shit. You'll see them on their phones giving this dealer or that dealer a heads up. It can get pretty tense. (Detective, Smallville)

There are people round here who hate the police more than the dealers. Hell, some of the dealers are like local celebrities in the estates. To them warrants are just another example of oppressive and discriminatory policing. (Detective, Metropolis)

For the most part, the detectives believed that successful raids were viewed in a positive light by law-abiding citizens and resulted in improved public confidence in the policing of drugs and enhanced satisfaction with the police. They also claimed that there was usually a slight increase in community intelligence in the immediate aftermath. That being said, it was also recognized that the control signals they transmitted could also be negative in their effects. The negative effect that bothered detectives the most was that unsuccessful raids undermined their authority and made them 'look like punks'. Other undesirable consequences that can be drawn from the above quotations are that raids can increase the fear of crime, fail to have any meaningful impact on entrenched drug markets, and come across as an unfair use of power that is disproportionately directed at marginal and low status groups. Interventions that are not seen as legitimate or 'good' policing are likely to increase tensions between the police and citizens and reduce community engagement and their normative commitment to formal controls (Bottoms and Tankebe 2012; Jackson et al. 2012).

The foremost advantage of the drug warrant was that it provided detectives with a 'quick, cheap, and easy' method of taking out their targets and racking up arrests and seizures. Where successful, suppliers were at least temporarily removed from the market and faced criminal justice penalties and economic disruption in the form of incomplete transactions or lost resources when their drugs and ill-gotten gains were confiscated. Raids also had broader goals in that they were used as a means of disrupting distribution networks, removing ready and available sources of drugs, and inconveniencing users by making it more difficult for them to make a purchase. However, the detectives were well aware of their limitations. Many said that using warrants as a stand-alone tactical resolution was only likely to bag the 'small fry' and thereby diverted police resources away from the key players. Smart dealers, it was assumed, and those operating above the retail level, were unlikely to have incriminating evidence at their home address or premises under their control and adopted risk management strategies that could only be penetrated through covert surveillance. Unsuccessful warrants and results that were not as good as expected were common causes of concern and criticism. 'Most of the time we don't come out with what we went in for.' There were days when the detectives went in for 'wholesale quantities' of heroin and left with just a few grams, others when a small amount of cannabis was all that could be salvaged, and those when nothing was found and they left empty handed. Suspects occasionally slipped through the net because they had no fixed address and were difficult to pin down or were simply not present when the warrant was executed. These outcomes were blamed on gaps or inaccuracies in the police intelligence picture. Unless intelligence was 'current, accurate, and ongoing' there was a significant risk of striking at the wrong time or place. 'A warrant is a blunt instrument,' said one detective. 'Sometimes they get the job done but sometimes all they do is fuck it up.' He explained that when a warrant was unsuccessful, the intelligence that justified the application stayed on the system but was temporarily rendered null and void. Consequently, they needed more intelligence to justify another operation. In the meantime, the dealer had been made aware of the investigation and would therefore alter their business patterns and become more wary of police activity. This slight disruption was not considered a result: no arrest, no seizure, and no prosecution. All it did was make it more difficult to make the case. Finally, the detectives recognized that unless they got lucky and 'struck big' a raid was not going to cause a major disruption to the larger market system or impact on levels of use, availability and price. They knew that distribution networks are adaptable, suppliers are easily replaced, and deterrent effects are transitory. Drug warrants are not designed to change the marketplace. Their objective is to uphold the law, bring offenders to justice, and send a message that something is being done.

Covert Operations

Covert investigation is widely viewed as an indispensable aspect of crime control and the only realistic means of gathering evidence to prosecute criminal activity that cannot be secured through overt policing (Harfield and Harfield 2012; Loftus and Goold 2012; Loftus et al. 2015; Marx 1988). It incorporates a range of investigative techniques which infringe upon the private life of people considered suspect, from simply following, watching, and listening to individuals and populations without their awareness, through the use of undercover police officers and other deceptive tactics, to electronic forms of surveillance, such as telephone tapping, email monitoring, and audio visual devices. Surveillance can provide high quality evidence that is tantamount to a confession without the need to interview. Generally speaking, such techniques are used to confirm suspicions, fill in the gaps or connect the dots of the intelligence picture, and detect crimes that are largely invisible to the untrained eye, those which take place behind closed doors between consenting individuals and have no party to the act who has an interest in being the plaintiff. More controversially, the 'invisibilities of policing' (Loftus and Goold 2012) are also used to manipulate the environment, perceptions, and behaviour of the suspect in order to entice them to commit an offence or enable an officer to infiltrate a criminal network. In some cases, the police let crimes happen without intervention or even participate in the very crimes that are under investigation. Much of the information collected through covert means remains intelligence, rather than becoming evidence used to support the case for the prosecution.

In many countries, the use of covert methods of investigation generates a profound sense of moral ambiguity and has been subject to heated academic, legal, and political debate (Brodeur 1992; Bronitt 2004; Fijnaut and Marx 1995; Hyland and Walker 2014; Ross 2008; Wachtel 1992). Some significant and well-founded concerns relate to abuses of power, threats to the principles of democracy, and the expansion of mass surveillance into the realms of everyday life. What has emerged from this discourse is that, if we are to be convinced that covert policing is indeed a 'necessary evil', it needs to balance public security with the protection of civil liberties and the integrity of the criminal justice system. To this end, considerable importance is placed upon police ethics and the effectiveness of appropriate forms of governance and accountability (Harfield 2010; Marx 1988).

The traditional dominance of reactive approaches to criminal investigation has meant that legal mechanisms for regulating investigative practice have focused almost entirely upon procedures surrounding searches, detention, and interrogation. Prior to RIPA, there was no statutory framework in the UK to regulate the use of covert techniques, with the exception of the interception of communications and surveillance involving an interference with property or wireless telegraphy. Individual investigators were subject only to the common law and Home Office and internal police guidelines. Maguire and John (1996: 320) note that the police were largely 'left alone to experiment with a "trial and error" approach, pushing at the limits of previously accepted practice and waiting to see whether the resultant evidence will be deemed admissible by the courts'. Formal regulation came about primarily in response to the need to ensure that the surveillance powers of the state were compliant with human rights law and subject to more stringent and transparent controls. There now exists a raft of legal powers, procedures and codes of practice about the conditions under which covert methods of investigation are justifiable, the kinds of limits that should be imposed on such activities, and the most effective ways of preventing officers from overstepping the boundaries of professionalism and fairness.

Surveillance

Covert investigative techniques were ordinarily used against those dealers who 'play hard to get'—organized, savvy, and risk-averse criminals who took measures to evade the long arm of the law. The Smallville drug squad focused their surveillance powers on heroin and cocaine dealers, who operated through closed distribution networks. Whilst they did come across the occasional 'kingpin', the vast majority of dealing enterprises subjected to investigation were small groups of loosely linked individuals and sole traders. Some bought in bulk and sold kilos and ounces to local dealers and 'out-of-towners', whereas others were retail level suppliers who sold small amounts directly to the end user. Violent street gangs were the number one priority for the Metropolis firearms team and occupied the bulk of their surveillance capacity. According to the intelligence picture, in the geographical territory of the gangs that they sought to dismantle and disrupt the drug trade was more or less controlled by gang members from wholesale to retail. The more established gangs were also known to have links to international traffickers and suppliers in other districts and cities across the country. With their surplus resources, the detectives would target 'middle market' heroin and crack but seldom powder cocaine dealers.

Part II of RIPA created a regulatory regime for 'directed' and 'intrusive' surveillance. In basic terms, directed surveillance involves watching or listening to people without their awareness in order to obtain private information. It may be conducted for the purpose of preventing or detecting any crime or offence and can take place anywhere except residential premises or a private vehicle. Surveillance becomes intrusive when it involves the presence of an officer on the premises or in the vehicle or is carried out by means of a 'bugging' device that gives information of the quality and detail that would be provided by a person in that property. Intrusive surveillance is limited to the investigation of 'serious' crime.[4] Before the commencement of a 'RIPA operation', the investigating officer was statutorily required to complete a standardized application form and obtain written authorization from an appropriate senior ranking officer.[5] This method of due process control meant that the majority of covert activities undertaken by the police were 'self-authorized' and only subject to judicial scrutiny if their lawfulness was challenged in court. Applications contained a detailed description of the planned operation and clearly set out the grounds on which the authority was being sought. The wording tended to be very precise as only conduct specified in the authority was authorized and therefore lawful. Authorization would only be granted if the authorizing officer was satisfied that the proposed activities were necessary in the circumstances and proportionate to the intended outcomes. Furthermore, the officer

---

[4] 'Serious' crime is defined as: (a) an offence for which, on first conviction, a person with no previous convictions could reasonably be expected to be sentenced to imprisonment for a term of three years or more; or (b) the conduct involves the use of violence, results in substantial financial gain, or is engaged in by a larger number of persons for a common purpose (s 81(3)).

[5] For directed surveillance, an authorization must be granted by an officer not below the rank of superintendent, whereas for intrusive surveillance the authorizing officer is the chief constable or commissioner and, save in urgent cases, will not take effect without the prior written approval of a surveillance commissioner.

seeking the authorization was also required to demonstrate that the activities were the most viable means of achieving the stated objectives, or that all other tactical options had been exhausted, and describe the precautions to be taken to minimise collateral intrusion into the privacy of third parties present in the surveillance arena. Authorizations lasted for three months and could be renewed. They were reviewed at monthly intervals or whenever there was a material change in circumstances affecting the validity of the authority.

Detectives were inclined to regard the authorization process as bureaucratically onerous and an impediment to their proactive investigative work. 'We have to jump through so many hoops to get authorization for surveillance jobs,' remarked one officer. 'It's like being a dog at Crufts.' The RIPA regime was invariably described as being constraining, time-consuming, and overly managerial. As with drug warrants, most experienced detectives had a draft copy of an application form saved on their computers and would change the specifics on a case-by-case basis. These shortcut documents included tried and tested explanations for why surveillance was necessary for the purpose of detecting drug supply offences and proportionate to both the extent of harm caused by the crimes being investigated and the value of the evidential product derived from the use of covert methods. In reality, however, such time-saving devices yielded little practical benefit, since, besides a few readily transferable phrases and sentences, the bulk of each application was case specific and therefore had to be written from scratch.

Despite their criticisms, observations revealed that detectives in both police forces prided themselves on knowing 'the ins and outs of the law' and took the administrative part of making cases very seriously. 'You've got to be good at paperwork to be a good detective', act like a 'professional' and make sure 'everything's above board'. The meeting of legal and organizational requirements was a way to demonstrate their ability to do the job well (Hobbs 1988; Skolnick 2011; Waddington 1999a). The majority of the detectives under study had undertaken a range of surveillance training courses and were familiar with the provisions of the relevant statutes and the need to consider human rights issues when planning operations. Well-thumbed copies of police textbooks and professional practice publications could be found scattered around the office, officers regularly debated the best way to carry out covert policing within legal limitations, and supervisors routinely provided 'tutoring sessions' and checked applications before they were submitted for authorization. 'If we want to use surveillance tactics to gather evidence that will stand up in court we need to comply with the law.' Indeed, the detectives were well aware that if the authorization process was not properly followed their case could be compromised as they risked a stay in proceedings or the exclusion of evidence from trial. Add to this, the risk of disciplinary proceedings and reputational damage. These findings indicate that the regulatory framework was viewed primarily as what Smith and Gray (1983: 171) call 'inhibitory rules', those 'which police officers take into account when deciding how to act and which tend to discourage them from behaving in certain ways in case they should be caught and the rule invoked against them'. In consequence, instead of being internalized as guiding principles of conduct, human rights compliance in relation to surveillance activities was first and foremost treated as a box-ticking administrative task.

Most of the covert operations observed during fieldwork were directed surveillance only and performed by the drug detectives alone. For the most part, they involved officers carrying out surveillance on foot and from unmarked police cars or specially equipped surveillance vans using non-intrusive technical aids. These technical aids included cameras and devices that were attached to vehicles in order to reveal their location and track their movements. Requests for directed surveillance authorization were seldom rejected. The main reasons for this remarkable success rate were that the paperwork was completed to a satisfactory standard and the proposed targets and covert methods of investigation met the statutory criteria. 'If you nail the application [authorizing officers] are bound to say yes,' confided one detective. 'I mean, why would they want to prevent us from investigating drug dealers?' It should also be noted that when authorizing officers did identify problems with applications they would typically provide the officer seeking the authorization with feedback and allow them to make revisions and then resubmit. In a sense, therefore, the application process can be equated to a system of internal peer review that is designed to address issues relating to rigour, reliability, and validity before deployment. This is a prime example of a police 'cover your ass' strategy. Moreover, whilst somewhat time-consuming, the application process could hardly be said to act as a significant constraint on drug detective work. The fact that authorization was relatively easy to obtain actually facilitated the use of surveillance as it rendered such activities legitimate and less open to challenge. On the handful of occasions when the detectives failed to obtain authorization for directed surveillance, it was because they were unable to secure the tactical or technical support needed to execute the proposed operation. They found it frustrating when their operational plans were thwarted by management but accepted that they were working in an organization of competing priorities and limited resources.

The need to prioritize the allocation of resources also explains why detectives rarely obtained authorization for intrusive surveillance. As a general rule, such techniques were reserved for operations against serious and organized criminals who operated across district or force boundaries. These targets fell within the occupational mandate of force-level specialist detective units, or what was then SOCA, and were not usually capable of being managed by local resources. Over the years, the Smallville drug squad had applied to use audio and visual probes for intrusive surveillance purposes and bid for the necessary technical support to force mangers on numerous occasions, but had only ever acquired it twice. In Metropolis, on the other hand, even though they had access to substantially more resources, both the detectives and the management team were of the opinion that drug supply was not a serious enough offence to justify anything more than directed surveillance unless the target was a suspected wholesaler or there was an associated firearms risk or threat to life. The firearms squad undertook intrusive surveillance operations on three separate occasions during fieldwork and said they averaged two or three per year.

Shortly after entering the field, the detectives informed me that they had recently started a RIPA operation against the 'Westside Towers Crew' (WTC), an established street gang based in and around the Metropolis Towers Estate. The members were all young IC3 males (African/Caribbean), who were associated with each other through a geographical peer group. Intelligence suggested that the gang was involved in the supply of Class A drugs, had ready access to firearms, and were willing to use as much violence as necessary to maintain respect, protect their interests, and stake a claim to their perceived territories.

'They're one of the most dangerous gangs in the city,' claimed the investigating officer.

The gang leaders—'Avon', 'Stringer' and 'D'—were suspected of being responsible for a series of shootings, threats with firearms, and serious assaults. There were over four hundred intelligence reports on Avon alone, who was suspected of leading both the criminal and rap music side of the gang. Upon viewing the gang's websites, it was clear that expressed through their music was the intent to glamorize gang violence and encourage younger and easily influenced males to join their criminal enterprise. Analytical products clearly showed that the area controlled by the WTC was a hotspot for serious violence, knife crime, firearms recoveries, and robbery within the district. The purpose of the operation was to reduce the harm caused by the gang through violence driven by the criminality and funding streams of the illegal drug business by targeting the key players and disrupting their criminal networks.

After going live, the first step for the detectives was to work closely with the intelligence unit to develop target profiles and a problem profile for the WTC. Within three months they had a detailed intelligence picture, had carried out a comprehensive police database check on all their targets, run financial, utilities, and welfare checks, and identified the phones they were believed to be using. Intelligence was actively sought through daily intelligence checks – search strings were created for the suspects, vehicles and phone numbers – and global tasking in order to obtain all possible sources of information from the available police databases. As the intelligence development stages progressed, the detectives learned that Avon and Stringer were involved in wholesale distribution as well as retail after a registered informer provided them with information suggesting that they were supplying drugs throughout Greater Metropolis and cities in the North West and West Midlands regions of England. 'This case has got legs,' remarked one of the detectives. The source also said that they were using local girls to store, transport and deal the drugs on their behalf, usually by train but sometimes by vehicles hired outside Metropolis. In consequence, the detectives broadened the scope of the operation and worked collaboratively with a number of Greater Metropolis BCUs and police forces in two other cities by sharing intelligence and coordinating tactical resolutions.

The detectives carried out directed surveillance upon their targets, initially focusing upon the Metropolis Towers Estate to identify the business patterns and associates of Avon, Stringer and D. They also used tracking and intrusive audio devices on the gangs' vehicles and monitored their movements using telephone data. After a few weeks of further intelligence gathering, the detectives decided to execute 'disruption' warrants against a number of street sellers and addresses that were suspected to be 'safe houses'. Following this, police officers carried out extensive sweeps of the estate and high visibility reassurance. This disruptive tactic stimulated the flow of intelligence and resulted in the arrest of ten gang affiliates for drug supply offences. 'It's got them all paranoid now,' said one of the detectives the morning after. 'It won't be much longer until our guys have to get their hands dirty to sort it out.' The detectives continued using the covert investigative techniques they were authorized to use, executing drug warrants, and making arrests whenever they had the intelligence or the evidence to justify it. Once all the opportunities for intelligence gathering and enforcement were exhausted, they arrested Avon, Stringer and D and searched the premises where they resided.

In the end, the operation led to the arrest of six key gang members and over twenty of their associates, including a suspected drug trafficker who was later removed from the UK for immigration offences. Seizures and confiscations included: one kilo of Class A drugs, one assault rifle, two pump action shotguns, two Baikal handguns, two smoke grenades, two bullet proof vests and a large quantity of blank birth certificates. Avon, Stringer and D were remanded for serious offences: attempted murder: possession of an illegal firearm: and possession with the intent to supply Class A drugs. However, during the course of the operation it became clear that the gang was highly organized and was connected with wider criminal networks, and so it continued to function despite the disruptions caused by the imprisonment of its leaders and many of its 'soldiers'. The potential harm to the local community was diminished, but firearms continued to be recovered around the Metropolis Towers Estate area and there continued to be drug supply offences and violent crime.

The first phase of a surveillance operation was to carry out reconnaissance of the immediate setting. Mapping the 'lie of the land' enabled detectives to pinpoint appropriate vantage points and plan how they were going to manipulate the environment in order to intrude into the private life of the targeted individual or group.

Before we go in we need to know where we can park our vehicles without drawing too much attention. We'll check out if there's a car park nearby, if it's pay and display or permit only for on street parking, that sort of thing. We don't want to get a ticket now do we [laughs]. (Detective, Metropolis)

When you're out on foot you need to give yourself a reason for being there. You can't just stand around or keep walking up and down or you'll end up being made. You give yourself a story and act like that's what you're doing. It might be that you're going to meet a friend at such and such a place, or going down the shop to buy a lottery ticket. If there's a bench you might want to take a load off or mess about with your phone or something. If there's a café you might fancy a cuppa or a read of the paper. The trick is to act normal and do what everybody else is doing. (Detective, Smallville)

You've got to find the observation points that will give you an uninterrupted view of the subject or the location under surveillance. In built-up areas this can be harder than you think. You need a place where you can sit tight for hours at a time without being noticed. Vehicles are too obvious if you ask me. They're too exposed. Buildings are better. The best strategy for static surveillance is to station yourself on a rooftop or inside the house across the street. (Detective, Metropolis)

Following the pre-surveillance recce, the detectives would set about constructing a detailed target profile by collecting and compiling the minutiae of their routine activities. This process was called 'researching' or 'lifestyling' (Loftus and Goold 2012; O'Neill and Loftus 2013). It essentially involved shadowing suspects in order to obtain information about their possibly illegal and mundane legal behaviours–appearance, associates, habits, movements, pastimes, and so on. 'You really get to know a person.' The aim was to get a 'feel' for the operation, identify the key players, the modus operandi of the network and any patterns of drug dealing activity. By gaining a deep enough understanding of the ordinary, the detectives were able to spot anything that was out of the ordinary. Once the research phase was exhausted, they would figure out how best to work up the case, finalize the tactical plan and complete what was known as an 'Operation Order' or 'Proactive Assessment and Tasking Proforma'. These documents were used to justify funding applications and included the current intelligence picture, operational strategy, and command structure.

When carrying out surveillance, officers attempted to appear 'natural', 'blend' into their surroundings, and render their work invisible (Loftus and Goold 2012). In order to go unnoticed they would carefully craft and manage their own appearance so that it corresponded with that of the local population. 'You don't want to stand out from the crowd.' Plain, inexpensive clothes with no branding were the norm, no 'mad' hairstyles, visible tattoos, or other distinguishing features. Cars were rentals and exchanged on a regular basis. Surveillance vans were made up to look like they belonged to builders, electricians, joiners, painters, plumbers, or other tradesmen. It was crucial that they remained inconspicuous and were not 'clocked' by their targets or inadvertently outed by members of the public. This was sometimes easier said than done.

We don't even bother with directed surveillance in some of the estates anymore because there are too many lookouts. They can spot a cop a mile off. They'll assume any car they don't recognize is an unmarked police car. And just look at me—I'm a big, fat white bloke. I'd stick out like a sore thumb even if I wasn't wearing a badge. (Detective Sergeant, Metropolis)

A problem we've got is a lot of the local dealers know who we are because we've had run-ins with them in the past. If they see us they'll guess something's up and take precautions…We've confiscated phones and found our numbers and pictures of us on them. It's a worry. (Detective, Smallville)

Stories about 'surveillance screw-ups' provided the officers with valuable lessons and amusing anecdotes to be shared during off-duty socializing (Loftus et al. 2015). There was the one about the time when the detectives got pulled over after a concerned citizen reported their suspicious activities to the police. Research participants told me that they had fallen asleep and missed criminal occurrences, forgotten their pen and been unable to record their observations, and found themselves so desperate to urinate that they were forced to go in a public place only to be scolded by a passer-by for their indecent behaviour. Targets waved at them, gave them a thumbs-up or flipped them off, and took them on wild-goose chases. A target once walked straight up to an unmarked police car, knocked on the window, and asked the detectives if they'd care to join him for dinner. These tales from the field highlight the fragility of surveillance work, the human elements, the operational dilemmas and the emphasis placed on learning through on-the-job experience and socialization.

Without exception, surveillance techniques were used to monitor targeted individuals and their associates in order to gather intelligence and evidence to support the case for the prosecution.

Photographs were taken, video footage was recorded and scrupulous surveillance logs were kept. Detectives were interested in who was involved in the drug dealing enterprise under investigation, how they were connected to each other, what roles they performed, and the ways in which they were prone to carry out care of business. They were interested in where the drugs were being stored and when and where 'buys' and 'drops' took place. Tell-tale signs of criminal activity included acting 'shifty', visiting people for a short period of time, and socializing with known drug offenders. The ultimate goal was to put together the pieces of a distribution network and be fully cognizant of its structure and operations. What they were looking for was the perfect opportunity to catch their targets in the act or in possession of self-incriminating evidence. The primary objective of the Smallville drug squad was to prosecute their targets for drug supply offences. In Metropolis, however, the detectives saw their function as dismantling and disrupting the drug trade by whatever means possible. Rather than focusing on drug offences in isolation, they were more inclined to view their targets as 'business criminals':

The approach we take is to treat it as a business. What we have to do is put them out of business in whatever way we can. Drugs is one way we can do this, but if we can get them for something else we will, like firearms, or money laundering, or violence against the person...or even tax evasion—the Al Capone method. (Detective, Metropolis)

In some cases, surveillance was used in a simple role to corroborate intelligence and inform a search warrant application. It established that the information provided was based on police observations and not exclusively on the word of a citizen or informer. Furthermore, when intelligence was lacking, it was argued that if a warrant were to be executed without the use of surveillance in the first instance officers would be entering the premises with very little knowledge of who or what was present. Without this prior knowledge there was a greater risk that no drugs would be recovered and the subject would be made aware of police interest in them. In other cases, the detectives spent days, weeks, and even months watching and waiting for a pattern to emerge before they could determine when, where, and how to strike. 'You've got to be patient. The longer you stay on someone the more you learn.' That being said, sometimes it was more down to serendipity than anything else.

We'd planned for a lengthy surveillance operation. Rumour had it these guys were backed by a neighbourhood gang leader so we wanted to work our way up the chain. On the first day, he shows up and walks straight into the flat we're watching. We thought about waiting it out; letting events take their course and all that. But then we thought fuck it. We arrested him as soon as he left and then raided the flat. He'd been making a drop-off. They usually use runners for drop-offs and pick-ups so it must have been our lucky day. He'd over a grand in small bills and another bag of rocks on him. (Detective, Metropolis)

It's all about being in the right place at the time... There was this job last year when we were seeing nothing for weeks. Our guy was a real smooth operator, as cautious as they come. The Super was about to pull us off so we upped the ante and started doing round the clock surveillance. On the second night, he goes for a stroll in the woods behind his house—he didn't take his dog; he didn't even use a torch. That's when we knew we had him. Turned out he had just shy of half a kilo buried back there! We hid in the bushes and used a couple of thermal imaging cameras to film him digging it up the next time... He didn't half run when we moved in on him. (Detective, Smallville)

Preventing drug offences from happening was not a primary concern during surveillance operations. In fact, detectives often allowed drug supply and possession offences to take place without intervention for evidentiary purposes. On the following occasion the justification for selectively enforcing the law was 'operational necessity':

The drug squad were nearly two weeks into an operation against members of a notorious Grandville gang, who had started dealing in their territory. Having already filmed three suspected transactions using their surveillance van, it was decided in the morning briefing that when the opportunity arose a 'punter' would be pulled after making a buy. At around 11am, Carver noticed a familiar figure approaching the potential crime scene—let's call her Dee-Dee the drug user. 'Looks like we're on lads,' he informed the others over the radio. She entered the alleyway where it was believed the drugs were being hidden, exited a minute or so later, and continued walking down the street. A young black male emerged from a nearby house, walked to the entrance of the alley, smoked a cigarette, entered the alley, exited a minute or so later and returned to the house. 'Just like clockwork,' said Herc with a knowing smile. 'Now let's go get our girl!'

As the car slowly pulled up alongside Dee-Dee the detectives unfastened their seatbelts. 'Stop! Police!' She froze like a deer in the headlights. Without any further words of warning Carver grabbed her by the throat to make sure she couldn't swallow then thrust his fingers into her mouth. No drugs. The detectives then falsely explained why they had stopped and searched her so as not to jeopardize the operation and told her that they would have to take her back to the station for an intimate body search. Upon entering the station Dee-Dee became noticeably more agitated and cagey; clearly the custody suite did not bring back fond memories, or maybe she had something to hide. The search yielded two £10 bags of heroin. The detectives seized the drugs and left her with the custody officers. They had what they wanted: the evidence. (Fieldnotes, Smallville)

Once a pattern had been determined and thoroughly documented, the detectives would either execute a search warrant when both the target and the drugs were present at a particular address or execute an arrest warrant when there was sufficient evidence to prove that they were involved in drug supply. On the other hand, if the surveillance seemed to be going nowhere and nothing evidential was forthcoming it would eventually be terminated, normally with a 'cold' warrant although sometimes the case was simply shelved and returned to at a later date.

Test purchase

Another tactical resolution that the detectives had in their operational toolkit was 'test purchase'. A test purchase or 'buy-bust' operation is where a plainclothes officer goes undercover and poses as a drug user in order to buy drugs from persons identified as potential dealers and thereby secure evidence of a supply offence. This tactic was deployed on a handful of occasions during fieldwork to tackle open-air markets and semi-open distribution systems based in the night-time economy. The buys were made by specially trained test purchase officers and monitored by means of directed surveillance and CCTV camera systems wherever possible. Their role was to do 'partial undercover' work in that they worked the street for a typical shift and became only marginally involved in a local drug scene. When a greater degree of immersion was required a specialist undercover officer was added to the mix. Such officers carry out 'deep undercover' work and adopt an identity and lifestyle that is maintained on a continuous basis for a lengthy period of time (Dorn et al. 1992; Pistone and Woodley 1988). Registered informers were never tasked with making supervised buys and seldom used to introduce an operative to a dealer. Whilst detectives admitted that such practices did occur, they considered them to be 'too risky' and overly complex in terms of logistics and the evidentiary paper trail. Nor did they use the controversial 'reverse sting' tactic, which involves officers posing as drug dealers and offering to supply or actually supplying drugs to their targets. In fact, the official position of the police was that no such operations take place. 'That's an American thing,' said one senior officer. 'It's not condoned in England and Wales and I would not authorize it under any circumstances.'

In contrast to surveillance, test purchase is not only covert but also deceptive in that the officer adopts a false persona with the intention of misleading the target into thinking that they are just another drug offender and then willingly incriminating themselves. Deception is essentially a form of lying that constitutes 'soft' coercion. It is arguably justifiable if the moral and social benefits of a successful operation outweigh the ethical costs. Closely connected to the issue of deception is the more serious problem of entrapment. A fundamental legal principle is that police must not act as *agents provocateurs* and incite a person to commit an offence which they would not otherwise have committed (Bronitt 2004; Maguire and John 1996; Squires 2006).

RIPA makes no specific provision for undercover deployments by the police. With regard to regulation, test purchase and undercover officers fall under the regulatory regime created for the use of covert human intelligence sources. Where the officer undertaking a test purchase was tasked with establishing a relationship with a dealer or group of dealers so as to maintain their cover and obtain information, the operation required prior authorization. However, if no such relationship was established, the police could act without authority.[6] Combined authorization for the use of a source and directed or intrusive surveillance was required where the officer used technical devices to record the transaction. The statute does not specifically permit the police to participate in a

[6] The Regulation of Investigatory Powers (Covert Human Intelligence Sources: Relevant Order) 2013 requires that all deployments of undercover officers must be authorized by an officer of at least assistant chief constable rank or equivalent.

criminal offence nor provide much supplementary guidance on the dividing line between acceptable and unacceptable conduct. What it does is give considerable latitude to authorizing officers and thus allow them to legitimize illegal activities that are deemed necessary and proportionate. As long as the activity does not amount to entrapment, case law confirms that police are entitled to enter a criminal conspiracy, take part in an offence already laid on, and provide an opportunity for a person to commit a crime by asking them to sell drugs (Harfield and Harfield 2012; Hyland and Walker 2014).

The town centre of Smallville was known to the police as a hotspot for heroin distribution. The current intelligence picture suggested that the market was growing and drug-related crime was on the rise. Patrol officers were running into more addicts on the streets than usual; they were carrying out more stops and searches and seizing more drugs. There was a slight increase in acquisitive crime, and more people were testing positive for opiates on arrest. Members of the public were making more complaints about drug use in public places, coming across more syringes, and other drug using paraphernalia. Informants were telling the police that the cause of the problem was the drug distribution network of the Stanfield family, who had recently branched out from their neighbourhood market in the Eastside of the district with the backing of a notorious Grandville street gang. After a month of intelligence development via the tasking of registered sources and directed surveillance, the drug squad decided that the best way to deal with the problem was to carry out a test purchase operation. 'Plus we'd never done one before so we were keen to give it a go,' said the investigating officer. The objective was to identify and take out the Stanfield network and thereby disrupt the heroin markets in the town centre and the Eastside.

The squad recruited two test purchase officers (TPOs) from police services in Southern England to ensure that they were not recognized by the local dealers. Each had their own unique 'legend' and style. For instance, the operative deployed in the town centre was a colourful character and skilled musician and so generally assumed the role of a busker when in the field. 'I can't believe how much they look like addicts,' confessed a bemused Carver. The squad were also working with a force-level surveillance unit and had been granted the resources to purchase a range of new technical surveillance devices for the district. Amongst these were the buttonhole cameras worn by the TPOs to record the transactions. In terms of officer numbers, not only did the detectives need sufficient manpower to be able to track the targets under surveillance, but in order to mitigate risks to the safety of the TPOs they too needed to be carefully monitored. 'They're doing a dangerous job and we need to be on hand to intervene if things go tits-up.' After a couple of weeks of acclimatization and further intelligence gathering, the busker was approached by a street seller, a purchase was made and the first piece of hard evidence acquired. A registered source was tasked with introducing the other operative into the Eastside market. The plan was for them to make at least two purchases from every dealer they came across, build up a rapport, and infiltrate the network. First buys were always sent off to forensics for analysis before a second buy was made, so that the TPO knew the purity and could comment on the quality—or not buy again if they were duped into buying a fake product. The detectives also noted the serial numbers of the banknotes used to buy the drugs in the hope of chasing the money and mapping the financial structure of the network. This stage of the operation lasted for six months.

When sufficient evidence had been gathered, the detectives unleashed a torrent of raids. The enforcement stage lasted for three weeks and led to the arrest of forty-five people for drug supply offences. Thirty of the arrestees were labelled as runners and street sellers; the rest were closed market dealers and included all of the Stanfields. 'Some of them actually handed themselves in because they were scared of what was coming,' bragged DS Daniels. Following the crackdown, there was a short period of high-visibility policing in the target areas, which was aimed at informing the public about the intervention and engaging the local drug-using population. The police worked in collaboration with drug treatment services, who, having been informed about the police action in advance, sent out workers with patrol officers to speak to their clients and users not yet in treatment. In addition, the operation also led to the clearing up of over twenty burglaries and contributed significantly to the intelligence picture of the stolen goods market. The operation was hailed as a success because of the mass arrests and convictions. It also succeeded in that the heroin market was noticeably absent from the town centre and the Eastside neighbourhood for several months and there was little evidence of displacement. 'We know the market hasn't completely disappeared,' explained Bunk. 'But at least the dealers we didn't catch have gone off somewhere else for a while'. They expected the market to adapt. Sure enough, in the end the forces of supply and demand proved to be more powerful than the deterrent effect of the police and intelligence reports started coming in suggesting that members of a certain Grandville street gang had entered the frame.

As Collison (1995: 134) observed, the use of test purchase 'is largely dictated by the nature of the drug market being targeted and only partially influenced by the predilections of detectives and their supervising officers'. It is very difficult if not impossible for police to infiltrate closed markets where access is limited to known and trusted participants or social network markets that are primarily based around friendship and existing acquaintances. Generally speaking, their only inroads into the drug world are through open markets that allow equal access to all and semi-open markets wherein sellers will generally do business without prior introduction, provided the buyer 'looks the part'. On top of appearing natural and blending into the surveillance setting, test purchase officers have to act like drug users, interact with real users and criminals and convince them that they are one and the same. They have to speak the same language, know the code of the street, and tell stories that illustrate their deviant lifestyle and overwhelming desire to score. They have to be police on the inside and anti-police on the outside. This challenging assignment is perfectly captured in the following interview excerpt:

You gotta become a crackhead, you know, look like them, act like them. People treat you like shit, and you gotta be ready for it; you gotta be able to take it. When I'm preparing for a job, I don't shower or shave, got greasy hair, spots, I wear dirty clothes – I fucking stink mate. I always carry a can of special brew, walk about all edgy. I've been spat on by people, pushed, told what a mess I am; can't react as I usually would though. You're in the crackhead mindset, you see. You gotta be a broken man. You gotta act like you need crack more than anything, like the dealers are doing you a favour, you know. "Oh go on, please, go on mate, please, go on mate sell us a rock." I've followed dealers for half a mile doing that before, until he finally dealt to me. The worst thing that can happen is when the drugs are plugged. Dealer takes it out of his arse and tells you to put it in your mouth. Fucking disgusting! But you've gotta do it, a crackhead would do it. (Detective, Metropolis)

A common view expressed during fieldwork was that 'it takes a particular type of person to do undercover work'. The qualities mentioned included being young, unattached, motivated, resourceful, resilient, and a little bit duplicitous and devil-may-care. As they involve close and often prolonged exposure to criminals, test purchase operations can be extremely demanding and potentially dangerous. This is precisely why RIPA makes additional provision for source management by requiring that handlers and controllers carry out risk assessments and take responsibility for security and welfare issues. The central concerns of operatives in a buy-bust scenario were blowing their cover, becoming victims of violence, or finding themselves in a situation where they were expected to consume drugs in the presence of others. 'When dealers don't know you, they sometimes force you to take it there and then to prove you're not a cop,' explained one test purchase officer. 'You've got to have a damn good reason for not taking it or things might turn nasty. I've had a few close calls myself. The best way out of it is to tell them you're going home to get high and do your missus. Get all graphic like, really lay it on thick until they're in stiches. Works like a charm.' The job was said to be an art form, a craft learnt through experience that takes a great deal of instinct, 'balls', and bravado. Role-play exercises carried out during training sessions helped with character development and working through various operational dilemmas but nothing could fully prepare an officer for the realities of going undercover.

Test purchase operations were used to target individual deal-ers, infiltrate drug distribution networks, or cast a wide net when the police were not really sure who was involved in local markets. The aim was invariably to collect evidence and identify and arrest offenders either on the spot or at a subsequent date after a warrant had been obtained. This latter enforcement plan had the advantages of protecting the identity of the operative and permitting a number of raids to be coordinated. Arrests were almost certain to result in conviction because the police witness the transactions and secure drugs and money as evi-dence. Indeed, operational activities were closely and constantly monitored by surveillance units to ensure that all of the buys were meticulously recorded and beyond refute. Take the follow-ing extract from a surveillance log as a typical example of this investigative process:

TPO deployed into Metropolis Town Centre and into Market Avenue. TPO met with IC1 male Market Avenue. This male was wearing a black Nike zip up top. TPO and the IC1 male engaged with an IC3 motor-cyclist. The motorcyclist was wearing a black crash helmet and a red and black bike jacket. He was riding a moped VRM XXXXXXX. The motorcyclist walked to Market Avenue and underneath the red awnings. He engaged with a male at that location and then returned to TPO and the IC1. He handed the IC1 male small packages. This male then departed. TPO then asked the motorcyclist if he could sort him out with the same, if he paid him £5. The motorcyclist agreed and TPO handed over £20. The motorcyclist walked to Market Avenue, again under the red awnings. He returned to TPO and supplied him with two white rocks. TPO gave the male £10 and received £5 change. The motorcyclist told TPO that he was in fact a drug dealer. The motorcyclist then departed along Market Lane towards Market Street. TPO then returned to a secure location.

The detectives under study opted for a stand-alone 'buy-bust' when they wanted a quick and easy result or did not have the resources to mount a lengthier operation. For example, on one occasion reactive CID officers used this tactic on a gang-affiliated ecstasy dealer who was overtly plying his trade in a Metropolis nightclub. The club manger had informed the police licensing officer about the individual but was reluctant to act for fear of reprisal.

Supposedly he never took his work home with him, which meant a search warrant unlikely to get us anywhere. One of our guys is a TPO, so we figured we'd take a team down to the club and see what was happening. We spotted him straight away, got ourselves into position and waited for him to get busy. He sold to our guy no questions asked. Fifty pills and a supply charge – not bad for a few hours' work. (Detective, Metropolis)

Alternatively, if the detectives had the resources, their goal was to take out a group of dealers or make buys from a dealer who was 'higher up the food chain' than the person from whom the first buys were made. An example of this escalation strategy was an operation against a bouncer who was suspected of selling ecstasy. The test purchase officer successfully made a number of small preliminary buys from the target, who then unwittingly asked if he was interested in buying in larger amounts. A week or so later, an undercover officer was introduced to the bouncer and an agreement to buy 25,000 pills was reached. The undercover officer was taken to an unknown address later that night where the arrest was made and 50,000 pills seized.

The Case for the Prosecution

Most of the detectives who participated in this study were proficient in the art and craft of constructing a case for the prosecution and conversant with courtroom procedures. After all, detective work is a case-focused enterprise and 'the case' is ultimately what justifies their investigations, reveals their skills as criminal investigators, and enables them to bring offenders to justice. 'I get a lot of satisfaction from building up a watertight case and watching them go down,' said a detective after his 'day in court'. Given that the end goal of the investigatory process was to prosecute and convict drug dealers, detectives would regularly spend more time compiling case dossiers in the station than gathering intelligence or performing operational police work on the streets.

The fact that the police are given responsibility for the general management of the prosecution file allows them to generate information and present it in particular ways and thereby exert considerable influence over the entire criminal justice process (McConville et al. 1991; Sanders et al. 2010). Although it was not popular within the culture, it was widely recognized that the ability to produce a convincing written record of events and manipulate the 'paper reality' so that it contains the elements necessary to convict any person arrested are core detective skills. This paperwork aspect of the detective function is what Dixon (1997) describes as the production of 'legalised' accounts which satisfy the requirements of a secure conviction and render police experiences into a version suitable for legal proceedings. In these accounts, the 'whole truth' is replaced by 'the facts of the case', police actions are validated, and offences are clear, exact, and unproblematic. Prosecution files were prepared, discussed, reworked, and rehearsed back stage in the squad room in order to ensure that there were no 'holes' in the case for the defence to exploit. As Hobbs (1988: 190) explains, the 'cross-examination of the police by the defence centres upon documentation prepared by the detective, seizing upon any incongruity and stressing the importance of competent paperwork'. The back stage was where narrative threads were seamlessly woven together, decisions about the non-disclosure of evidence were made, and suspects were characterized as 'violent gang members', a 'plague on the local community', or the 'main player in a highly organised criminal operation that bought and sold drugs on a commercial scale'.

In both police forces, detectives had confidence in their collective grasp of the legal and regulatory context within which they operated. Pragmatic comprehension was said to come with experience of making cases. Furthermore, over half of those who considered themselves drug law enforcement specialists had undertaken both the National Drugs Course and the Drug Expert Witness Course.[7] This level of expertise meant that detectives rarely felt the need to communicate with the Crown Prosecution Service (CPS) in the early stages of their investigations. When they did, it was because they were unfamiliar with a particular issue and needed advice on general points of law or the legal or evidential elements to be addressed for an operational matter.

I've been working drugs for two years so I've got a pretty decent knowledge of the relevant law and procedures. But I'm the first to admit that I'm no legal expert. I don't have a law degree. When I'm not sure of something I'll ask the Serg or speak to the CPS. (Detective, Smallville)

It's near enough impossible for us to stay on top of legal developments, especially new case law. That's what the CPS are there for. (Detective Sergeant, Metropolis)

For the most part, detectives tended only to engage with prosecutors towards the end of the investigatory process for guidance on a charging decision. What they wanted from these interactions was confirmation that their activities were in accordance with the law and the facts of the case were strong enough to meet the legal

---

[7] By speaking with officers who had completed the National Drug Course and reading the associated paperwork, I learned that it consisted of classroom-based learning and was designed to provide the police with the information and basic training needed to enforce drug laws. The course consisted of the following modules: the Misuse of Drugs Act 1971 and the Drugs Act 2005; drugs case law; powers of entry, search and seizure; methods of searching persons, vehicles and premises, and the planning and briefing of a drugs raid; general drugs guide and the physical and psychological aspects of drug abuse; a guide to Part II of the Regulation of Investigatory Powers Act 2000 and Part III of the Police Act 1997; a brief insight into the 'use' and 'conduct' of covert human intelligence sources; and the Proceeds of Crime Act 2002. The Drug Expert Witness Course enabled officers to become a drug expert witness and provide evidence in court on a wide range of drug-related issues: street, wholesale and bulk values of controlled drugs, including valuations, which form the basis of a financial investigation; consumption methods and details of substance abuse; interpretation of drug slang terminology; details of information contained within phones or other electronic media owned by the dealer; drugs trends, packaging and distribution methods; and the interpretation of items used in connection with drug abuse.

standards of proof for whichever offence they decided to proceed with. The police have total control over which cases enter the criminal justice system but the power to charge lies with the prosecution. Be that as it may, observations revealed that drug investigations were generally tailored with a specific charge in mind, and when discussing possible charges with prosecutors the detectives were able to hold sway over charging decisions. 'It's not that we do anything improper to get our way,' said one detective. 'We just let the evidence speak for itself.' Prosecutors routinely accepted police explanations and presumed that earlier decisions were properly made and should not be overturned. As McConville et al. (1991: 142) also found, in practice they 'almost invariably defer to the police on questions of policy and public interest on the basis that the close involvement of the police with the community makes them the best arbiters of local needs'.

Detectives saw themselves as performing the roles of both investigator and prosecutor and thus saw prosecutors as extensions of the detective function and representatives of themselves. Needless to say, when the detectives came across a sympathetic ally, a prosecutor who shared police values, working rules, and conviction-oriented goals and uncritically accepted their authority and legitimacy, they welcomed them as an honorary team member and endeavoured to maintain a good working relationship. Relationships between detectives and prosecutors were largely harmonious. Despite their different roles and responsibilities in the criminal justice process, they were normally 'singing from the same hymn sheet'. That being said, differences in opinion, conflicts of interest, and inconsistent evidentiary requirements did result in occasional tensions and feelings of resentment.

Given that operational success was often measured in terms of sentence outcomes, detectives were inclined to push for the charge that would lead to the most years in prison. Prosecutors, on the other hand, were more likely to opt for the charge that was most likely to win them the case. Discrepancies between what detectives considered 'case-worthy' evidence and what prosecutors considered 'court-worthy' caused disagreements about what story to tell the judge. Only once during fieldwork did a prosecutor decide to drop a case on the grounds of insufficient evidence. The Metropolis firearms team had recovered an ounce of crack following a raid on the address of a suspected drug dealer and were pushing for a possession charge. However, it had been discovered buried in a shared garden and they were unable to prove that the suspect had both knowledge and control of the drugs. Only once did a prosecutor consider evidence to be inadmissible. The Smallville drug squad were relying on evidence contained on a mobile phone handset to support a charge of possession with intent to supply but had failed to obtain the authorization to physically examine the phone or view the information beforehand. The detectives wanted to 'chance it' but the prosecutor refused. On other occasions when the evidence was judged to be lacking, prosecutors would try to convince the detectives to go for a lesser charge in order to enhance the prospect of a guilty plea or verdict. Suspected dealers were routinely charged with possession when there was a lack of relevant circumstantial evidence to prove possession with intent to supply. This was seen as 'letting them off lightly' and depriving the detectives of results. They had a strong stake in the outcome of their cases and did not like to settle for compromises when they were certain of a suspect's guilt. For supply charges, some prosecutors required proof of two transactions, whereas others would only proceed with a case if there was evidence of three transactions and corroborating witness statements. A common belief was that drug law enforcement would be more effective if the standard of proof was 'the balance of probabilities' rather than 'beyond reasonable doubt'.

To say that detectives did not exactly see eye to eye with defence solicitors is something of an understatement. In the police world-view, the defence are on the side of criminals, they are immoral, irresponsible, and inherently antithetical to the pursuit of justice. They are also a threat to the police in that they have the power to challenge their authority and unmask their activities (Holdaway 1983; McConville et al. 1991).

They're just doing their job. I get that. Everyone has a right to a fair trial and what have you. But sometimes they try and make out like we're the bad guys. They'll be all like "the police did this, that and the other wrong". Then they'll lay it on thick with the mitigating circumstances and argue for some mickey mouse sentence. (Detective, Smallville)

Upon entering the courtroom, the case that the detectives had painstakingly constructed was laid bare and out of their hands. They expected the legal system to support them in their decisions but knew that there were no guarantees. When the judge or jury delivered a guilty verdict and handed down a custodial sentence, it was viewed as a triumph for law and order and an affirmation of a job well done. The Smallville drug squad took tremendous pride in securing sentences totalling more than 145 years against dealers between April 2008 and March 2009, covered the walls of their office with newspaper clipping of their best busts and chalked up prison terms on their operations board. When they failed to convict, however, or the sentencing was inappropriately lenient, the detectives felt cheated and downtrodden. Unsuccessful cases served to highlight that the dice are 'loaded in favour of the criminal fraternity' (Daly and Sampson 2013: 145).

Conclusion

This chapter has explored the ways in which the key aspects of drug investigations were socially organized, the everyday realities of how detectives enforced the law, produced results, resolved uncertainties, negotiated dilemmas, and constructed cases within legal and organizational frameworks. Moreover, it has looked into some outcomes of current mechanisms designed to regulate investigative practice and covert policing in particular.

After a case became operational, detectives were concerned with little else other than figuring out how best to penetrate the drug world and gather sufficient evidence to implicate their targets in specific offences for which they could be prosecuted. Anyone who made it onto their hit list was guilty until proven guilty. They were acting out their sense of what is good and proper police work, endeavouring to uphold the law, rid the streets of serious criminals, disrupt drug distribution networks, and display control over the drug problem. They were acting with a great deal of discretion, making decisions about how to work the case, when to intervene, and what to include in the written record. When things went according to plan, the detectives had all the evidence they needed to secure a conviction at the point of arrest. Interviews were somewhat superfluous, a means of gathering more information and fleshing out the case dossier that might yield the added bonus of a confession. The challenge was getting the timing right under conditions of uncertainty, striking when a dealer was in possession of a substantial quantity of drugs, or being present when they were conducting transactions. Much of their time was spent playing the waiting game, as they were reluctant to pounce unless convinced of a positive outcome. Another challenge was maintaining the invisibilities of policing up until the point when the watchers came out of the shadows and in a short, sharp burst of highly visible power, turned into pursuers.

Drug law enforcement is habitually described as the epitome of the proactive approach to detective work in the sense that investigations are initiated from within police organizations in response to intelligence. Whilst this remains an accurate description of the initiation of drug detective work, the findings presented here show that the distinction between reactive and proactive should not be treated as a rigid dichotomy. Detectives often acted in a reactive manner and responded to external triggers. Raids, for example, provided them with a 'quick, cheap, and easy' method of taking out their targets and racking up arrests and seizures. Many of the warrants executed during fieldwork were nothing more than an immediate response to a 'tip off', ad hoc interventions that involved very little intelligence analysis or strategic planning. Detectives were frequently working with only a partial picture of their targets and had no clear understanding of how the market operated or the links in the supply chain. When conducting covert operations, therefore, they were reliant on luck and persistence, spent a large amount of their time on speculative work, searching for signs of drug dealing activity, establishing patterns based on suspicion and responding to unexpected and unpredictable situations. They were reacting to incidents and followed lines of inquiry as and when they emerged from the drug world. Their perceptions of the environment and situational rationality shaped their enforcement practices. Drug law enforcement also lends itself to strategically driven proactive policing interventions, operations which incorporate aspects of community policing and partnership engagement in order to deliver diverse and multi-pronged approaches to tackling drug problems. The detectives were partially receptive to such strategies, especially when dealing with entrenched drug markets, but tended to view them as optional operational 'bolt-ons' that were designed to further their crime control agenda. Taking a holistic approach to the policing of drugs remained an exception to the norm.

Drug investigations incorporate a range of investigative techniques which infringe upon the private life of people considered suspect and generate a profound sense of moral ambiguity. There is, then, a need to balance public security with the protection of civil liberties and the integrity of the criminal justice system. To this end, search warrants require prior authorization, and the legal framework established by RIPA is designed to protect human rights and prevent officers from overstepping the boundaries of professionalism and fairness. Detectives were inclined to regard authorization processes as bureaucratically onerous and an impediment to their work. Yet, despite their criticisms, observations revealed that they prided themselves on knowing the law and took the administrative part of making cases very seriously. The majority had undertaken training courses and regularly debated the best way to carry out investigations within legal limitations. Those officers who botched the paperwork were rebuked by their supervisors and disparaged by their peers for being unprofessional, compromising the reputation of the team, and risking a stay in proceedings or the exclusion of evidence from trial. The findings presented in this chapter also reveal that requests for authorization were seldom rejected. Magistrates tended to 'rubber stamp' warrant applications and rarely asked probing questions or contested what officers said under oath. With regard to surveillance, when authorizing officers identified problems with applications they would typically provide the officer seeking the authorization with feedback and allow them to make revisions and then resubmit. This virtual police self-certification is a classic crime control provision. Whilst somewhat time-consuming, the fact that authorization was relatively easy to obtain actually facilitated drug detective work because it rendered their activities legitimate and less open to challenge.

9

Detecting Change and the Future of Drug Law Enforcement

It's been almost four years since I left the field. Not that you ever truly leave. If you do research right it sticks; it becomes part of who you are. Being 'there' becomes close to home. And the words on the page are a permanent reminder. Time flies, writing is slow, and the song remains the same.

Joe hadn't aged a day since we last met. 'You look older,' he said. Thanks. I feel it. Being back in Metropolis brought back some fond memories. Research may well be business, but it can also be profoundly personal. I was here to catch up with friends and return a few favours. Researchers tend to rack up a lot of debt and I've got many more IOUs to work off.

The detectives who had read my work were generally of the opinion that 'it tells it like it is'. For an ethnographer, now that's a mighty fine compliment. Sure, there were various suggestions for improvement and interpretations about which we agreed to disagree, but my nerves had been somewhat settled. What was even more reassuring was their confirmation that the account was as true today as it was then. The membership of what was now the 'gang squad' had changed almost beyond recognition, there had been some restructuring at the organizational level, and senior management were floating some new ideas about their 'vision' for policing, but the detectives were still taking care of business as usual. 'Same shit, different day.' As might have been expected, what became very apparent from the conversation was that the government and their public sector cuts were the biggest problem facing the police at present. 'If things keep going the way they are we're not going to have the resources to police drugs like we're supposed to.' So, I thought, maybe it's time to rewrite the rules of the drug game?

(Fieldnotes, Metropolis)

Far from being static, the field of policing is in a constant state of change, not least because of the need to react to the often conflicting and arguably insatiable demands and expectations that have come to be attached to the police service (Loader and Mulcahy 2003; Mawby 1999). Reiner (1992) describes the police as like a 'litmus-paper' reflecting the unfolding dynamics of society. They are, in other words, pushed and pulled by the shifting social, economic, and political tides with and against which we all swim. This monograph has critically examined some of the most pertinent legislative initiatives, organizational reforms, and shifts in thinking about the values, objectives, and norms of policing that have occurred over recent decades, which, between them, have contributed to some significant changes in the ways that detectives are trained and investigations are controlled and carried out. In particular, it has explored how these changes have impacted on the work of detectives who specialize in investigating drug markets and making cases against suspected drug dealers. What is clear from this exploration is that the implementation of various reform agendas and patterns of change in the wider policing landscape have had a dramatic effect on the nature of drug investigations, the role of police detectives, and their occupational mandate. What is also clear is that, whilst there have been important breaks with the past, the fundamentals of the detective role remain unchanged and 'the manifest continuities with older patterns should not be overlooked' (Loftus 2009: 188).

In this final chapter, I want to pull together some key findings in order to consider the extent to which detective practices were affected by the formal structural context of policing and explain why some behaviours and aspects of their culture were susceptible to change whereas others proved resistant and enduring. The discussion then moves on to make some recommendations for potentially workable alternatives to traditional enforcement strategies that are designed to stimulate further research and reconfigure the evolution of the policing of drugs. By applying regulatory theory to drug detective work, it is argued that one way forward is for the police to use their powers to beneficially shape drug markets according to the standards and purposes of harm reduction.

Detecting Change

Before progressing any further with the discussion, it is worth reminding ourselves of what the existing literature tells us about police reform and cultural change. Importantly, organizational studies suggest that change cannot be forced but will happen when an organization is ready, either because of an external crisis or internal impetus and imperatives (Schein 2004). Reforms are implemented in large part by the people to whom they are addressed. More often than not, therefore, unless police reformers enlist the support of the lower ranks, their efforts will not succeed in fundamentally changing policing on the frontline. Police officers must believe there is a need to change, be convinced that the proposed policies of reform are both necessary and appropriate, and be properly motivated and equipped to introduce and maintain support for the changes in their everyday activities. The question of how to do this begins with chief officers understanding the nature of the occupational cultures in their organization and the ways in which they can inhibit or facilitate change. Legislators and policymakers can define new working models that will gradually alter values, beliefs, and basic assumptions if they are of practical benefit and provide meaning to the social experience of police officers. As a general rule, however, this will occur only if new ways of working are considered to work better than existing practices and make more sense than traditional understandings. Police studies have repeatedly shown that reform agendas have failed to override the conservative culture of the police when they conflict with accepted wisdoms. Changes to the status quo are resisted or adopted superficially when they challenge existing worldviews, require officers to break from their established routines, and do not accord with their intuitive common sense (Chan 1997; Loftus 2009; Skogan 2008).

Drug detective work

What little empirical research has been undertaken on the everyday realities of detective work has tended to depict it as something of a cultural craft. From this perspective, the craft of the detective is learnt predominantly through on-the-job experience and characterized by a specific set of investigative skills and unwritten understandings about the rules of the game (Collison 1995; Ericson 1981; Hobbs 1988; Jackall 2005; Maguire and Norris 1992; Manning 2004; Simon 1991; Skolnick 2011). The detective role enables officers to operate with a significant degree of autonomy and freedom from organizational constraint. Generally speaking, their activities are difficult to control on account of the low visibility of plain-clothes work, the individualistic nature of casework, and the entrenched belief that supervision is principally based on trust. Given the victimless nature of drug offences, drug detective work has been portrayed as a particularly discretionary form of policing, whereby the conduct of drug investigations is largely dependent on the decisions, resources, and craftsmanship of the investigating officers (Collison 1995; Manning 2004; Skolnick 2011). Without exception, detective work is shown to be a case-focused enterprise, in that efforts are organized and framed by the current caseload and performance is measured on the basis of clearance rates. Case knowledge, valuable informants, and intelligence are regarded as personal resources, a kind of property that is not easily shared with others. The ability to possess and retain knowledge unknown by others represents the supreme affirmation of the detective craft. This cultural trait contributes to the secretive, suspicious, and somewhat uncooperative nature of their working environment. Another commonly identified feature of detective culture is their willingness to work the system, bypass formal supervisory mechanisms, and bend or break rules that get in the way of efficient criminal investigations and desirable outcomes. Previous generations routinely constructed cases against suspect populations, did not pursue all reasonable lines of inquiry, overlooked evidence that contradicted police versions of events, and applied techniques that violated the rights of citizens (Maguire 2008; McConville et al. 1991; Sanders et al. 2010; Waddington 1999a). Whilst not impervious to change, Skogan (2008) notes that detectives are often able to avoid getting involved in efforts to innovate policing that require them to change their traditional ways and means.

The empirical studies referred to above relate to past policing contexts and police organizations that no longer exist in exactly the same form or function in exactly the same way. Indeed, the drug detectives of Metropolis and Smallville worked in markedly different environments, which had been changed by, amongst other things, legislative reforms and attempts to improve the delivery of policing through the adoption of new bureaucratic structures, management techniques, and accountability mechanisms.

The rise of intelligence-led policing and the implementation of the NIM altered the relationship between detectives and the organizational frameworks within which their formative intelligence and investigative practices were constructed and performed. Intelligence became an organizational resource. Much of the autonomy detectives previously had to develop information into actionable intelligence and set operational targets was eroded by the centrality of intelligence units to the police intelligence function. Furthermore, police managers were, in varying degrees, able to systematically preside over key decision-making processes, prioritize crime and disorder problems, and allocate resources accordingly for both strategic and tactical purposes. Some officers were resolutely committed to the NIM ideal and believed that it facilitated smarter policing and the targeting of resources where they could be expected to yield the best results. In Metropolis, for example, the leadership within the firearms squad was central to garnering and sustaining this commitment. Others, especially in Smallville, resented the erosion of their autonomy by the managerialist agenda and the somewhat tedious micromanagement of the NIM business process. Yet, despite widespread feelings of resentment, such officers said they complied with procedure because they were 'professionals' and did not want their reputations to be compromised. This understanding of professionalism is perhaps best viewed as a cultural response to the reforms, a way of adapting to accommodate new structures, experiences, and ideologies, in the sense that it allowed detectives to reconfigure their practices without substantially departing from their old dispositions.

That being said, policies are rarely, if ever, directly or straightforwardly implemented as their architects anticipate. Indeed, reform efforts are often renegotiated or transformed to reflect 'real world' demands as they are constituted in interactions in practice on the ground. Senior officers did not appear to be wholeheartedly committed to implementing the model to the letter. They took a 'NIM-lite approach', encouraged the rank-and-file to comply with the rules whilst exercising discretion, and accepted that certain 'personalities' would never report all of the information in their possession or listen to the recommendations of civilian analysts and use analytical products to proactively plan their operations. There were a range of accepted justifications for not following policy and procedure, and circumstances in which detectives could work the system or compliance was deemed situationally inappropriate to the exigencies of criminal investigation. The ability to generate intelligence and make cases remained central to the craft of the effective detective and their sense of elitism and territorial instincts made them much more inclined to trust, prioritize, and act upon intelligence that was under their control. Furthermore, despite being essential to the organizational effectiveness of the NIM business process, detectives rarely collaborated with analysts on knowledge production or integrated analysis into their operational endeavours. Analytical products did not sit well with traditional understandings of knowledge as being something that is gained through experience and officers would usually discount intelligence concerned with enhancing their understanding of crime and disorder issues as having little relevance to their everyday work.

In terms of investigative techniques, the legal framework established by RIPA sets out the conditions under which covert methods are justifiable under human rights law and aims to prevent officers from overstepping the boundaries of professionalism and fairness. Perhaps the most significant change brought in by the new regime is that informers have been divorced from frontline detectives and are now dealt with exclusively by specially trained handlers and controllers working in dedicated source units. This change should not be underestimated as traditionally the ability to identify, cultivate, and handle informers was considered a requisite of an effective detective and 'very much the "bread and butter" of drug policing' (Dorn et al. 1992: 135). Moreover, before the commencement of directed or intrusive surveillance, investigating officers are now statutorily required to obtain written authorization from an appropriate senior ranking officer. Only conduct specified in the authority is lawful and the authorizing officer must be satisfied that the proposed activities are necessary in the circumstances and proportionate to the intended outcomes. Detectives in both police forces prided themselves on knowing the law and took the administrative part of making cases very seriously. They also agreed that the current system is much more accountable and corrupt practices have diminished as a result. As Loftus et al. (2015: 15) found in their ethnographic study of covert policing, the logics, remit, and method of covert work foster the development of a distinctly 'erudite' working culture that 'operates in isolation from what might be regarded as the clichéd cultural expressions that have long been the focus of much scholarship'.

However, on the whole the changes had been poorly received by detectives engaged in proactive investigative work and were thought to have had a negative effect on operational efficiency. From the point of view of the drug detectives, the fact that they were no longer able to directly handle their own informers had stifled the craft of drug law enforcement and detrimentally affected their ability to effectively police drug markets. In response to the strains of the job, they had developed a number of informal practices to circumvent the constraints of their regulatory controls. An accepted practice was for detectives to extract as much information as possible from potential sources on a one-off basis before notifying the source unit. They still made use of unregistered sources, pushed the boundaries of what officially constituted tasking, and gathered intelligence vicariously through handlers by getting them to ask informers questions on their behalf. Detectives were inclined to regard the surveillance authorization process as bureaucratically onerous and an impediment to their work. Yet, despite their criticisms, requests were seldom rejected. The main reasons for this remarkable success rate were that the paperwork was completed to a satisfactory standard and the proposed targets and covert methods of investigation met the statutory criteria. Additionally, when authorizing officers identified problems with applications they would typically provide the officer seeking the authorization with feedback and allow them to make revisions and then resubmit. Whilst somewhat time-consuming, the fact that authorization was relatively easy to obtain actually facilitated drug detective work because it rendered their activities legitimate and less open to challenge. Once they had obtained authorization, detectives were more or less free to act out their sense of what is good and proper police work with a great deal of discretion, making decisions about how to work the case, when to intervene, and what to include in the written record.

In effect, the detectives under study acted within their legal and organizational parameters because it had become impossible for them to make cases outside them. Reforms had altered practice by limiting decision-making autonomy through a concerted top-down programme of statutory regulation and the imposition of new organizational policies and procedures. These changes in the 'field', Chan (1997) argues, the formal rules governing policing, inevitably alter the way the game is played, since 'habitus', the informal norms, values, and beliefs of police officers, interacts with the field. Be that as it may, reform initiatives might be deemed successful by virtue of them bringing about changes in formal practice and explicit philosophy, but unless they can alter the bedrock of police culture meaningful change will not occur. Whilst detectives accepted the need to play by, or at least pay lip service to, the rules, they were above all viewed as how policing *must* be done rather than how it *should* be done. Consequently, when the rules were not enforced, were seen as unenforceable, or allowed for the exercise of discretion, the detectives—especially the older generation— expressed themselves and acted in ways that resonated with the traditional themes of their occupational culture. They strove for freedom from organizational constraint, disliked bureaucracy, engaged in informal working practices, believed that strict adherence to the rules had a negative impact on operational efficiency, and exhibited strong territoriality towards *their* informers, intelligence, and cases. In short, the NIM business process and the framework established by RIPA had been relatively successful in changing the formal practices, processes, and procedures of criminal investigation without substantially changing the ingrained attitudes and behaviours of detective culture.

The formal and informal aspects of the police were interconnected, overlapped, and were at times indistinguishable from one another. Informality was a deliberate choice for the detectives, a necessity for doing police work in ways that were seen as practical, just, and flexibly responsive to the challenges and changing contexts in which they operated. It also enabled them to evade, resist, and exploit the governmental structures of the state and the police organization. Since informal decisions and behaviours were to some extent designed to circumvent the constraints and consequences of formality, they proved to be highly resilient and adaptable to regulatory mechanisms. The informal aspects of policing can equally be viewed as a sign of the incapacity, or perhaps the lack of will, of politicians, policymakers, and police management to control everything officers do in the station and on the streets.

Drug law enforcement

The 'war on drugs' has dominated conceptions of drug control for decades and is central to any discussion on the policing of the drug problem. Broadly speaking, the drug war is a demonizing rhetorical strategy in the social campaign against certain people who use or sell those psychoactive substances deemed to be 'dangerous' that is designed to elicit support for repressive drug prohibition policies that emphasize enforcement and punishment. Drug law enforcement has traditionally focused on reducing the size of illegal drug markets by seeking to eradicate or significantly reduce the production, supply, and use of drugs through arrests and seizures. Yet, if the purpose of prohibition is to stifle the illegal drug business and ultimately create a 'drug free society', most people would concede that it has not only failed but cannot succeed. Despite the vast amount of public resources that have been spent on enforcement to date, it has neither eliminated the market nor had any significant and sustainable impact on supply or demand (Mazerolle et al. 2007; McSweeney et al. 2008). Another strong criticism of the drug war is that it actually causes a range of significant harms in its own right. Indeed, the damaging impact on aspects of crime, security, civil liberties, human rights, public health, and social inequality has been extensively documented (Rolles et al. 2012). Against this backdrop, the concept of 'harm reduction' has moved to the foreground of drug control and some policing agencies appear to be choosing to rethink and redevelop their enforcement strategies and tactics to focus on managing drug markets in a way that minimizes the various associated harms (Caulkins and Reuter 2009; Felbab-Brown 2013; Stevens 2013; UKDPC 2009).

Despite the complicated, contested, and counterproductive realties of drug control policy and practice, the detectives of Metropolis and Smallville had a remarkably clear understanding of their role in the global prohibition regime. Above all else, they saw themselves as elite crime fighters and considered the detection, arrest, and successful conviction of those involved in the drug business to be the core justification for the policing of drugs. This was the task to which the detectives had been assigned by the organization, the means through which they made a difference, and helped 'keep the lid on' the local drug problem. This long-standing war-like mentality is what the police knew and all many of them understood. It has provided them with a job, a sense of mission, and a justification for making use of and augmenting some of their most powerful and invasive crime control tools and tactics. Detectives accepted the need for a multifaceted approach to drug control, appreciated that enforcement alone was never a silver bullet, and advocated the benefits of partnership initiatives in tackling both supply and demand, but for them it was essentially about disrupting markets by making cases against suspected drug dealers. Generally speaking, they viewed community policing and multi-agency partnerships as 'soft' policing activities and low priorities in the drug control agenda of the police because they departed from 'proper' images of police work. Save for diverting drug-using offenders into treatment, a common feeling amongst the police officers under study was that demand reduction has 'nothing to do with policing'.

Whilst detectives rarely questioned the authority of the law, believed they were making a positive difference, and remained motivated by operational successes on a case-by-case basis, their efforts were accompanied by a sense of futility and doubt. Many officers had a cynical outlook, they were defeatist, pessimistic about the future of policing drugs, and disheartened by their failure to stop things getting worse. However, even though there was widespread acknowledgement that the current system is not exactly working as intended, the majority of police officers remained faithful supporters of the status quo and resistant to change. Prohibition was seen as the only morally legitimate and feasible policy option. The more authoritarian and closed-minded officers were of the opinion that the drug problems of today are the result of the failure to enforce fully and properly the external ordering imposed by the criminal law. Arguments for reform, such as decriminalization or legal regulation, were generally viewed with scepticism or given zero weight when they appeared irrelevant or repugnant. The detectives were particularly dismissive of claims that enforcement was a waste of resources and actually exacerbated drug problems. On the other hand, a significant minority sat at the opposite end of the drug policy spectrum, said they would welcome fundamental change, and were well aware of the unintended consequences of prohibition. Some of these officers believed that the criminalization of recreational users was overly punitive, that contemptuous 'othering' was inhumane, stigmatizing, and counterproductive, and that the disproportionate use of stop and search on young people of black and other minority ethnic origins had severely damaged police legitimacy and police–community relations. Then there were the agnostics, those who were open to change but remained on the fence as they were unaware of the evidence or uncertain about the practical application and likely outcomes of alternative policy options.

Although an explicit priority in strategy documents and official mission statements, during fieldwork it was found that drug law enforcement had been unofficially deprioritized and was regularly downplayed when there were deemed to be more serious and pressing issues to deal with. The police were essentially attempting to 'manage' the market by keeping it from growing or causing too many problems locally (Dorn and Lee 1999; Parker 2006). Furthermore, police managers frequently asserted that they struggled to justify using their limited resources to rigorously enforce drug laws when there were 'statistically significant' victims of crime in need of police services. Public sector budget cuts and austerity measures have exacerbated this challenge and drug-related policing expenditure is expected to fare worse than other police activities (UKDPC 2011). The detectives readily acknowledged that enforcement is a marginal activity of limited capacity and dwindling resources. They were working within their limits to manage the drug trade and reduce the collateral damage. For the most part therefore, proactive investigations targeted the drugs, dealers, and marketplaces that emerged from the police intelligence picture as being the most harmful in terms of crime and disorder. Focused deterrence strategies and selective targeting of law enforcement enable the police to 'do more with less' and have produced impressive results in reducing the harms associated with drug markets (Braga and Weisburd 2012; Felbab-Brown 2013; Mazerolle et al. 2007; Stevens 2013; UKDPC 2009).

The idea of applying harm reduction principles to drug law enforcement emerged during the fieldwork period and remains a relatively new movement that is gathering momentum but still exists almost entirely in academic discourse and occasional dialogue between drug researchers, policymakers, and practitioners. It was all but unheard of in the police organizations under study. Albeit down to economics rather than ethics, the fact that the principal role of proactive drug investigations was to target the most harmful elements of the drug trade might be taken to indicate that there was some degree of support for rethinking and redeveloping enforcement strategies and tactics to focus on managing drug markets in a way that minimizes the various associated harms. Then again, it could equally be perceived as business as usual, in the sense that detectives have always responded to the more serious crimes and made cases against the most serious and organized criminals. The views expressed by the majority were certainly not indicative of an all-embracing harm reduction philosophy.

On the surface, 'harm reduction' was central to national drug policies, had been incorporated into police drug strategy documents, and was regularly used as a justification for policing drugs in management meetings, operational planning, and paperwork. There was, however, a lack of clarity over the definition of harm and little discussion about what a harm reduction approach to policing drug markets actually involved or how success might be measured. As Skogan (2008: 26) makes clear, abstract concepts 'must be turned into lists of practical, day-to-day activities and then enshrined in enforceable orders to which officers in the field can fairly be held accountable'. Moreover, there had been no change in what Sackmann (1991) calls 'axiomatic knowledge', which represents the fundamental assumptions about 'why things are done the way they are' in the organization. The theory and practice of harm reduction had not been clearly explained or effectively disseminated through professional practice publications or training sessions. For the most part, 'harm' reduction was thought of as being synonymous with 'crime' or 'supply' reduction, or in terms of public health initiatives that focus on harms associated with drug use. The detectives did not take a broad approach to reducing the entire suite of harms generated by drug markets and drug control efforts or think beyond blanket prohibition and traditional enforcement interventions. It was generally assumed that arrests for drug offences and drug seizures would automatically have a positive impact on individuals and communities. These were the ultimate measures of good drug detective work in an organization focused on reducing crime and bringing offenders to justice. This much was common sense and there was no reason compelling enough for them to break from their established routines. Police reform at a cultural level is difficult to achieve without structural change to the police environment (Chan 1997).

Notwithstanding the apparent failure and unintended consequences of the war on drugs, at present there are no external pressures in the drug policy arena or internal forces that are powerful enough to trigger the seismic shift that seems to be needed to significantly reform the role of the police in the policing of drugs. Calls for change are loud and persuasive but have a tendency to fall on deaf ears. Being a heavily politicized policy area, evidence is all too often jettisoned in favour of an overriding need to appear 'tough on drugs' and 'send the right message' (MacGregor 2011, 2013; Monaghan 2011; Stevens 2011). If there is any hope of walking further down the path towards a more effective and just approach to drug law enforcement, the wider policing landscape must be ripe for organizational change to occur. Police forces around the world are beginning to break from the drug war mentality and experiment with innovative strategies and tactics that are yielding positive results. Some officers would welcome fundamental change and others are open to persuasion and debate. As MacGregor (2011: 41) points out, research which 'challenges an accepted consensus tends to have less immediate impact on policy *per se* but over time it can be seen to help to develop alternative perspectives and, in alliance with other forces, may lead then to a further policy shift when a "window of opportunity" arises'. It pays to be optimistic. The day will come when the evidence can no longer be ignored and forces for change will tip the balance and bring out transformation.

Regulating the Drug Trade

Once it is accepted that suppression of the illegal drug business is an impossible mandate the task of policing inevitably becomes its regulation (Curtis and Wendel 2007; Dorn and South 1990; Maher and Dixon 1999; Murji 1998). With this in mind, when thinking about the ways in which the police could, or should, intervene in drug market activity, policing is best conceived as largely analogous to social and economic regulation (Gill 2000, 2002). Rather than defining regulation in a narrow sense, as the actions of the state to govern through laws, systematic monitoring, and the enforcement of sanctions for their breach, it is defined here as all attempts to steer the course of events according to explicit standards or purposes with the intention of producing specific outcomes (Black 2002; Braithwaite 2008). Taking a broad approach to drugs as a regulation problem heightens our awareness and understanding of the forms and functions of regulation in diverse fields. Moreover, Seddon (2010: 100–21) argues that it also highlights the need to look 'beyond the state', decentring it both in our analyses and in our prescriptions for action, and 'beyond the law', as managing the course of events requires a much wider range of tools than just legal instruments. In what follows, drug law enforcement is considered through the lens of regulation in order to broaden the field and build upon the ideas of those who have applied regulatory theory to drug control policy and practice. Much can be learned from regulatory scholarship that will help us rethink the policing of drugs and develop more effective, compassionate, and creative responses to drug markets and their associated harms (Ritter 2010; Rolles 2009; Seddon 2010, 2013).

Instead of falling back on the myriad well-founded criticisms of prohibition and advocating reform through the decriminalization or legal regulation of drugs, the recommendations for change made below are relatively modest by comparison and do not require a radical overhaul of the current drug control system. Besides, providing a 'blueprint' for regulation is outside the scope of this study and has already been superbly undertaken by others elsewhere (Rolles 2009; Rolles and Murkin 2013). Whilst I am a vehement supporter of drug policy reform, the aim here is simply to ever so slightly loosen the straitjacket of the law and propose some potentially workable alternatives to traditional enforcement strategies that build on current trends in practice and might reconfigure the evolution of the policing of drugs. Right-minded people must continue the campaign to change the terms of the drug policy debate and mobilize support for an end to the failed war on drugs (Nadelmann 2004; Rolles et al. 2015). However, given that there is no immediate prospect of liberalization in the UK, the next best solution for the foreseeable future is to find ways of making prohibition work better through smarter, more pragmatic enforcement interventions and criminal justice policies (MacCoun and Reuter 2011; Shiner 2006; UKDPC 2009, 2012). Government ministers and policymakers are overwhelmingly obtuse and politically stunted when it comes to the subject of drugs, repeatedly ignore, misunderstand, or misuse the evidence base, and continue to collude in the fiction that blanket prohibition is working (MacGregor 2013; Nutt 2012; Stevens 2011). The police, on the other hand, despite their flaws, generally recognize that blanket prohibition cannot be enforced, especially 'zero tolerance' approaches against low-level offenders; routinely exercise discretion when translating policy from its written form into action; and are increasingly making decisions on the basis of 'what works' in policing and crime reduction. Thus, although it is regrettable that prohibition is here to stay, there are opportunities to change the ways in which it is enacted on the frontline.

By applying regulatory theory to drug detective work, I would argue that one way forward is for the police to use their powers, or not, to beneficially shape drug markets according to the standards and purposes of harm reduction (Caulkins and Reuter 2009; Felbab-Brown 2013; Stevens 2013; UKDPC 2009). A key argument of this book is that much of what drug detectives do in terms of the intelligence-led policing of drugs can be conceived as attempts to shape the nature and extent of the drug trade by steering the course of events through enforcement interventions. In other words, drug detectives are already performing a regulatory function, and there is no essential difference between the investigation of illegal drug markets and the regulation of legal markets. However, albeit a step in the right direction, there is still a long way to go down the path of applying harm reduction principles to the investigation of drug offences and offenders. The cornerstone of the proposition outlined here is that the law is a resource that can be enforced as a means of promoting order and reducing harms to members of the public rather than a rule that must be mechanistically followed as an end in itself. Drug laws should only be enforced when drug offenders become 'out of order' and beyond less formal mechanisms of control. Such an approach to enforcement might be criticized for flying in the face of the rule of law, 'sending the wrong message', and being 'soft on drugs', but if one works on the assumption that the drug trade is a constant and policing is a marginal activity of limited capacity and dwindling resources, there are few alternatives if drug policy remains situated within a criminal law framework. One could also argue that, if the wider purpose of drug laws is harm reduction, the police, by exercising enforcement discretion in order to reduce harm, are acting in the spirit of the law. Another rebuttal to the critics is that harm reduction is being 'smart' not 'soft' on drugs and that prohibition 'has become discredited to such an extent that any usefulness in setting a moral position has in many situations become largely ineffectual' (UKDPC 2012: 119).

Under the prohibition regime it is of course not possible to regulate drug markets using conventional economic mechanisms like taxation and trading standards, so what I am proposing here is an approach based on the principles of 'responsive regulation' (Ayres and Braithwaite 1992; Braithwaite 2002, 2008; Seddon 2010). For Braithwaite (2008: 88), the basic rationale of responsive regulation 'is that regulators should be responsive to the conduct of those they seek to regulate in deciding whether a more or less interventionist response is needed'. At the heart of this approach lies the 'regulatory pyramid', which provides a useful and dynamic model for determining when to punish and when to persuade. The idea is that, even with the most serious offences, any response should begin with dialogue at the base of the pyramid, and only when these efforts fail or are deemed inappropriate should the regulators progress to the next, more punitive, level. This is not how drug investigations work in practice. Once the intelligence reports are in and the operational target is set, the primary objective of detectives is to start and finish at the apex of the pyramid, with arresting, charging and ultimately prosecuting drug dealers being their first and last resort. They have yet to embrace the logic that to beneficially shape drug markets and reduce the associated harms it is not always necessary to punish offenders or reduce the quantity of drugs being sold or used. Instead, it might actually be possible for them to persuade offenders to cease their illegal activities, or at least alter their business practices, by using the law as leverage but without resorting to criminal sanctions. Drug markets are markets much like any other and can therefore be manipulated through various strategies of regulation.

To bring drug investigations more into line with the principles of harm reduction and responsive regulation the following changes could be made. These recommendations for change are intended to stimulate debate, to highlight ways to frame and reframe the policing of drugs, rather than end it altogether through the provision of a 'how to' guide for 'the solution'.

Rather than tasking detectives to execute warrants or covertly investigate suspected drug dealers with the intention of gathering evidence for their prosecution, wherever possible and appropriate, the first step of any intervention should always be restorative justice (Braithwaite 2002). A restorative approach to justice views crime as an act against another person and the community, not simply an act against the state, shifts the focus away from punishing the offender, and aims to bring all those involved together to consider what has happened, what effects it has had, and what can be done to repair the harm and prevent recurrence (Johnstone 2011; Zehr and Mika 1998). Restorative justice processes take various forms, including family group conferences, healing and sentencing circles, victim and offender mediation, victim awareness courses, citizens' panels and community boards. Offenders should enter the process voluntarily, accept responsibility for their actions, and be sufficiently motivated to change. Engaging the community through structured, deliberative processes could help to develop a stronger understanding of the problems caused by drug markets and the options available to alleviate them. Furthermore, discovering what should be done about a particular injustice through deliberation in a supportive context is generally seen as more legitimate and procedurally fair than retributive punishment and can build normative commitment to making amends and complying with the law or social norms (Braithwaite 1989; Tyler 1990, 2006).

The victimless nature of drug offences creates conceptual and practical issues for restorative justice resolutions in the sense that they are inappropriate for offences that create no victim or source of injustice. Who, if not the state, does the drug offender violate? Who, in other words, should participate in the restorative justice process? To explore these issues further it is necessary to differentiate between supply and possession for personal use. Although it is difficult to quantify with existing data, 'it is likely that many if not most drug users *never* do wrongful harm to others as a result of their using careers—bearing in mind that the majority of these careers are limited in duration and intensity' (MacCoun and Reuter 2001: 61). In consequence, unless they are to be held responsible for the externalities of their behaviour using degrees of separation logic, such offenders are not suitable candidates for restorative justice. Dependent drug users, however, typically commit crimes that have a victim and cause genuine harms to family, friends, and the communities in which they live, and so Braithwaite (2001) and Shiner (2006) argue that restorative justice provides a potentially fruitful remedy for addressing their problematic behaviour and supporting rehabilitation and recovery. Sidestepping philosophical questions of whether it is right or wrong to punish drug use per se, Braithwaite (2001: 229) submits that if drug use 'is part of the story of injustice, part of what it is important to understand to come to terms with the injustice, then both the substance abuse and the injustice it causes are likely to be among the things participants will wish to see healed in the restorative process'. Furthermore, by blurring the boundaries and viewing drug users themselves as victims, he also points out that another thing they might want to see healed is hurt and injustice arising from the punishment and stigmatization of drug use. 'Citizens are given a space where they can contest laws they believe to be unjust or laws that might be just in some abstract sense but unjust in the practice of their enforcement in a particular context' (p230).

Many drug dealers are 'relatively ordinary individuals, with ordinary thoughts, feelings and even morals' (Coomber 2006: 167). And many do not commit any crimes other than drug supply offences. Be that as it may, although transactions are usually consensual, all drug dealers knowingly sell substances that cause varying degrees of harm to drug users. When they sell to dependent drug users, it could also be argued that they are indirectly responsible for their problematic behaviour. Moreover, violence, insecurity, and neighbourhood decline are just a few of the negative effects that drug markets can have on individuals, families, and communities. But even for the most serious drug offences criminal sanction is not necessarily the answer. 'A person might have committed some act we deplore,' Christie (2004: 40) professes, 'but he also has other sides. When one is open to this, it is not quite so easy to see the other person as a monster, even if we think some aspects of his or her behaviour might be particularly unacceptable'. If drug dealers are prepared to accept responsibility for their actions and are committed to making amends, restorative justice might just work. As Braithwaite (2008: 98) humanely states, one should '[n]ever dismiss the possibility that having the right kinds of conversations might persuade you to reframe the normative objectives that should be salient in the situation'. If the restorative approach fails, or there is a lack of compliance, the police can simply escalate up through more and more punitive regulatory options. Restorative processes could be initiated pre-arrest, by directly communicating their targeting decisions to targets, making them understand why they are being targeted, and facilitating access to relevant services—or, if this inceptive dialogue fails, post-arrest but pre-charge. By keeping their activities secret until the point of arrest, the police deprive themselves of the prospect of persuasive communication and those affected by the offences under investigation of a stake in the resolution. Intervening prior to arrest would also reduce the impact of drug offences on the criminal justice system.

A variation of restorative justice that has been used to deal with local drug dealers is the 'pulling levers' focused deterrence strategy, which has been experimented with by a number of US and Latin American police departments in order to close open drug markets, reduce serious gang violence and restore the community (Braga and Weisburd 2012; Corsaro et al. 2010, 2012; Kennedy and Wong 2009). Generally speaking, the police start by selecting a particular crime problem and conduct investigations to identify the key offenders. Taking a problem-oriented policing approach, they also convene a multi-agency partnership and engage family, friends, and other 'influential' community members. This enables them to understand, define, and interpret the norms and narratives of the involved parties. A detailed understanding of the harms arising from the particular drug problem and the ways in which these arise is best gained through discussion with all the stakeholders. In some operations, such as the High Point Drug Market Intervention Strategy (Kennedy and Wong 2009), officers gather sufficient evidence to prosecute their targets, 'bank' the cases, and then show the dealers in question that they will face punishment unless they stop or transform their criminal behaviour. The most violent offenders and those on parole are prosecuted as examples. For deterrence by threatening punishment to work, the threat needs to be perceived as outweighing the benefits of committing crime and contain an assurance that if offenders do not undertake a particular activity they will not be punished. The next stage of the operation is the 'call-in'. Targeted dealers are invited to attend a meeting at which the police, service providers, and community members explain the purpose of the intervention, make them understand why they are receiving this special attention, and deliver an uncompromising message about what behaviours are liable to receive a more punitive response. Victims are given an opportunity to describe the harms they have suffered and discuss the problems they would like to see solved. Offenders are encouraged to explain themselves, take responsibility for the harms they have caused, and make amends. Defining the problem together and considering harms to all parties provides a platform for developing coordinated action to deal with the issues. Crucially, in recognizing that selling drugs is often a consequence of addiction or socio-economic deprivation, partner agencies also facilitate access to drug treatment, education, housing assistance, job training, employment, and a range of other opportunities that might help deflect offenders away from crime. Braga and Weisburd (2012) conclude that pulling levers strategies seem to be effective in reducing crime and increasing the legitimacy of police actions and the collective efficacy of communities. However, they urge caution in interpreting these results because of the lack of more rigorous randomized controlled trials in the existing body of scientific evidence.

When restorative justice is deemed inappropriate on the grounds that the drug offender has not created obvious victims or easily identifiable sources of injustice, the 'most direct way in which the police can reduce harm is to stop imposing criminal records and other punishments which harm people' (Stevens 2013: 6). 'We should oppose a strategy of casting the net of criminality so widely,' contends Husak (2002: 123) in his case for decriminalizing drugs. 'We should not turn vast numbers of people into criminals in order to prevent the misdeeds of a few.' Having critically discussed possible good answers to the basic question of why people should be punished for using some drugs for recreational purposes, he concludes that criminalization is fundamentally unjust and that deterrence ignores the crucial role of justice in favour of an attempt to coerce by legal threat. Decriminalization operates reasonably comfortably inside the confines of the UN drug control conventions. Indeed, there is greater scope to provide health care or social support instead of punishment for people caught up in minor offences related to personal use or socio-economic necessity (Bewley-Taylor and Jelsma 2012). The growing support and adoption of various decriminalization policies around the world demonstrates that such approaches are a viable and successful policy option for many countries (Home Office 2014; Rosmarin and Eastwood 2012).

In practice, until there are specific legal reforms, police forces in England and Wales could effectually decriminalize drugs by ending the official policy of making arrests for minor drug offences and adopting a *de facto* model of decriminalization through the non-enforcement of laws that technically remain in place. The 'Lambeth cannabis experiment' indicates that the police can play an important role in the campaign for reform and police drugs effectively and economically by reconfiguring policing priorities (Adda et al. 2014; Crowther-Dowey 2007). Although it is carried out in an uneven fashion—with some groups of users being targeted in an unfair and discriminatory way and thereby subject to more strict action and penalties than others, most notably those from ethnic minorities and deprived neighbourhoods (Eastwood et al. 2013; Rolles et al. 2012)—such an approach to policing drugs would not require a marked departure from what is already happening on the streets and in the courts. According to the UKDPC (2012: 118), the law bears little relationship to what police and prosecution authorities actually do, so much so in fact that 'simple drug possession offences have increasingly become depenalised, except for repeat offences, and in a few relatively isolated instances'. Despite the penalties in the Misuse of Drugs Act 1971, the status of cannabis as a Class B drug and the enduring political rhetoric, Monaghan and Bewley-Taylor (2013: 11) illustrate that 'the overall policy trend regarding possession and minor cases involving cultivation, production and even the importation of cannabis has become increasingly relaxed', especially since the introduction of 'Cannabis Warnings' and the inclusion of the offence of cannabis possession in the 'Penalty Notice for Disorder' (PND) scheme. Many police officers routinely 'turn a blind eye' to cannabis use and drug offences in the night-time economy (Bacon 2013c; Warburton et al. 2005). Furthermore, to promote compliance and obtain information, Lister et al. (2008) found that, where appropriate, officers would foster relationships with problem drug users and keep encounters as informal as possible, which meant offenders were not necessarily subject to the formal use of police powers.

Those commentators who advocate decriminalization almost invariably restrict it to possession of small quantities of drugs for personal use. 'Social supply' among peer networks and small-scale cannabis production are occasionally included in such discussions. If the police are to truly apply the principles of responsive regulation to drugs policing, however, there is no good reason why it should not at least be considered for drug dealers as well. There is no denying the fact that dealers are purveyors of substances that carry a recognized risk of harm. Yet, that alone is not necessarily sufficient grounds for criminal sanction, especially when one acknowledges that cannabis, ecstasy, LSD, and numerous other controlled drugs are less harmful to both the individual user and wider society than alcohol and tobacco (Nutt 2012; Nutt et al. 2007, 2010). A largely unquestioned assumption in the drug policy debate is that drug supply is a serious criminal offence and suppliers should therefore be targeted through aggressive enforcement and treated on a par with people who commit aggravated burglaries, armed robberies, grievous bodily harm and rape in terms of sentencing. This seems somewhat disproportionate as it does not reflect the nature of a great many supply offences or the behaviour of many drug offenders. In particular, it fails to acknowledge that some dealers are relatively harmless in that they do not create obvious victims or easily identifiable sources of injustice. By selling drugs they know they might cause harm to others but they do not intentionally do so.

Where to draw the line between a harmful dealer and a relatively harmless dealer is an issue that requires further theoretical and empirical exploration. It might, for instance, be necessary to established threshold quantities, differentiate between offenders at different levels of the supply chain, and take into account the harmfulness of the drugs they are supplying. Aggravating factors, such as employing young people to distribute drugs, cutting drugs with harmful substances, and carrying out acts of violence or intimidation, would also increase the seriousness of the offence. The answers will depend on many factors specific to context and come with different costs, benefits, and trade-offs. For the time being however, if we can accept the notion that there is such a thing as a relatively harmless drug dealer, we might also be able to accept that the police should treat them as minor offenders when regulating the drug trade. Under a *de facto* model of decriminalization, the 'policy of escalation' for the policing of cannabis and khat possession provides a framework that might be used for all minor drug offences (ACPO 2009, 2014). According to this approach, relatively harmless dealers would have their drugs seized and be given a warning for a first offence, a fine for a second and only face arrest and possible jail time for a third. They could also be referred to drug awareness sessions run by a public health body, or, if there is a demonstrable need, to a drug treatment programme. At each stage of the intervention, the police could make the offender understand why they are being targeted and explain that if they reoffend or behave in an unacceptable manner they will receive a more punitive response.

At the risk of coming across as being overly radical, perhaps serious thought should also given to the pros and cons of allowing the police to officially permit 'well-behaved' dealers to continue selling drugs without much interference in exchange for the provision of information and the upholding of harm reduction principles in the marketplace. Given that many registered informers are known or suspected to be actively involved in or on the periphery of the drug world, the prospect of licensing dealers is actually not a far cry from reality. If we accept that the licensing of criminals is an inescapable aspect of the police informer system and covert policing more generally, it might be prudent to reconceptualize the relationship between the police and their sources as one that is based on contract-like agreements and draw insights from the socio-legal literature on the 'contractual governance' of deviant behaviour (Bacon and Seddon 2013; Crawford 2003).

The body of literature on contractual governance discusses how social relationships between state agencies and citizens are being regulated more and more through a variety of mechanisms that resemble contracts. These have emerged across a very diverse set of domains, from 'young offender contracts' in youth justice to behaviour contracts in public housing. In both appearance and effect, these social control strategies constitute distinctive new forms of contract, as their purpose is neither to facilitate economic exchange nor to regulate the provision of services but rather to modify and control specific behaviours. More specifically, they are aimed at governing the conduct of individuals who are viewed as socially problematic because certain elements of their behaviour breach social norms. As a mode of behavioural control, what is common to these forms of contractual governance is that they operate under a strategy of 'responsibilisation' and are informed by the principles of 'regulated self-regulation' (Grabosky 1995; O'Malley 1992). This indicates that a central function of contractual governance is to communicate social values, norms, and expectations. In this way, contracts act as directive codes of practice that set out how citizens should behave in any given context and how they should contribute to the maintenance of social order.

From this perspective, a 'dealing contract' might set out the responsibilities and requirements placed on dealers, as well as what the police service commits to providing for them in return. Rather than being limited to the provision of information in exchange for money or some other benefit, such contracts could broaden the scope of the police informer system by requiring registered dealers to apply the principles of harm reduction to their criminal activities. They could also require them to communicate such principles to other drug offenders in order to make them aware of which practices are considered unacceptably harmful and thereby liable to trigger a punitive response if detected. Altering behaviours in this way would undoubtedly make a positive contribution to the self-regulation of the illegal drug business.

Any attempt to regulate the drug trade will be less than perfect. The fundamental dilemma facing policymakers and practitioners today is how best to reconcile the good, the bad, and the ugly aspects of the drug problems that affect the individuals and communities under their watch. There is no silver bullet. Every gun makes its own tune. In the absence of foolproof answers, maybe the time has come for us to break with the past and start experimenting with different approaches to drug control and the policing of drugs.

References

ACPO (1985) *Final Report of the Working Party on Drugs Related Crime (Broome Report)*, London: ACPO.

ACPO (2005) *Guidance on the National Intelligence Model*, Wyboston: NCPE.

ACPO (2007) *Practice Advice: Introduction to Intelligence-Led Policing*, Wyboston: NCPE.

ACPO (2009) *ACPO Guidance on Cannabis Possession for Personal Use (Revised Intervention Framework)*, London: ACPO.

ACPO (2014) *National Policing Guidelines on KHAT Possession for Personal Use Intervention Framework (England & Wales Only)*, London: ACPO.

Adda, J., McConnell, B., and Rasul, I. (2014) 'Crime and the Depenalization of Cannabis Possession: Evidence from a Policing Experiment', *Journal of Policing Economy*, 122(5): 1130–1202.

Adler, P. (1993) *Wheeling and Dealing: An Ethnography of an Upper-Level Drug Dealing and Smuggling Community* (2nd edn.), Oxford: Columbia University Press.

Aldridge, J. and Décary-Hétu, D. (2014) 'Not an "Ebay for Drugs": The Cyptomarket "Silk Road" as a Paradigm Shifting Criminal Innovation', *available at Social Science Research Network (SSRN)*.

Aldridge, J., Measham, F., and Williams, L. (2011) *Illegal Leisure Revisited: Changing Patterns of Alcohol and Drug Use in Adolescents and Young Adults*, London: Routledge.

Amey, P., Hale, C., and Uglow, S. (1996) *Development and Evaluation of a Crime Management Model* (Police Research Series Paper 18), London: Home Office.

Anderson, E. (1999) *The Code of the Street: Decency, Violence and the Moral Life of the Inner City*, New York: William W Norton & Co.

Ascoli, D. (1979) *The Queen's Peace*, London: Hamish Hamilton.

Atkinson, C. (2013) *Beyond Cop Culture: The Cultural Challenge of Civilian Intelligence Analysis in Scottish Policing*, PhD: University of Glasgow.

Atkinson, P., Coffey, A., Delamont, S., Lofland, J., and Lofland, L. (eds.) (2001) *Handbook of Ethnography*, London: Sage.

Audit Commission (1993) *Helping With Enquiries: Tackling Crime Effectively*, London: Audit Commission.

Ayres, I. and Braithwaite, J. (1992) *Responsive Regulation: Transcending the Deregulation Debate*, New York: Oxford University Press.

Babor, T., Caulkins, J., Edwards, G., Fischer, B., Foxcroft, D., Humphreys, K., Obot, I., Rehm, J., Reuter, P., Room, R., Rossow, I., and Strang, J. (2010) *Drug Policy and the Public Good*, Oxford: Oxford University Press.

Bacon, M. (2013a) 'Endangered Species', *Druglink*, 28(1): 12–13.

Bacon, M. (2013b) 'The Informal Regulation of an Illegal Trade: The Hidden Politics of Drug Detective Work', *Etnografia e Ricerca Qualitativa*, 1/2013: 61–80.

Bacon, M. (2013c) 'Dancing Around Drugs: Policing the Illegal Drug Markets of the Night-Time Economy in the UK', in Saitta, P., Shapland, J., and Verhage, A. (eds.), *Getting Rich or Getting By? The Formal, Informal and Criminal Economy in a Globalised World*, The Hague: Eleven International Publishers, 261–283.

Bacon, M. (2014) 'Police Culture and the New Policing Context', in Brown, J. (ed.) *The Future of Policing*, London: Routledge, 103–19.

Bacon, M. and Sanders, T. (2016) ' "Risky" Research and Discretion in Pursuing the Criminological Imagination', in Jacobsen, M. and Walklate, S. (eds.) *Liquid Criminology: Doing Imaginative Criminological Research*, Aldershot: Ashgate (forthcoming).

Bacon, M. and Seddon, T. (2013) 'The Contractual Governance of Drug Users in Treatment', *International Journal of Drug Policy*, 24(5): 379–84.

Banton, M. (1964) *The Policeman in the Community*, London: Tavistock.

Barratt, M. (2012) 'Silk Road: eBay for Drugs', *Addiction*, 107(3): 683.

Barratt, M., Ferris, J., and Winstock, A. (2014) 'Use of *Silk Road*, the Online Drug Marketplace, in the United Kingdom, Australia and the United States', *Addiction*, 109(5): 774–83.

Barton, A. (2011) *Illicit Drugs: Use and Control*, Abingdon: Routledge.

Barton, M. (2013) 'Why Ending the War on Drugs Will Cut Crime', *The Guardian* (28 September).

Bayley, D. (1994) *Police for the Future*, New York: Oxford University Press.

Bayley, D. (2002) 'Law Enforcement and the Rule of Law: Is There a Tradeoff?', *Criminology & Public Policy*, 2(1): 133–54.

Bean, P. and Billingsley, R. (2001) 'Drugs, Crime and Informers', in Billingsley, R., Nemitz, T., and Bean, P. (eds.) *Informers: Policing, Policy, Practice*, Cullompton: Willan, 25–37.

Beattie, J. (2012) *The First English Detectives: The Bow Street Runners and the Policing of London, 1750–1840*, Oxford: Oxford University Press.

Becker, H. (1963) *Outsiders: Studies in the Sociology of Deviance*, Glencoe, IL: Free Press.

Beckert, J. and Wehinger, F. (2013) 'In the Shadow: Illegal Markets and Economic Sociology', *Socio-Economic Review*, 11(1): 5–30.

Beetham, D. (1991) *The Legitimation of Power: Issues in Political Theory*, Basingstoke: Palgrave Macmillan.

Berridge, V. (2005) *Temperance: Its History and Impact on Current and Future Alcohol Policy*, York: Joseph Rowntree Foundation.

Berridge, V. and Edwards, G. (1981) *Opium and the People*, London: Allen Lane.

Bewley-Taylor, D. (2012) *International Drug Control: Consensus Fractured*, Cambridge: Cambridge University Press.

Bewley-Taylor, D. and Jelsma, M. (2012) *The UN Drug Control Conventions: The Limits of Latitude*, Transnational Institute and International Drug Policy Consortium, Series on Legislative Reform of Drug Policies (No. 18).

Billingsley, R. (2001a) *Informers*, PhD: University of Loughborough.

Billingsley, R. (2001b), 'Informers' Careers: Motivations and Change', in Billingsley, R., Nemitz, T., and Bean, P. (eds.) *Informers: Policing, Policy, Practice*, Cullompton: Willan, 81–97.

Billingsley, R. (2004) 'Process Deviance and the Use of Informers: The Solution', *Police Research & Management*, 6(2): 67–87.

Billingsley, R. (ed.) (2009) *Covert Human Intelligence Sources: The 'Unlovely' Face of Police Work*, Hampshire: Waterside Press.

Billingsley, R., Nemitz, T., and Bean, P. (eds.) (2001) *Informers: Policing, Policy, Practice*, Cullompton: Willan.

Bittner, E. (1970) *The Functions of the Police in Modern Society*, Washington DC: US Government Printing Office.

Bittner, E. (1990) *Aspects of Police Work*, Boston: Northeastern University Press.

Black, J. (2002) 'Critical Reflections on Regulation', *Australian Journal of Legal Philosophy*, 27(1): 1–36.

Bottoms, A. (2008) 'The Relationship between Theory and Empirical Observations in Criminology', in King, R. and Wincup, E. (eds.) *Doing Research on Crime and Justice* (2nd edn.), Oxford: Oxford University Press, 75–116.

Bottoms, A. and Tankebe, J. (2012) 'Beyond Procedural Justice: A Dialogic Approach to Legitimacy in Criminology', *Journal of Criminal Law and Criminology*, 102: 119–70.

Bourdieu, P. (1990) *The Logic of Practice*, Stanford, CA: Stanford University Press.

Bourgois, P. (2003) *In Search of Respect: Selling Crack in El Barrio* (2nd edn.), Cambridge: Cambridge University Press.

Bovenkerk, F., Siegel, D. and Zaitch, D. (2003) 'Organized Crime and Ethnic Reputation Manipulation', *Crime, Law & Social Change*, 39(1): 23–38.

Bowling, B. (2010) *Policing the Caribbean: Transnational Security Cooperation in Practice*, Oxford: Oxford University Press.

Boyatzis, R. (1998) *Transforming Qualitative Information: Thematic Analysis and Code Development*, Thousand Oaks, CA: Sage.

Bradford, B., Jackson, J., and Hough, M. (2014) 'Police Futures and Legitimacy: Redefining "Good Policing", in Brown, J. (ed.) *The Future of Policing*, London: Routledge, 79–99.

Braga, A. and Weisburd, D. (2012) 'The Effects of Focused Deterrence Strategies on Crime: A Systematic Review and Meta-Analysis of the Empirical Evidence', *Journal of Research in Crime and Delinquency*, 49(3): 323–58.

Braithwaite, J. (1989) *Crime, Shame and Reintegration*, Cambridge: Cambridge University Press.

Braithwaite, J. (2001) 'Restorative Justice and a New Criminal Law of Substance Abuse', *Youth and Society*, 33(2): 227–48.

Braithwaite, J. (2002), *Restorative Justice and Responsive Regulation*, Oxford: Oxford University Press.

Braithwaite, J. (2008) *Regulatory Capitalism: How it Works, Ideas to Make it Work Better*, Cheltenham: Edward Elgar.

Brodeur, J.-P. (1992) 'Undercover Policing in Canada: Wanting What is Wrong', *Crime, Law and Social Change*, 18(1–2): 105–36.

Brodeur, J.-P. (2010) *The Policing Web*, Oxford: Oxford University Press.

Brodeur, J.-P. and Dupont, B. (2006) 'Knowledge Workers or "Knowledge" Workers', *Policing and Society*, 16(1): 7–26.

Brogden, M. and Ellison, G. (2013) *Policing in the Age of Austerity: A Post Colonial Perspective*, London: Routledge.

Bronitt, S. (2004) 'The Law and Undercover Policing: A Comparative Study of Entrapment and Covert Interviewing in Australia, Canada and Europe', *Common Law World Review*, 33(1): 35–80.

Bronitt, S. and Stenning, P. (2011) 'Understanding Discretion in Modern Policing', *Criminal Law Journal*, 35(6): 319–32.

Brown, J. (1996) 'Police Research: Some Critical Issues', in Leishman, F., Loveday, B., and Savage, S. (eds.) *Core Issues in Policing*, London: Macmillan, 179–90.

Brown, R., Roe, J., Hall, A., and Evans, E. (2008) *Evaluation of Operation Reduction*, Glasgow: Evidence Led Solutions.

Buchanan, J. (2010) 'Drug Policy Under New Labour 1997–2010: Prolonging the War on Drugs', *Probation Journal*, 57(3): 250–62.

Bullock, K. (2013) 'Community, Intelligence-Led Policing and Crime Control', *Policing and Society*, 23(2): 125–44.

Burgess, R. (1984) *In the Field: An Introduction to Field Research*, London: Unwin Hymann.

Cain, M. (1973) *Society and the Policeman's Role*, London: Routledge and Kegan Paul.

Campeau, H. (2015) 'Police Culture at Work: Making Sense of Police Oversight', *British Journal of Criminology*, 55(4): 669–87.

Caulkins, J. and Reuter, P. (1998) 'What Price Data Tell Us About Drug Markets', *Journal of Drug Issues*, 28(3): 593–612.

Caulkins, J. and Reuter, P. (2009) 'Towards a Harm-Reduction Approach to Enforcement', *Safer Communities*, 8(1): 9–23.

Caulkins, J., Johnson, B., Taylor, A., and Taylor, L. (1999) 'What Drug Dealers Tell Us About Their Costs of Doing Business', *Journal of Drug Issues*, 29(2): 323–40.

Caulkins, J., Reuter, P., Iguchi, M., and Chiesa, J. (2005) *How Goes the War on Drugs? An Assessment of US Drug Problems and Policy*, Santa Monica: Rand Corporation.

Chan, J. (1997) *Changing Police Culture: Policing in a Multicultural Society*, Cambridge: Cambridge University Press.

Chan, J (2001) 'The Technology Game: How Information Technology is Transforming Police Practice', *Criminal Justice*, 1(2): 139–59.

Chatterton, M. (1979) 'The Supervision of Patrol Work Under the Fixed Points System', in Holdaway, S. (ed.) *The British Police*, London: Edward Arnold, 83–101.

Chatterton, M. (1992) *Controlling Police Work: Strategies and Tactics of the Lower Ranks–Their Past and Future Relevance*, Social Order in Post Classical Sociology, University of Bristol.

Chatterton, M. (2008) *Losing the Detectives: Views from the Frontline*, London: Police Federation.

Choongh, S. (1997) *Policing as Social Discipline*, Oxford: Oxford University Press.

Christie, N. (2004) *A Suitable Amount of Crime*, London: Routledge.

Clark, D. (2007) 'Covert Surveillance and Informer Handling', in Newburn, T., Williamson, T., and Wright, A. (eds.) *Handbook of Criminal Investigation*, Cullompton: Willan, 426–49.

Clayman, S. and Skinns, L. (2012) 'To Snitch or Not to Snitch? An Exploratory Study of the Factors Affecting Active Youth Co-operation with the Police', *Policing and Society*, 22(2): 1–21.

Cockcroft, T. (2012) *Police Culture: Themes and Concepts*, London: Routledge.

Cohen, S. (1985) *Visions of Control*, Cambridge: Polity Press.

Collin, M. (1997) *Altered State: The Story of Ecstasy Culture and Acid House*, Serpent's Tail.

Collison, M. (1995) *Police, Drugs and Community*, London: Free Association Books.

Collison, M. (1996) 'In Search of the High Life: Drugs, Crime, Masculinities and Consumption', *British Journal of Criminology*, 36(3): 428–44.

Coomber, R. (2006) *Pusher Myths: Re-Situating the Drug Dealer*, London: Free Association Books.

Coomber, R. and Moyle, L. (2014) 'Beyond Drug Dealing: Developing and Extending the Concept of "Social Supply" of Illicit Drugs to "Minimally Commercial Supply"', *Drugs: Education, Prevention and Policy*, 21(2): 157–64.

Coomber, R., Measham, F., McElrath, K., and Moore, K. (2013) *Key Concepts in Drugs and Society*, London: Sage.

Cope, N. (2004), 'Intelligence Led Policing or Policing Led Intelligence? Integrating Volume Crime Analysis into Policing', *British Journal of Criminology*, 44(2): 188–203.

Corsaro, N., Brunson, R., and McGarrell, E. (2010) 'Evaluating a Policing Strategy Intended to Disrupt an Illicit Street-Level Drug Market', *Evaluation Review*, 34(6): 513–48.

Corsaro, N., Hunt, E., Hipple, N., and McGarrell, E. (2012) 'The Impact of Drug Market Pulling Levers Policing on Neighborhood Violence', *Criminology & Public Policy*, 11(2): 167–99.

Courtwright, D. (2001) *Forces of Habit: Drugs and the Making of the Modern World*, Cambridge, MA: Harvard University Press.

Crank, J. (2004) *Understanding Police Culture* (2nd edn.), Cincinnati, OH: Anderson.

Crawford, A. (2003) ' "Contractual Governance" of Deviant Behaviour', *Journal of Law and Society*, 30(4): 479–505.

Crawford, A. (2008) 'The Pattern of Policing in the UK: Policing Beyond the Police', in Newburn, T. (ed.) *Handbook of Policing* (2nd edn.), Cullompton: Willan, 147–81.

Crimestoppers (2014) *Annual Report and Accounts 2012/13*, London: Crimestoppers.

Crowther-Dowey, C. (2007) 'The Police and Drugs' in Simpson, M., Shildrick, T., and MacDonald, R. (eds.) *Drugs in Britain: Supply, Consumption and Control*, London: Palgrave, 108–24.

Curtis, R. and Wendel, T. (2000) 'Toward the Development of a Typology of Illegal Drug Markets', in Natarajan, M. and Hough, M. (eds.), *Illegal Drug Markets: From Research to Prevention Policy* (Crime Prevention Studies, Vol. 11), New York: Criminal Justice Press, 121–52.

Curtis, R. and Wendel, T. (2007) ' "You're Always Training the Dog": Strategic Interventions to Reconfigure Drug Markets', *Journal of Drug Issues*, 37(4): 867–91.

Daly, M. and Sampson, S. (2013) *Narcomania: How Britain Got Hooked on Drugs*, London: Windmill Books.

Decker, S. and Chapman, M. (2008) *Drug Smugglers on Drug Smuggling*, Philadelphia: Temple University Press.

Decorte, T. (2000) *The Taming Of Cocaine: Cocaine Use in European and American Cities*, Brussels: VUB University Press.

Degenhardt, L., Conroy, E., Gilmour, S., and Collins, L. (2005) 'The Effect on a Reduction in Heroin Supply in Australia Upon Drug Distribution and Acquisitive Crime', *British Journal of Criminology*, 45(1): 2–24.

Dixon, D. (1997) *Law in Policing: Legal Regulation and Police Practices*, Oxford: Oxford University Press.

Dorn, N. and Lee, M. (1999) 'Drugs and Policing in Europe: From Low Streets to High Places', in South (ed.) *Drugs: Culture, Controls and Everyday Life*, London: Sage, 86–102.

Dorn, N. and South, N. (eds.) (1987) *A Land Fit for Heroin? Drug Policies, Prevention and Practice*, London: Macmillan.

Dorn, N. and South, N. (1990) 'Drug Markets and Law Enforcement', *British Journal of Criminology*, 30(2): 171–88.

Dorn, N., Levi, M., and King, L. (2005) *Literature Review on Upper Level Drug Trafficking* (Home Office Online Report 22/05), London: Home Office.

Dorn, N., Murji, K., and South, N. (1992) *Traffickers: Drug Markets and Law Enforcement*, London: Routledge.

Dorn, N., Oette, L., and White, S. (1998) 'Drugs Importation and the Bifurcation of Risk: Capitalization, Cut Outs and Organized Crime', *British Journal of Criminology*, 38(4): 537–60.

Drug Policy Alliance (2015a) *Marijuana Legalization in Colorado After One Year of Retail Sales and Two Years of Decriminalisation*, New York: Drug Policy Alliance.

Drug Policy Alliance (2015b) *Marijuana Legalization in Washington After 1 Year of Retail Sales and 2.5 Years of Legal Possession*, New York: Drug Policy Alliance.

Duffy, M., Schafer, N., Coomber, R. O'Connell, L. (2007) *It's A Social Thing: Cannabis Supply and Young People*, York: Joseph Rowntree Foundation.

Dunnighan, C. (1992) 'Reliable Sources', *Police Review*, 14 August: 1496–7.

Dunnighan, C. and Norris, C. (1996) 'A Risky Business: Exchange, Bargaining and Risk in the Recruitment and Running of Informers by English Police Officers, *Police Studies*, 19(2): 1–25.

Dunnighan, C. and Norris, C. (1999) 'The Detective, the Snout, and the Audit Commission: The Real Costs in Using Informants', *Howard Journal of Criminal Justice*, 38(1): 67–86.

Eastwood, N., Shiner, M., and Bear, D. (2013) *The Numbers in Black and White: Ethnic Disparities in the Policing and Prosecution of Drug Offences in England and Wales*, London: Release.

Edmunds, M., Hough, M., and Urquia, N. (1996) *Tackling Local Drug Markets*, Crime Prevention and Prevention Series (Paper 80), London: Home Office.

Ellis, A. (2015) *Men, Masculinities and Violence: An Ethnographic Study*, London: Routledge.

EMCDDA (2013) *Drug Squads: Units Specialised in Drug Law Enforcement in Europe*, Lisbon: EMCDDA.

Emerson, R., Fretz, R., and Shaw, L. (2001) 'Participant Observation and Fieldnotes', in Atkinson, P., Coffey, A., Delamont, S., Lofland, J., and Lofland, L. (eds.) *Handbook of Ethnography*, London: Sage, 352–68.

Emsley, C. (1996) *The English Police: A Political and Social History* (2nd edn.), Harlow: Longman Pearson.

Engel, R. and Peterson, S. (2014) 'Leading by Example: The Untapped Resource of Front-Line Police Supervisors', in Brown, J. (ed.) *The Future of Policing*, London: Routledge, 398–413.

Ericson, R. (1981) *Making Crime: A Study of Detective Work*, Toronto: Butterworth.

Ericson, R. (2007) 'Rules in Policing: Five Perspectives', *Theoretical Criminology*, 11(3): 367–401.

Ericson, R. and Haggerty, K. (1997) *Policing the Risk Society*, Oxford: Oxford University Press.

Escohotado, A. (1999) *A Brief History of Drugs: From the Stone Age to the Stoned Age*, Rochester: Park Street Press.

Farrall, S., Bottoms, A. and Shapland, J. (2010) 'Social Structures and Desistance from Crime', *European Journal of Criminology*, 7(6): 546–70.

Farrell, G. (1998) 'Routine Activities and Drug Trafficking: The Case of the Netherlands', *International Journal of Drug Policy*, 9(1): 21–32.

Fassin, D. (2013) *Enforcing Order: An Ethnography of Urban Policing*, Cambridge: Polity.

Felbab-Brown, V. (2013) *Focused Deterrence, Selective Targeting, Drug Trafficking and Organised Crime: Concepts and Practicalities*, London: International Drug Policy Consortium.

Fielding, N. (1989) 'Police Culture and Police Practice', in Weatheritt, M. (ed.) *Police Research: Some Future Prospects*, Aldershot: Avebury, 77-87.

Fielding, N. (1994) 'Cop Canteen Culture', in Newburn, T. and Stanko, E. (eds.), *Just Boys Doing Business: Men, Masculinities and Crime*, London: Routledge, 46–63.

Fielding, N. (1995) *Community Policing*, Oxford: Clarendon Press.

Fielding, N. (2008) 'Ethnography', in Gilbert, N. (ed.), *Researching Social Life* (3rd edn.), London: Sage, 145–63.

Fijnaut, C. and Marx, G. (eds.) (1995) *Undercover: Police Surveillance in Comparative Perspective*, The Hague: Kluwer Law International.

Garland, D. (2001) *The Culture of Control: Crime and Social Order in Contemporary Society*, Oxford: Oxford University Press.

Geertz, C (1973) 'Thick Description: Toward an Interpretive Theory of Culture', in Geertz, C. (ed.) *The Interpretation of Cultures: Selected Essays*, New York: Basic Books, 3–30.

Gill, P. (2000) *Rounding Up The Usual Suspects? Developments in Contemporary Law Enforcement Intelligence*, Aldershot: Ashgate.

Gill, P. (2002) 'Policing and Regulation: What is the Difference?' *Social and Legal Studies*, 11(4): 523–46.

Gilling, D. (2012) 'Reasons to be Cheerful? Addressing Public Perceptions through National Tackling Drugs Week', *Criminology and Criminal Justice*, 12(1): 41–60.

Global Commission on Drug Policy (2011) *War on Drugs: Report of the Global Commission on Drug Policy* (http://www.globalcommission-ondrugs.org/wp-content/themes/gcdp_v1/pdf/Global_Commission_Report_English.pdf)

Goffman, E. (1959) *The Presentation of Self in Everyday Life*, Harmondsworth: Penguin.

Gold, R. (1958) 'Roles in Sociological Fieldwork', *Social Forces*, 36(3): 217–223.

Goldstein, P. (1985) 'The Drugs/Violence Nexus: A Tripartite Conceptual Framework', *Journal of Drug Issues*, 15(4): 493–506.

Gossop, M. (2007) *Living with Drugs* (6th edn.), Aldershot: Ashgate.

Grabosky, P. (1995) 'Using Non-Governmental Resources to Foster Regulatory Compliance', *Governance*, 8(4): 527–50.

Greenwood, P., Chaiken, J., and Petersilia, J. (1977) *The Criminal Investigation Process*, Lexington, MA: D.C. Heath.

Greer, S. (1995) 'Towards a Sociological Model of the Police Informant', *British Journal of Sociology*, 46(3): 509–27.

Griffiths, B. and Murphy, A. (2001) 'Managing Anonymous Informants Through Crimestoppers', in Billingsley, R., Nemitz, T., and Bean, P. (eds.) *Informers: Policing, Policy, Practice*, Cullompton: Willan, 141–52.

Griffiths, P., Evans-Brown, M., and Sedefov, R. (2013) 'Getting Up to Speed with the Public Health and Regulatory Challenged Posed by New Psychoactive Substances in the Information Age', *Addiction*, 108(10): 1700–3.

Hadfield, P. (2006) *Bar Wars: Contesting the Night in Contemporary British Cities*, Oxford: Oxford University Press.

Hadfield, P., Lister, S., and Traynor, P. (2009) ' "This Town's a Different Town Today": Policing and Regulating the Night-Time Economy', *Criminology & Criminal Justice*, 9(4): 465–85.

Hale, C., Heaton, R., and Uglow, S. (2004) 'Uniform Styles? Aspects of Police Centralisation in England and Wales', *Policing and Society*, 14(4): 291–312.

Hales, G., Lewis, C., and Silverstone, D. (2006) *Gun Crime: The Market In and Use of Illegal Firearms*, Home Office Research Findings 279, London: Home Office.

Hall, S., Winlow, S., and Ancrum, C. (2008) *Criminal Identities and Contemporary Culture: Crime, Exclusion and the New Culture of Narcissism*, Cullompton: Willan.

Hammersley, M. and Atkinson, P. (2007), *Ethnography: Principles in Practice* (3rd edn.), London: Routledge.

Harfield, C. (2009) 'The Regulation of CHIS', in Billingsley, R. (ed.) (2009) *Covert Human Intelligence Sources: The 'Unlovely' Face of Police Work*, Hampshire: Waterside Press, 43–56.

Harfield, C. (2010) 'The Governance of Covert Investigation', *Melbourne University Law Review*, 34: 773–803.

Harfield, C. and Harfield, C. (2012) *Covert Investigation* (3rd edn.), Oxford: Oxford University Press.

Hewitt, S. (2010) *Snitch! A History of the Modern Intelligence Informer*, London: Continuum Books.

Hill, M. (2009) *The Public Policy Process*, Harlow: Pearson Longman.

HM Government (1995) *Tackling Drugs Together: A Strategy for England 1995–1998*, HMSO: London.

HMIC (1997) *Policing with Intelligence: Criminal Intelligence—A Thematic Inspection on Good Practice*, London: HMIC.

Hobbs, D. (1988) *Doing the Business: Entrepreneurship, The Working Class and Detectives in the East End of London*, Oxford: Oxford University Press.

Hobbs, D. (1991) 'A Piece of Business: The Moral Economy of Detective Work in the East End of London', *British Journal of Sociology*, 41(4): 597–608.

Hobbs, D. (1995) *Bad Business: Professional Crime in Britain*, Oxford: Oxford University Press.

Hobbs, D. (1998) 'Going Down the Glocal: The Local Context of Organised Crime', *The Howard Journal*, 37(4): 407–422.

Hobbs, D. (2001) 'The Firm: Organizational Logic and Criminal Culture on a Shifting Terrain', *British Journal of Criminology*, 41(4): 549–60.

Hobbs, D. (2013) *Lush Life: Constructing Organized Crime in the UK*, Oxford: Oxford University Press.

Hobbs, D. and Antonopoulos, G. (2013) 'Endemic to the Species: Ordering the 'Other' via Organised Crime', *Global Crime*, 14(1): 27–51.

Hobbs, D. and May, T. (eds.) (1993) *Interpreting the Field: Account of Ethnography*, Oxford: Oxford University Press.

Hobbs, D., Hadfield, P., Lister, S. and Winlow, S (2003) *Bouncers: Violence and Governance in the Night-Time Economy*, Oxford: Oxford University Press.

Holdaway, S. (1983) *Inside the British Police*, Oxford: Basil Blackwell.

Holdaway, S. (1989) 'Discovering Structure: Studies of the British Police Occupational Culture', in Weatheritt, M. (ed.) *Police Research: Some Future Prospects*, Aldershot: Avebury, 55–75.

Home Affairs Select Committee (2012) *Drugs: Breaking the Cycle*, London: House of Commons.

Home Office (1998) *Tackling Drugs To Build A Better Britain: The Government's Ten Year Strategy for Tackling Drug Misuse*, London: Home Office.

Home Office (2002) *Updated Drug Strategy 2002: Tackling Drugs*, London: Home Office.

Home Office (2008) *Drugs: Protecting Families and Communities: The 2008–2018 Drug Strategy*, London: Home Office.

Home Office (2014) *Drugs: International Comparators*, London: Home Office.

Hornsby, R. and Hobbs, D. (2007) 'A Zone of Ambiguity: The Political Economy of Cigarette Bootlegging', *British Journal of Criminology*, 47(4): 551–71.

Hoyle, C. (1998) *Negotiating Domestic Violence: Police, Criminal Justice and Victims*, Oxford: Oxford University Press.

Husak, D. (1992) *Drugs and Rights*, Cambridge, England: Cambridge University Press.

Husak, D. (2002) *Legalize This! The Case for Decriminalizing Drugs*, London: Verso.

Huxley, A. (1956) *The Doors of Perception and Heaven and Hell*, London: Penguin.

Hyland, K. and Walker, C. (2014) 'Undercover Policing and Underwhelming Laws', *Criminal Law Review*, 8: 555–74.

Ignatieff, M. (1979) 'Police and People: The Birth of Mr. Peel's Blue Locusts', *New Society*, 49(882): 443–5.

Innes, M. (2000) 'Professionalising the Role of the Police Informant: The British Experience', *Policing and Society*, 9(4): 357–84.

Innes, M. (2003a) *Investigating Murder: Detective Work and the Police Response to Criminal Homicide*, Oxford: Oxford University Press.

Innes, M. (2003b) *Understanding Social Control*, Maidenhead: Open University Press.

Innes, M. (2014a) 'Reinventing the Office of Constable: Progressive Policing in an Age of Austerity', in Brown, J. (ed.) *The Future of Policing*, London: Routledge, 64–78.

Innes, M. (2014b) *Signal Crimes: Social Reactions to Crime, Disorder, and Control*, Oxford: Oxford University Press.

Innes, M., Fielding, N. and Cope, N. (2005) 'The Appliance of Science? The Theory and Practice of Criminal Intelligence Analysis', *British Journal of Criminology*, 45(1): 39–57.

Ipsos MORI (2013) *Public Attitudes to Drugs Policy*, London: Social Research Institute.

Jacinto, C., Duterte, M., Sales, P. and Murphy, S. (2008) ' "I'm Not A Real Dealer": The Identity Process of Ecstasy Sellers', *Journal of Drug Issues*, 38(2): 419–44.

Jackall, R. (2005) *Street Stories: The World of Police Detectives*, Cambridge, MA: Harvard University Press.

Jackson, J., Bradford, B., Stanko, E., and Hohl, K. (2012) *Just Authority? Trust in the Police in England and Wales*, London: Routledge.

Jacobs, B. (1996) 'Crack Dealers and Restrictive Deterrence: Identifying Narcs", *Criminology*, 34(3): 409–31.

Jacobs, B. (1999) *Dealing Crack: The Social World of Streetcorner Selling*, Boston: Northeastern University Press.

Jacobs, B. (2000) *Robbing Drug Dealers: Violence Beyond the Law*, New York: Aldine de Gruyter.

Jacobs, B., Topalli, V., and Wright, R. (2000) 'Managing Retaliation: Drug Robbery and Informal Sanction Threats', *Criminology*, 38(1): 171–98.

James, A. (2013) *Examining Intelligence-Led Policing: Developments in Research, Policy and Practice*, Basingstoke: Palgrave Macmillan.

Jay, M. (2000) *Emperors of Dreams: Drugs in the Nineteenth Century*, London: Dedalus.

Jermier, J., Slocum, J., Fry, L., and Gaines, J. (1991), 'Organizational Subcultures in a Soft Bureaucracy: Resistance Behind the Myth and Façade of an Official Culture', *Organizational Science*, 2(2): 170–94.

John, T. and Maguire, M. (2003) 'Rolling Out The National Intelligence Model: Key Challenges', in Bullock, K. and Tilley, N. (eds.) *Crime Reduction and Problem-Oriented Policing*, Cullompton: Willan, 38–68.

John, T. and Maguire, M. (2004), *The National Intelligence Model: Key Lessons From Early Research* (Home Office Online Report 30/04), London: Home Office.

John, T. and Maguire, M. (2007) 'Criminal Intelligence and the National Intelligence Model', in Newburn, T., Williamson, T., and Wright, A. (eds.) *Handbook of Criminal Investigation*, Cullompton: Willan, 199–225.

Johnson, B. and Natarajan, M. (1995) 'Strategies to Avoid Arrest: Crack Sellers' Response to Intensified Policing', *American Journal of Police*, 14(3/4): 49–69.

Johnson, B., Goldstein, P., and Preble, E. (1985), *Taking Care of Business: The Economics of Crime by Heroin Abusers*, Lexington, MA: Lexington Books.

Johnson, B., Dunlap, E., and Tourigny, S. (2000) 'Crack Distribution and Abuse in New York', in Natarajan, M. and Hough, M. (eds.), *Illegal Drug Markets: From Research to Prevention Policy* (Crime Prevention Studies, Vol. 11), New York: Criminal Justice Press, 19–58.

Johnston, L. and Shearing, C. (2003) *Governing Security*, London: Routledge.

Johnstone, G. (2011) *Restorative Justice: Ideas, Values and Debates* (2nd edn.), London: Routledge.

Jones, T. and Newburn, T. (eds.) (2006) *Plural Policing: A Comparative Perspective*, London: Routledge.

Katz, J. (1988) *Seductions of Crime: Moral and Sensual Attractions in Doing Evil*, New York: Basic Books.

Kennedy, D. and Wong, S. (2009) *The High Point Drug Market Intervention Strategy*, Washington: US Department of Justice, Office of Community Oriented Policing.

Kerr, T., Small, W. and Wood, E. (2005) 'The Public Health and Social Impacts of Drug Market Enforcement: A Review of the Evidence', *International Journal of Drug Policy*, 16(4): 210–20.

King, S. (2000) *On Writing: A Memoir of the Craft*, London: Hodder and Stoughton.

Kingdon, J. (2003) *Agendas, Alternatives and Public Policies*, New York: Addison-Wesley.

Kleemans, E. and van de Bunt, H. (2008) 'Organised Crime, Occupations and Opportunity', *Global Crime*, 9(3): 185–97.

Kleiman, M., Caulkins, J., and Hawken, A. (2011) *Drugs and Drug Policy: What Everyone Needs to Know*, Oxford: Oxford University Press.

Klein, A. (2008) *Drugs and the World*, London: Reaktion.

Klockars, C. (1985) *The Idea of Police*, Beverly Hills, CA: Sage.

Kohn, M. (1992) *Dope Girls: The Birth of the British Drug Underground*, London: Lawrence & Wishart.

Kuykendall, J. (1986) 'The Municipal Detective: A Historical Analysis', *Criminology*, 24(1): 175–202.

Laville, S. and McDonald, H. (2013) 'Top Police Chiefs Warn Mike Barton: Be Careful About Message on Drugs', *The Guardian* (29 September).

Layder, D. (1998) *Sociological Practice: Linking Theory and Social Research*, London: Sage.

Lee, M. and South, N. (2008) 'Drugs Policing', in Newburn, T. (ed.) *Handbook of Policing* (2nd edn.), Cullompton: Willan, 497–521.

Levitt, S. and Dubner, S. (2005) *Freakonomics: A Rogue Economist Explores the Hidden Side of Everything*, London: Penguin Books.

Levitt, S. and Venkatesh, S. (2000) 'An Economic Analysis of a Drug-Selling Gang's Finances', *The Quarterly Journal of Economics*, 15(3): 755–89.

Lister, S., Seddon, T., Wincup, E., Barrett, S., and Traynor, P. (2008) *Street Policing of Problem Drug Users*, York: Joseph Rowntree Foundation.

Loader, I. and Mulcahy, A. (2003) *Policing and the Condition of England*, Oxford: Oxford University Press.

Lofland, J. and Lofland, L. (1995) *Analyzing Social Settings: A Guide to Qualitative Observation and Analysis* (3rd edn.), Belmont, CA: Wadsworth.

Loftus, B. (2009) *Policing Culture in a Changing World*, Oxford: Oxford University Press.

Loftus, B. and Goold, B. (2012) 'Covert Surveillance and the Invisibilities of Policing', *Criminology and Criminal Justice*, 12(3): 275–88.

Loftus, B., Goold, B., and Mac Giollabhui, S. (2010) 'Covert Policing and the Regulation of Investigatory Powers Act 2000', *Archbold Review*, 8: 3–9.

Loftus, B., Goold, B., and Mac Giollabhui, S. (2015) 'From a Visible Spectacle to an Invisible Presence: The Working Culture of Covert Policing', *British Journal of Criminology*, azv076

London, J. (2007) *The People of the Abyss*, Teddington: The Echo Library.

Loveday, B. (2000) 'Managing Crime: Police Use of Crime Data as an Indicator of Effectiveness', *International Journal of the Sociology of Law*, 28(3): 215–37.

Lowe, D. (2011) 'The Lack of Discretion in High Policing', *Policing and Society*, 21(2): 233–47.

Lucy, W. (1989) 'Contract as a Mechanism of Distributive Justice', *Oxford Journal of Legal Studies*, 9(1): 132–47.

Lupton, R., Wilson, A., May, T., Warburton, H., and Turnbull, J. (2002) *A Rock and a Hard Place: Drug Markets in Deprived Neighbourhoods* (Home Office Research Findings 167), London: Home Office.

MacCoun, R. and Reuter, P. (2001) *Drug War Heresies—Learning From Other Vices, Times and Places*, Cambridge: Cambridge University Press.

MacCoun, R. and Reuter, P. (2011) 'Assessing Drug Prohibition and its Alternatives: A Guide for Agnostics', *Annual Review of Law & Social Science*, 7: 61–78.

MacGregor, S. (2011) 'The Impact of Research on Policy in the Drugs Field', *Methodological Innovations Online*, 6(1): 41–57.

MacGregor, S. (2013) 'Barriers to the Influence of Evidence on Policy: Are Politicians the Problem?' *Drugs: Education, Prevention and Policy*, 20(3): 225–33.

Madoff, R. (1997) 'Unmasking Undue Influence', *Minnesota Law Review*, 81: 571–629.

Maguire, M. (2000) 'Policing by Risks and Targets: Some Dimensions and Implications of Intelligence-Led Crime Control', *Policing and Society*, 9(4): 315–36.

Maguire, M. (2008) 'Criminal Investigation and Crime Control', in Newburn, T. (ed.) *Handbook of Policing* (2nd edn.), Cullompton: Willan, 430–64.

Maguire, M. (2012) 'Criminal Statistics and the Construction of Crime', in Maguire, M., Morgan, R. and Reiner, R. (eds.) *The Oxford Handbook of Criminology* (5th edn.), Oxford: Oxford University Press, 206–44.

Maguire, M. and John, T. (1995) *Intelligence, Surveillance and Informants: Integrated Approaches* (Police Research Group, Crime Detection and Prevention Series Paper 64), London: Home Office.

Maguire, M. and John, T. (1996) 'Covert and Deceptive Policing in England and Wales: Issues in Practice and Regulation', *European Journal of Crime, Criminal Law and Criminal Justice*, 4: 316–34.

Maguire, M. and John, T. (2006) 'Intelligence-Led Policing, Managerialism and Community Engagement: Competing Priorities and the Role of the National Intelligence Model in the UK', *Policing and Society*, 16(1): 67–85.

Maguire, M. and Norris, C. (1992) *The Conduct and Supervision of Criminal Investigations: The Royal Commission on Criminal Justice* (Research Report No. 5), London: HMSO.

Maher, L. and Dixon, D. (1999) 'Policing and Public Health: Law Enforcement and Harm Minimization in a Street-level Drug Market', *British Journal of Criminology*, 39(4): 488–512.

Manning, P. (1977) *Police Work: The Social Organization of Policing*, Cambridge, MA: MIT Press.

Manning, P. (1980) *The Narcs' Game: Organizational and Informational Limits on Drug Law Enforcement*, Cambridge: MIT Press.

Manning, P. (1997) *Police Work: The Social Organization of Policing* (2nd edn.), Illinois: Waveland Press.

Manning, P. (2004) *The Narcs' Game: Organizational and Informational Limits on Drug Law Enforcement* (2nd edn.), Illinois: Waveland Press.

Manning, P. (2007) 'Detective Work/Culture', in Greene, J. (ed.) *The Encyclopedia of Police Science*, London: Routledge, 390–7.

Manning, P. (2008a) 'Goffman on Organizations', *Organization Studies*, 29: 677–99.

Manning, P. (2008b) *The Technology of Policing: Crime Mapping, Information Technology, and the Rationality of Crime Control*, New York: New York University Press.

Manning, P. (2014) 'Ethnographies of the Police', in Reisig, M. and Kane, R. (eds.) *The Oxford Handbook of Police and Policing*, New York: Oxford University Press, 518–47.

Manning, P. and Hawkins, K. (1989) 'Police Decision Making', in Weatheritt, M. (ed.) *Police Research: Some Future Prospects*, Aldershot: Avebury, 139–56.

Mark, R. (1978) *In the Office of Constable*, London: Collins.

Marks, M. (2004) 'Researching Police Transformation: The Ethnographic Imperative', *British Journal of Criminology*, 44(6): 866–88.

Martin, J. (2014) *Drugs on the Dark Net: How Cryptomarkets are Transforming the Global Trade in Illicit Drugs*, Basingstoke: Palgrave Macmillan.

Marx, G. (1988) *Undercover: Police Surveillance in America*, Berkeley: University of California Press.

Massari, M. (2005) 'Ecstasy in the City: Synthetic Drug Markets in Europe', *Crime, Law and Social Change*, 44(1): 1–18.

Matrix Knowledge Group (2007) *The Illicit Drug Trade in the United Kingdom*, Home Office Online Report 20/07, London: Home Office.

Matza, D. (1964) *Delinquency and Drift*, New York: Wiley.

Mawby, R. C. (2007) 'Criminal Investigation and the Media', in Newburn, T., Williamson, T., and Wright, A. (eds.) *Handbook of Criminal Investigation*, Cullompton: Willan, 146–69.

Mawby, R. C. and Wright, A. (2008) 'The Police Organisation', in Newburn, T. (ed.) *Handbook of Policing* (2nd edn.), Cullompton: Willan, 224–52.

Mawby, R. I. (ed.) (1999) *Policing Across the World: Issues for the Twenty-First Century*, London: UCL Press.

May, T. and Hough, M. (2004) 'Drug Markets and Distribution Systems', *Addiction Research and Theory*, 12(6): 549–63.

May, T., Harocopos, A., Turnbull, P., and Hough, M. (2000) *Serving Up: The Impact of Low-Level Police Enforcement on Drug Markets*, Police Research Series (Paper 133), London: Home Office.

May, T., Duffy, M., Few, B., and Hough, M. (2005) *Understanding Drug Selling in Communities: Insider or Outsider Trading?* York: Joseph Rowntree Foundation.

May, T., Duffy, M., Warburton, H., and Hough, M. (2007) *Policing Cannabis as a Class C Drug: An Arresting Change*, York: Joseph Rowntree Foundation.

May, T., Warburton, H., Turnbull, P., and Hough, M. (2002) *Times They Are A-changing: Policing of Cannabis*, York: Joseph Rowntree Foundation.

Mazerolle, L., Soole, D., and Rombouts, S. (2007), 'Drug Law Enforcement: A Review of the Evaluation Literature', *Policing Quarterly*, 10(2): 115–53.

McAllister, W. (2000) *Drug Diplomacy in the Twentieth Century*, London: Routledge.

McBarnet, D. (1981) *Conviction: Law, the State and the Construction of Justice*, London: Macmillan.

McCarthy, D (2013) 'Gendering "Soft" Policing: Multi-Agency Working, Female Cops, and the Fluidities of Police Culture/s', *Policing and Society*, 23(2): 262–78.

McCarthy, D. (2014) *'Soft' Policing: The Collaborative Control of Anti-Social Behaviour*, Basingstoke: Palgrave Macmillan.

McConville, M., Sanders, A., and Leng, R. (1991) *The Case for the Prosecution: Police Suspects and the Construction of Criminality*, London: Routledge.

McKeganey, N. (2011) *Controversies in Drug Policy and Practice*, Basingstoke: Palgrave Macmillan.

McLaughlin, E. (2007) *The New Policing*, London: Sage.

McSweeney, T., Turnbull, P., and Hough, M. (2008), *Tackling Drug Markets and Distribution Networks in the UK: A Review of the Recent Literature*, London: UKDPC.

Measham, F. and Brain, K. (2005) ' "Binge" Drinking, British Alcohol Policy and the New Culture of Intoxication', *Crime Media Culture*, 1(3): 262–83.

Moeller, K. and Hessee, M. (2013) 'Drug Market Disruption and Systemic Violence: Cannabis Markets in Copenhagen', *European Journal of Criminology*, 10(2): 206–21.

Monaghan, G. and Bewley-Taylor, D. (2013) *Practical Implications for Policing Alternatives to Arrest and Prosecution for Minor Cannabis Offences*, London: International Drug Policy Consortium.

Monaghan, M. (2011) *Evidence Versus Politics: Exploiting Research in UK Drug Policy Making?* Bristol: Policy Press.

Morris, B. (2007) 'History of Criminal Investigation', in Newburn, T., Williamson, T., and Wright, A. (eds.) *Handbook of Criminal Investigation*, Cullompton: Willan, 15–40.

Morselli, C. (2008) *Inside Criminal Networks*, New York: Springer.

Morselli, C. and Petit, K. (2007) 'Law-Enforcement Disruption of a Drug Importation Network', *Global Crime*, 8(2): 109–30

Murji, K. (1998) *Policing Drugs*, Aldershot: Ashgate.

Murji, K. (2007) 'Hierarchies, Markets and Networks: Ethnicity/Race and Drug Distribution', *Journal of Drug Issues*, 37(4): 781–804.

Murphy, S., Waldorf, D., and Reinarman, C. (1990) 'Drifting into Dealing: Becoming a Cocaine Seller', *Qualitative Sociology*, 13(4): 321–43.

Nadelmann, E. (2004) 'Criminologists and Punitive Drug Prohibition: To Serve or to Challenge?' *Criminology & Public Policy*, 3(3): 1001–10.

Natarajan, M. (2000) 'Understanding the Structure of a Drug Trafficking Organization: A Conversational Analysis', in Natarajan, M., and Hough, M. (eds.), *Illegal Drug Markets: From Research to Prevention Policy* (Crime Prevention Studies, Vol. 11), New York: Criminal Justice Press, 273–98.

Natarajan, M. (2006) 'Understanding the Structure of a Large Heroin Distribution Network: A Quantitative Analysis of Qualitative Data', *Journal of Quantitative Criminology*, 22(2): 171–92.

NCIS (2000) *The National Intelligence Model*, London: National Criminal Intelligence Service.

Norris, C. and Dunnighan, C. (2000) 'Subterranean Blues: Conflict as an Unintended Consequence of the Police Use of Informers', *Policing and Society*, 9(4): 385–412.

Nutt, D. (2012) *Drugs Without the Hot Air: Minimising the Harms of Legal and Illegal Drugs*, Cambridge: UIT Press.

Nutt, D., King, L. A., Saulsbury, W., and Blakemore, C. (2007) 'Development of a Rational Scale to Assess the Harm of Drugs of Potential Misuse', *The Lancet*, 369(9566): 1047–53.

Nutt, D., King, L., and Philips, L. (2010) 'Drug Harms in the UK: A Multicriteria Decision Analysis', *The Lancet*, 376(9752): 1558–65.

O'Malley, P. (1992) 'Risk, Power and Crime Prevention', *Economy and Society*, 21(3): 252–75.

O'Malley, P. And Valverde, M. (2004) 'Pleasure, Freedom and Drugs: The Uses of "Pleasure" in Liberal Governance of Drug and Alcohol Consumption', *Sociology*, 38(1): 25–42.

O'Neill, M. and Loftus, B. (2013) 'Policing and the Surveillance of the Marginal: Everyday Contexts of Social Control', *Theoretical Criminology*, 17(4): 437–54.

O'Neill, M. and McCarthy, D. (2014) '(Re) Negotiating Police Culture through Partnership Working: Trust, Compromise and the "New" Pragmatism', *Criminology and Criminal Justice*, 14(2): 143–59.

Oakensen, D., Mockford, R., and Pascoe, C. (2002) 'Does There Have to be Blood on the Carpet? Integrating Partnership, Problem-Solving and the National Intelligence Model in Strategic and Tactical Police Decision-Making Processes', *Police Research and Management*, 5(4): 51–62.

Palmiotto, M. (2013) *Criminal Investigation*, FL: CRC Press.

Paoli, L. and Reuter, P. (2008) 'Drug Trafficking and Ethnic Minorities in Western Europe', *European Journal of Criminology*, 5(1): 13–37.

Pardo, B. (2014) 'Cannabis Policy Reforms in the Americas: A Comparative Analysis of Colorado, Washington and Uruguay', *International Journal of Drug Policy*, 25(4): 727–35.

Parker, H. (2000) 'How Young Britons Obtain Their Drugs: Drugs Transactions at the Point of Consumption', in Natarajan, M. and Hough, M. (eds.), *Illegal Drug Markets: From Research to Prevention Policy* (Crime Prevention Studies, Vol. 11), New York: Criminal Justice Press, 59–82.

Parker, H. (2006) 'Keeping the Lid On: Policing Drug-Related Crime', *Criminal Justice Matters*, 63(6): 7–38.

Parker, H., Aldridge, J., and Measham F. (1998), *Illegal Leisure: The Normalization of Adolescent Recreational Drug Use*, London: Routledge.

Pearson, G. (1987) *The New Heroin Users*, Oxford: Basil Blackwell.

Pearson, G. and Hobbs, D. (2001) *Middle Market Drug Distribution*, Home Office Research Study No. 224, London: Home Office.

Pistone, J. and Woodley, R. (1988) *Donnie Brasco: My Undercover Life in the Mafia*, London: Pan.

Potter, G. (2010) *Weed, Need and Greed: A Study of Domestic Cannabis Cultivation*, London: Free Association Books.

Pritchard, M. and Laxton, E. (1978) *Busted! The Sensational Life Story of an Undercover Hippy Cop*, London: Mirror Books.

Punch, M. (1979) *Policing the Inner City: A Study of Amsterdam's Warmoesstraat*, London: Macmillan.

Ratcliffe, J. (2008) *Intelligence-Led Policing*, Cullompton: Willan.

Redhead, S. (ed.) (1993) *Rave Off: Politics and Deviance in Contemporary Youth Culture*, Aldershot: Avebury Press.

Reiner, R. (1978) *The Blue-Coated Worker*, Cambridge: Cambridge University Press.

Reiner, R. (1992) 'Policing a Postmodern Society', *Modern Law Review*, 55(6): 761–81.

Reiner, R. (2010) *The Politics of the Police* (4th edn.), Oxford: Oxford University Press.

Reiner, R. (2015) 'Revisiting the Classics: Three Seminal Founders of the Study of Policing: Michael Banton, Jerome Skolnick and Egon Bittner', *Policing and Society*, 25(3): 308–27.

Reiner, R. and Newburn, T. (2008) 'Police Research', in King, R. and Wincup, E. (eds.) *Doing Research on Crime and Justice* (2nd edn.), Oxford: Oxford University Press, 343–74.

Reuter, P. (1983a) *Disorganized Crime: Illegal Markets and the Mafia*, Cambridge, MIT Press.

Reuter, P. (1983b) 'Licensing Criminals: Police and Informants', in Caplan, G. (ed.) *ABSCAM Ethics: Moral Issues and Deception in Law Enforcement*, Cambridge, MA: Ballinger, 100–17.

Reuter, P. (2009) 'Systemic Violence in Drug Markets', *Crime, Law and Social Change*, 52(3): 275–84.

Reuter, P. and Greenfield, V. (2001) 'Measuring Global Drug Markets: How Good Are the Numbers and Why Should We Care About Them?' *World Economics*, 2(4): 159–73.

Reuter, P. and Kleiman, M. (1986) 'Risks and Prices: An Economic Analysis of Drug Enforcement', *Crime and Justice*, 7: 289–340.

Reuter, P. and Stevens, A. (2007) *An Analysis of UK Drug Policy: A Monograph Prepared for the UK Drug Policy Commission*, London: UK Drug Policy Commission.

Rice, L. (2016) *The Wrong Side of the Frontline: Exploring the Utilisation of Civilian Investigators by Police Forces Across England and Wales*, PhD: University of Sheffield.

Ritter, A. (2010), 'Illicit Drugs Policy Through the Lens of Regulation', *International Journal of Drug Policy*, 21(4): 265–70.

Roberts, C. and Innes, M. (2009) 'The "Death" of Dixon? Policing Drug Crime and the End of the Generalist Police Constable in England and Wales', *Criminology and Criminal Justice*, 9(3): 337–57.

Rolles, S. (2009) *After the War on Drugs: Blueprint for Regulation*, Bristol: Transform Drug Policy Foundation.

Rolles, S. and Murkin, G. (2013) *How to Regulate Cannabis: A Practical Guide*, Bristol: Transform Drug Policy Foundation.

Rolles, S., Murkin, G., Powell, M., Kushlick, D., and Slater, J. (2012) *The Alternative World Drug Report: Counting the Costs of the War on Drugs*, Bristol: Transform Drug Policy Foundation.

Rolles, S., Sanchez, L., Powell, M., Kushlick, D., and Murkin, G. (2015) *Ending the War on Drugs: How to Win the Global Drug Policy Debate*, Bristol: Transform Drug Policy Foundation.

Rosmarin, A. and Eastwood, N. (2012) *A Quiet Revolution: Drug Decriminalization Policies in Practice Across the Globe*, London: Release.

Ross, J. (2008) 'Undercover Policing and the Shifting Terms of Scholarly Debate: The United States and Europe in Counterpoint', *Annual Review of Law and Social Science*, 4(1): 239–73.

Rubinstein, J. (1973) *City Police*, New York: Farrar Straus and Giroux.

Ruggiero, V. (1993) 'Brixton, London: A Drug Culture without a Drug Economy?' *International Journal of Drug Policy*, 4(2): 83–90.

Ruggiero, V. (2000) *Crime and Markets*, Oxford: Oxford University Press.

Ruggiero, V. and Khan, K. (2006) 'British South Asian Communities and Drug Supply Networks in the UK: A Qualitative Study', *International Journal of Drug Policy*, 17(6): 473–83.

Ruggiero, V. and South, N. (1995) *Eurodrugs: Drug Use, Markets and Trafficking in Europe*, London: UCL Press.

Sackmann, S. (1991) *Cultural Knowledge in Organizations*, Newbury Park, CA: Sage.

Saitta, P., Shapland, J., and Verhage, A. (eds.) (2013) *Getting By or Getting Rich? The Formal, Informal and Criminal Economy in a Globalised World*, The Hague: Eleven International Publishing.

Sandberg, S. (2012) 'The Importance of Culture for Cannabis Markets: Towards an Economic Sociology of Illegal Drug Markets', *British Journal of Criminology*, 52(6): 1133–51.

Sandberg, S. and Pedersen, W. (2009) *Street Capital: Black Cannabis Dealers in a White Welfare State*, Bristol: Policy Press.

Sanders, W. (1977) *Detective Work: A Study of Criminal Investigations*, New York: Free Press.

Sanders, A., Young, R., and Burton, M. (2010) *Criminal Justice* (4th edn.), Oxford: Oxford University Press.

Savage, S. (2007) *Police Reform*, Oxford: Oxford University Press.

Schein, E. (2004) *Organizational Culture and Leadership* (3rd edn.), San Francisco, CA: Jossey-Bass.

Seddon, T. (2010) *A History of Drugs: Drugs and Freedom in the Liberal Age*, London: Routledge.

Seddon, T. (2013) 'Regulating Global Drug Problems', *RegNet Research Paper No. 2013/6*.

Seddon, T. (2014) 'Drug Policy and Global Regulatory Capitalism: The Case of New Psychoactive Substances', *International Journal of Drug Policy*, 25(5): 1019–24.

Seddon, T., Ralphs, R., and Williams, L. (2008) 'Risk, Security and the "Criminalization" of British Drug Policy', *British Journal of Criminology*, 48(6): 818–34.

Seddon, T., Williams, L., and Ralphs, R. (2012) *Tough Choices: Risk, Security and the Criminalization of Drug Policy*, Oxford: Oxford University Press.

Shapland, J. and Ponsaers, P. (eds.) (2009), *The Informal Economy and Connections with Organised Crime: The Impact of National Social and Economic Policies*, The Hague: BJu Legal Publishers.

Shapland, J., Albrecht, H., Ditton, J., and Godefroy, T. (eds.) (2003) *The Informal Economy: Threat and Opportunity in the City*, Germany: Imprime en Allemagne.

Shapland, J., Bottoms, A., and Muir, G. (2013) 'Perceptions of the Criminal Justice System Among Young Adult Would-Be Desisters', in Losel, F., Bottoms, A., and Farrington, D. (eds.) *Young Adult Offenders: Lost in Transition?* London: Routledge, 128–45.

Shearing, C. and Ericson, R. (1991) 'Culture as Figurative Action', *British Journal of Sociology*, 42(4): 481–506.

Sheptycki, J. (2004) 'Organisational Pathologies in Police Intelligence Systems: Some Contributions to the Lexicon of Intelligence-Led Policing', *European Journal of Criminology*, 1(3): 307–32.

Shiner, M. (2006) 'Drugs, Law and the Regulation of Harm' in Hughes, R. Lart, R., and Higate, P. (eds.) *Drugs: Policy and Politics*, Maidenhead: Open University Press, 59–74.

Shiner, M. (2013) 'British Drug Policy and the Modern State: Reconsidering the Criminalisation Thesis', *Journal of Social Policy*, 42(3): 623–43.

Shpayer-Makov, H. (2011) *The Ascent of the Detective: Police Sleuths in Victorian and Edwardian England*, Oxford: Oxford University Press.

Simon, D. (1991) *Homicide: A Year on the Killing Streets*, Boston: Little, Brown.

Sklansky, D. (2007) 'Seeing Blue: Police Reform, Occupational Culture, and Cognitive Burn-In', in O'Neill, M., Marks, M., and Singh, A. (eds.) *Police Occupational Culture: New Debates and Directions*, Amsterdam, The Netherlands: Elsevier, 19–46.

Sklansky, D. (2014) 'The Promise and the Perils of Police Professionalism', in Brown, J. (ed.) *The Future of Policing*, London: Routledge, 343–54.

Skogan, W. (2008) 'Why Reforms Fail', *Policing and Society*, 18(1): 23–34.

Skogan, W. and Frydl, K. (eds.) (2004) *Fairness and Effectiveness in Policing: The Evidence*, Washington DC: National Research Council: National Academies Press.

Skolnick, J. (1966), *Justice Without Trial: Law Enforcement in Democratic Society*, New York: Macmillan.

Skolnick, J. (2008) 'Enduring Issues of Police Culture and Demographics', *Policing and Society*, 18(1): 35–45.

Skolnick, J. (2011), *Justice Without Trial: Law Enforcement in Democratic Society* (4th edn.), New York: Macmillan.

Smith, D. and Gray, J. (1983) *Police and People in London: The Police in Action*, London: Policy Studies Institute.

Smith, S. (1997) 'Contracting Under Pressure: A Theory of Duress', *Cambridge Law Journal*, 56(2): 343–73.

South, N. (1999) 'Debating Drugs and Everyday Life: Normalisation, Prohibition and "Otherness" ', in South (ed.) *Drugs: Culture, Controls and Everyday Life*, London: Sage, 1–15.

Squires, D. (2006) 'The Problem with Entrapment', *Oxford Journal of Legal Studies*, 26(2): 351–76.

Stelfox, P. (2007) 'Professionalizing Criminal Investigation', in Newburn, T., Williamson, T., and Wright, A. (eds.) *Handbook of Criminal Investigation*, Cullompton: Willan, 628–51.

Stelfox, P. (2009) *Criminal Investigation: An Introduction to Principles and Practice*, Cullompton: Willan.

Stevens, A. (2011) *Drugs, Crime and Public Health: The Political Economy of Drug Policy*, London: Routledge.

Stevens, A. (2013) *Applying Harm Reduction Principles to the Policing of Retail Drug Markets*, London: International Drug Policy Consortium.

Stimson, G. (2000) ' "Blair Declares War": The Unhealthy State of British Drug Policy', *International Journal of Drug Policy*, 11(5): 259–64.

Sutherland, E. (1947) *Principles of Criminology* (4th edn.), Philadelphia: J.P. Lippincott.

Taylor, M. and Potter, G. (2013) 'From "Social Supply" to "Real Dealing": Drift, Friendship, and Trust in Drug Dealing Careers', *Journal of Drug Issues*, 43(4): 392–406.

Thornton, S (1995) *Club Cultures: Music, Media and Subcultural Capital*, Hanover, NH: Wesleyan University Press.

Tilley, N. (2008) 'Modern Approaches to Policing: Community, Problem-Oriented and Intelligence-Led', in Newburn, T. (ed.) *Handbook of Policing* (2nd edn.), Cullompton: Willan, 373–403.

Tong, S. (2009) 'Introduction: A Brief History of Criminal Investigation', in Tong, S., Bryant, R., and Horvath, M. (eds.) *Understanding Criminal Investigation*, Chichester: Wiley, 1–12.

Tong, S. and Bowling, B. (2006) 'Art, Craft and Science in Detective Work', *The Police Journal*, 79(4): 323–330.

Topalli, V., Wright, R., and Fornango, R. (2002) 'Drug Dealers, Robbery and Retaliation: Vulnerability, Deterrence and the Contagion of Violence', *British Journal of Criminology*, 42(2): 337–51.

Tyler, T. (1990) *Why People Obey the Law: Procedural Justice, Legitimacy, and Compliance*, New Haven, CT: Yale University Press.

Tyler, T. (2006) 'Restorative Justice and Procedural Justice: Dealing with Rule Breaking', *Journal of Social Issues*, 62(2): 307–26.

UKDPC (2009) *Refocusing Drug-Related Law Enforcement to Address Harms*, London: UKDPC.

UKDPC (2011) *Drug Enforcement in an Age of Austerity: Key Findings from a Survey of Police Forces in England*, London: UKDPC.

UKDPC (2012) *A Fresh Approach to Drugs: The Final Report of the UK Drug Policy Commission*, London: UKDPC.

UNODC (2005) *World Drug Report 2005*, Vienna: United Nations.

van Duyne, P. and Levi, M. (2005) *Drugs and Money: Managing the Drug Trade and Crime-Money in Europe*, London: Routledge.

van Hulst, M. (2013) 'Storytelling at the Police Station: The Canteen Culture Revisited', *British Journal of Criminology*, 53(4): 624–42.

Van Maanen, J. (1978a) 'On Watching the Watchers', in Manning, P. and Van Maanen, J (eds.) *Policing: A View from the Street*, Santa Monica, CA: Goodyear, 309–50.

Van Maanen, J. (1978b) 'The Asshole', in Manning, P. and Van Maanen, J (eds.) *Policing: A View From The Street*, Santa Monica, CA: Goodyear, 221–38.

Van Maanen, J. (1983) 'The Boss: First-Line Supervision in an American Policy Agency', in Punch, M. (eds.) *Control in the Police Organization*, Cambridge, MA: MIT Press, 275–317.

Van Maanen, J. (1984) 'Making Rank: Becoming an American Police Sergeant', *Urban Life*, 13(2–3): 155–76.

Van Maanen, J. (1988) *Tales of the Field: On Writing Ethnography*, Chicago, IL: University of Chicago.

Van Maanen, J. (ed.) (1995), *Representation in Ethnography*, Thousand Oaks, CA: Sage.

Venkatesh, S. (2006) *Off the Books: The Underground Economy of the Urban Poor*, Cambridge, MA: Harvard University Press.

Venkatesh, S. (2013) *Floating City: A Rogue Sociologist Lost and Found in New York's Underground Economy*, New York: Penguin Books.

Wachtel, J. (1992) 'From Morals to Practice: Dilemmas of Control in Undercover Policing', *Crime, Law and Social Change*, 18(1): 137–58.

Waddington, P. (1999a) *Policing Citizens*, London: UCL Press.

Waddington, P. (1999b) 'Police (Canteen) Sub-culture: An Appreciation', *British Journal of Criminology*, 39(2): 287–309.

Walsh, C. (2011) 'Drugs, the Internet and Change', *Journal of Psychoactive Drugs*, 43(1): 55–63.

Warburton, H., May, T., and Hough, M. (2005) 'Looking the Other Way: The Impact of Reclassifying Cannabis on Police Warnings, Arrests and Informal Action in England and Wales', *The British Journal of Criminology*, 45(2): 113–28.

Weatherburn, D., Jones, C., Freeman, K., and Makkai, T. (2003) 'Supply Control and Harm Reduction: Lessons from the Australian Heroin "Drought"', *Addiction*, 98(1): 83–91.

Weatheritt, M. (1986) *Innovations in Policing*, Croom Helm: Kent.

Werb, D., Rowell, G., Guyatt, G., Kerr, T., Montaner, J., and Wood, E. (2011) 'Effect of Drug Law Enforcement on Drug Market Violence: A Systematic Review', *International Journal of Drug Policy*, 22(2): 87–94.

Westley, W. (1970) *Violence and the Police: A Sociological Study of Law, Custom and Morality*, Cambridge, MA: MIT Press.

Westmarland, L. (2013) ' "Snitches get Stitches": US Homicide Detectives' Ethics and Morals in Action', *Policing and Society*, 23(3): 311–27.

Williams, C. (2004) *Cash-in-Hand Work: The Underground Sector and the Hidden Economy of Favours*, Basingstoke: Palgrave Macmillan.

Williams, C. and Windebank, J. (1998) *Informal Employment in the Advanced Economies: Implications for Work and Welfare*, London: Routledge.

Williams, R. (2012) 'Britain is Losing War on Drugs on an Industrial Scale, Amid a "Conspiracy of Silence" Over Policy Failings, says Nick Clegg', *The Independent* (14 December).

Wilson, J. Q. (1978) *The Investigators: Managing FBI and Narcotics Agents*, New York: Basic Books.

Winlow, S. (2001) *Badfellas: Crime Tradition and New Masculinities*, Oxford: Berg.

Wolcott, H. (1990) 'Making a Study "More Ethnographic"', *Journal of Contemporary Ethnography*, 19(1): 44–72.

Wood, E., Werb, D., Marshall, B., Montaner, J., and Kerr, T. (2009) 'The War on Drugs: A Devastating Public-Policy Disaster', *The Lancet*, 373: 989–90.

Woodiwiss, M. (1988) *Crime, Crusades and Corruption: Prohibitions in the United States, 1900–1987*, London: Pinter.

Woodiwiss, M. and Hobbs, D. (2009) 'Organized Evil and the Atlantic Alliance: Moral Panics and the Rhetoric of Organized Crime Policing in America and Britain', *British Journal of Criminology*, 49(1): 106–28.

Wright, A., Waymont, A. and Gregory, F. (1993) *Drug Squads: Law Enforcement Strategies and Intelligence in England and Wales*, London: The Police Foundation.

Young, J. (1971) *The Drugtakers: The Social Meaning of Drug Use*, London: Paladin.

Young, M. (1991) *An Inside Job: Policing and Police Culture in Britain*, Oxford: Oxford University Press.

Young, M. (1995) 'Black Humour—Making Light of Death', *Policing and Society*, 5(2): 151–68.

Zaitch, D. (2002) *Trafficking Cocaine: Colombian Drug Entrepreneurs in the Netherlands*, Kluwer Law International: The Hague.

Zedner, L. (2006) 'Policing Before the Police', *British Journal of Criminology*, 46(1): 78–96.

Zehr, H. and Mika, H. (1998) 'Fundamental Concepts of Restorative Justice', *Contemporary Justice Review*, 1(1): 47–55.

Zinberg, N. (1984) *Drug, Set and Setting: The Basis for Controlled Intoxicant Use*, New Haven: Yale University Press.

Index